Caribbean Series, 15

Sidney W. Mintz, Editor

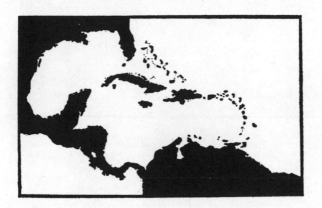

CREOLE DRUM

An Anthology of Creole Literature in Surinam

Edited by Jan Voorhoeve and Ursy M. Lichtveld

with English Translations by Vernie A. February

New Haven and London   Yale University Press

1975

Library of Congress catalog card number: 74-19575
International standard book number: 0-300-01661-1

Designed by John O. C. McCrillis
and set in Press Roman type.
Printed in the United States of America by
The Murray Printing Co., Forge Village, Massachusetts.

Published in Great Britain, Europe, and Africa by
Yale University Press, Ltd., London.
Distributed in Latin America by Kaiman & Polon,
Inc., New York City; in India by UBS Publishers'
Distributors Pvt., Ltd., Delhi; in Japan by John
Weatherhill, Inc., Tokyo.

Contents

Preface

Surinam Creole (called Negro-English, Taki-Taki, and Nengre or more recently also Sranan and Sranan tongo) has had a remarkable history. It is a young language, which did not exist before 1651. It served as a contact language between slaves and masters and also between slaves from different African backgrounds and became within a short time the mother tongue of the Surinam slaves. After emancipation in 1863 it remained the mother tongue of lower-class Creoles (people of slave ancestry), but it served also as a contact language or lingua franca between Creoles and Asian immigrants. It gradually became a despised language, an obvious mark of low social status and lack of proper schooling. After 1946, on the eve of independence, it became more respected (and respectable) within a very short time, owing to the great achievements of Creole poets: Cinderella kissed by the prince.

In this anthology we wish to give a picture of the rise and glory of the former slave language. The introduction sketches the history of Surinam Creole in its broad outlines, starting from the first published text in 1718. The texts are presented in nine chronologically ordered chapters starting from the oral literature, which is strongly reminiscent of the times of slavery, and ending with modern poetry and prose. Each chapter is introduced by some general remarks that present all the relevant information necessary to appreciate and understand the texts. Footnotes clarify minor points.

The title of the anthology—*Creole Drum* (*krioro dron*)—requires some explanation. The name comes from a certain part in the traditional *banya* play in Surinam (see chapter 1), in which participants have the opportunity of commenting in song on past events. Through this book we too comment on past events. In the real *krioro dron* ridicule is most prominent, but our book is more in the nature of a song of praise. This is not due primarily to the design of the editors but rather to the quality of the works themselves.

This book might be regarded as a modern counterpart of an earlier book by the same authors, called *Suriname: spiegel der vaderlandse kooplieden. Een historisch leesboek* (Surinam: mirror of the Dutch traders. A historical reader) (Zwolle, 1958). The texts there, mostly in Dutch, illustrate the history of Surinam. Here we illustrate the history of the Creole language of Surinam.

The limited purpose of the anthology excludes specimens of the Dutch literature of Surinam, which has become more important during the last ten years. Before that there was only one Creole author, Albert Helman (pseudonym of Lou Lichtveld), who considered himself more a Dutch author with a Creole background. In a poetry contest in 1960, it was quite clear that the Dutch poems by Surinam authors represented a markedly lower level of accomplishment than their Creole poems. The situation has since changed. Johan Ferrier and Bea Vianen have published remarkable novels in Dutch and have found Dutch editors sufficiently interested to publish their work. Another group of authors working and living in Surinam publish in Dutch and in Creole or in a sort of local Dutch. They wish to publish and distribute their work locally, and it is rather difficult to obtain it outside Surinam. They employ quite original marketing techniques, selling their products on street corners and attracting customers with a local band. They also recite their works in schools and at public meetings. In this way they try to keep in touch with their own people. One of the most productive authors of this group, which is named after its periodical, *Moetete,* is Dobru, pseudonym of Robin Ravales.

The Moetete group has more than local interest. The most serious problem of the Caribbean writer using a European language seems to be that he is often more appreciated and read in Europe than in his home country, which is also the case with African writers. He constantly faces the threat of losing contact with his audience. The use of local idioms is subconsciously screened by European editorial policies. Publishing in Surinam means that one has to be satisfied with reaching a small audience. Every author publishing in Surinam, and especially one who writes in Creole, knows beforehand that his work will be sold only on a very small scale.

The editors of this volume have different backgrounds, which is sometimes revealed by the way their opinions are formulated in different chapters. Ursy M. Lichtveld, a Surinam Creole, composed chapter 5 and had a prominent part in the composition of chapter 9. Jan Voorhoeve, who is Dutch, wrote the introduction and prepared the first three chapters, using much firsthand material which he taped in Surinam in close cooperation with H. C. van Renselaar. Vernie A. February, born in South Africa, is responsible for the translations of the texts, which also means that he took part in their interpretation. These three names are mentioned on the title page, indicating that they share responsibility for the entire work.

We wish to acknowledge the help of many others. Richard Price

read the first draft of the manuscript and gave valuable advice about
the composition and presentation of the work for an American audience.
At a later stage he carefully checked the manuscript once more.
Douglas McRae Taylor went over the manuscript with the editors
in search of errors in the translations. He has an intimate knowledge
of the Surinam Creole language and culture and was able to interpret
the texts and to determine whether they were rendered faithfully
into English. In two instances Douglas and his son Jacques tried out
completely new translations, which were gladly accepted by the
authors and incorporated in the text. H. F. de Ziel prepared the text
of chapter 4 and assisted in interpreting modern poems. The Surinam
students following the lectures of Jan Voorhoeve at Leiden University
during the academic years 1969-70 and 1970-71 contributed valuable
suggestions. The Netherlands Foundation for Cultural Cooperation
with Surinam and the Netherlands Antilles (STICUSA) made possible
the translation of the texts into English. The same institution granted
Jan Voorhoeve a one-month period in Surinam in February 1970 to
renew contacts with the Surinamese authors. The Netherlands Foundation for the Advancement of Tropical Research (WOTRO) did the
same for Ursy M. Lichtveld. Many storytellers, singers, and authors
contributed toward giving this anthology its present form. We feel
honored to be entrusted with this task.

University of Leiden   Jan Voorhoeve
Bureau of Linguistic Research in Suriname,
University of Amsterdam   Ursy M. Lichtveld
Africa Study Centre, Leiden   Vernie A. February

Introduction

The Country and Its Inhabitants

Surinam is the middle of the three Guianas, which with Venezuela
form the upper northern ridge of the mainland of South America. We
may assume that it was sparsely populated by different Indian tribes
(mainly of Carib and Arawak stock) before 1651, when permanent
European settlement began. Early in its European history, in 1667,
it became a possession of the Netherlands, producing sugar, coffee,
and cacao for the world market. Surinam in those days consisted
of no more than the coastal area along the borders of the Surinam
River and its affluents, Commewijne and Para. The remaining part of
the area between the borders of present-day Surinam remained un-
cultivated and largely unknown for a long time. The far western part
was unoccupied until 1800, when the most northerly ridge was
cultivated. Beyond the coastal area chaos reigned, in the eyes of the
Europeans. The eastern part became the domain of bands of fugitive
slaves, called maroons, who remained dependent for their subsistence
on the coastal area, which they raided in search of iron, arms, am-
munition, salt, and women. These bands organized themselves in
different bushnegro communities—Matuari, Saramaccan, Djuka, and
others. Beyond the coast and the more inland fugitive settlements
wandered the often nomadic remnants of the former masters of the
land, the Indians.

The Early History of Surinam

Three different stages of European contact with Surinam followed each other. The first might be called the period of trade
colonies. European traders bought products from the Indians and
shipped them to Europe. During the second period—plantation
settlement—European farmers themselves started to cultivate the
most valued products (mainly tobacco) with the help later on of
some African and American Indian slave labor. The farmers in this
period were settlers who intended to stay if conditions were favorable.
In tropical Surinam, they were not. Moreover, the introduction of
the sugar industry eventually led to a completely different type of
colony—the slave colony—in which a few whites directed the labor
of a great many African slaves. The three stages were not clearly dis-

1

tinct from each other. Traders, for example, continued their activity
during the period of plantation settlement. The last two phases
especially overlapped to a considerable extent, though the ratio of
masters to slaves (.31 in 1661 and .08 in 1702) reveals a definite trend
in the direction of a slave colony.

Surinam was occupied by different and successive groups of
Europeans before Francis, Lord Willoughby, governor of Barbados,
planted a colony in 1651, called originally after him Willoughby Land.
French settlements were established in 1626 and 1639, and an English
settlement under Captain Marshall in 1645 was "cut off in one
day" (Rens 1953:13f.). There is no evidence that survivors of any
of these settlements remained in 1651. Willoughby was appointed governor of Barbados at a time when the expanding sugar
industry created a shortage of land there. He explored new possibilities'
and in 1651 sent a hundred men to settle a new colony in Surinam.
Fifty more people came the following year. Slaves are not mentioned
as part of the oldest settlement, but it seems highly unlikely that the
first settlers did not take with them a few African slaves. There could
not have been many, however, because Barbados itself had a shortage
of slaves at that time.

The English influence was of rather short duration, increasing
until 1665 and then rapidly diminishing from 1666 onward, but it was
more powerful than any other during the time of slavery. The white
masters were almost completely English speaking up to 1665. In that
year a group of 200 Portuguese Jews got permission to settle in Surinam
and later became one of the most important and stable components
of the society. The colony was captured by the Dutch in 1667, recaptured by Barbados the same year, but handed back to the Dutch
in 1668 in accordance with the peace treaty of 1667 between England
and Holland. Before the colony was handed over to the Dutch, 67
of the most important English planters left the colony with 412 slaves.
In 1671 a group of 517 people left, followed in 1675 by 250 whites
with 980 slaves. In 1680 the last group of 102 Englishmen and slaves
left, leaving only 39 Englishmen behind. The English planters were
not allowed to take with them the slaves acquired under Dutch rule,
which means that it was principally the old, experienced slaves who
left.

On the basis of historical documents, both English and Dutch, and
of old maps (see Rens 1953 and 1954, Voorhoeve 1964(b), Renselaar
1966), the following table can be constructed.

| | Europeans | | Africans | | American | | Ratio Eur./ |
	British	Non-British	Old	New	Indians	Total	Non-Eur.
1652	200		200		90	490	.41
1661	1,000		2.000		230	3,230	.31
1665	1,500		3,000		400	4,900	.31
1666	2,000	200	2,400		400	4,200	.33
1668	820	250	1,850		300	3,170	.34
1671	500	300	1,300	1,200	410	3,710	.22
1675	200	350	200	1,600	350	2,700	.20
1679	60	400	100	900	100	1,560	.29
1680	38	400	10	1,000	50	1,498	.29
1684	30	700		4,000	50	4,780	.15
1702	20	700		7,500	50	8,270	.08

This population table can be supplemented with relevant information of a different nature. During the English period the influence of
indentured servants on the slaves was even more important than that
of the white masters. "The main contact of the Negro slaves was
with these indentured servants and poor whites, who acted as bookkeepers and overseers on the plantations, rather than with the
planters themselves" (*Dictionary* 1967:xii). The indentured servants
were English speaking before 1668. (The institution of indentured
labor was not known in Holland.) In the English period also the
plantations were scattered over a wider area (Renselaar 1966),
which favored contact between slaves and whites.

Slave Society

The slaves had different ethnic backgrounds, but this did not
mean that they arrived in Surinam without any means of communication. The existence of an Afro-Portuguese pidgin on the African
coast in the sixteenth century is amply documented. Its influence
may have been diminishing during the seventeenth century, but there
is no evidence that it had disappeared. We may assume that Africans
from different ethnic backgrounds made some use of this language,
acquired at home, in the slave depots, or on the ships. The first
mention of the language used by the slaves in Surinam dates from
1693. A Dutch traveler reported that they spoke English (Voorhoeve
1973:140). There are still traces of Portuguese in the Creole language.
The Swadesh 200-item list, a widely used list of basic vocabulary
items first used by Morris Swadesh, shows 118 items of English origin,
25 of Dutch origin, 7 of Portuguese origin, and 4 of African origin.

The Portuguese items may have come into the language through
the Portuguese Jewish masters. The Saramaccan bushnegro language,
however, shows 72 items of English origin, 6 of Dutch origin, 50 of
Portuguese origin, and 6 of African origin. The high proportion of
Portuguese items cannot be explained by the linguistic influence of
the Portuguese Jews (Herskovits 1930).

Masters and Slaves

A slave colony is essentially a two-caste society of masters and
slaves. In 1702 the slaves in Surinam outnumbered their masters in
a ratio of 92 to 8. This 8 percent of the population forced 92 percent
to hard labor without offering much reward. The two-caste society
was one of the most effective means of keeping the slaves under control. The entire society was based on the conception that slaves could
never become masters and masters never slaves. One was born a slave
and thus had to work for the man who was born a master. The
society tried very hard to make the slaves accept this state of affairs
as inevitable. The cultural policy therefore discouraged assimilation,
and the two groups were kept as distinct as possible. Slaves had to
speak a different language, wear different clothes, believe in a different
god, perform different jobs, enjoy a different kind of music, and so
forth. Cultural assimilation would have constituted the greatest
threat to the slave colony.

The clearest example is to be found in religion. In a slave colony,
missionary activities are well-nigh impossible. A slave had to remain
a pagan and could never become a Christian. This attitude is seen
clearly in events surrounding the life of the Protestant minister Kals,
who arrived in Surinam in 1731 and was sent home in 1733 as unworthy of the ministry. He came to Surinam with the ardent wish to
preach the gospel to the slaves. When he expressed his wish before
the church council of Paramaribo, he got—according to his own
description—the following reaction:

> They interrupted my speech in the middle, jumped up in rage,
> ran away, ridiculed me, and screamed at me: Well Pastor! Let
> us convert those who have the same skin as we, and are of the
> same color as we, and . . . let the cursed children of Ham go to
> the devil; they have been created in order to plant coffee and
> sugar for us.

The institution of manumission is an anomaly in this type of society,
because it creates a group of colored people who are neither slaves nor

real masters. Yet it was unavoidable. In general one employed youthful Europeans in the lower ranks as overseers or bookkeepers or even
as craftsmen. They were not allowed to bring wives and children to
the plantation. They could not afford them, in any case, on the low
salaries they earned. Even directors could not marry before they had
served on the plantation for some years. Sexual intercourse between
masters and slaves was therefore a regular phenomenon. The master's
concubine occupied a special position on the plantation and had a
special name, *sisi*. She was the natural intermediary between the
slaves and the plantation director. Complaints came to the master
via his concubine. The first story in chapter 3 shows that a married
director could also have a *sisi*.

   Children, however, received the status of the mother. Thus in
many cases children of the master were born slaves. The only solution
to this problem for the master was to buy the freedom of his own
children and leave the mother a slave or to free the mother before the
children were born. The practice of manumission created a group of
free colored men in the colony, who should have been considered part
of the group of masters but were not in fact accepted by them on an
equal basis. A case in point is that of the rich free black woman
Nanette Samson, who married a European of rather low social standing in 1767. The colonial administration was at a loss what to do.
There were no laws prohibiting such a marriage. Therefore they sent
a letter to the directors in Holland in a last effort to prevent it. In
this letter they stated their case as follows:

> The objection against such a marriage is that it is repugnant and
> repulsive, utterly disgraceful for a white person, whether out of
> sexual perversion or for food, to enter into such a marriage,
> which has always been despised here. It is also true that, in
> order to maintain our upright position in the middle of such
> a perverted and twisted people, we must rely more on the feel-
> ing of the negroes for our preeminence over them, as if we are
> of a better and nobler nature, than on our real power. What will
> they believe about that excellent nature if they see that they
> need only to be free in order to join with us in a solemn bond
> of marriage and thus have their children the companions of our
> own? Should not the laxity of whites who so debase themselves
> be singled out for criticism? (Lichtveld and Voorhoeve 1958:
> 177-78)

The directors in Holland did not agree with this reasoning, thus

giving Nanette Samson the distinction of being the first colored
woman to marry a white man. The letter to the directors, however,
shows clearly how the two-caste society operated to keep masters
and slaves apart and what the basic reasoning behind the system was.

The two-caste society had great influence on the formation of
a Creole culture. As a slave language Creole remained relatively pure
and did not undergo a destructive influx of Dutch lexical items and
grammatical constructions. A new religion was constructed in relative
isolation without overt signs of syncretism. A new culture came into
being with an extensive oral literature, reflecting the conditions
of slavery (see chapters 1, 2, and 3). In the later stages there was also
a clear contribution from the free colored people, who often held
important positions in Creole cultural societies and could devote
time and energy to them. We also have the impression that the more
elaborate cultural forms originated in the capital, Paramaribo. There
the slaves (often house slaves or craftsmen) had more leisure time
and more money to spend than on the plantations.

Toward Emancipation

The two-caste society gradually disintegrated after 1800. Before
that date, as we have seen, missionaries could barely reach the slaves.
It is said that the Moravian Mission bought slaves in order to be able
to preach the gospel. In reality, most missionary activities before
1800 were directed toward the American Indians and, after the
peace treaties of 1761, also toward the bushnegro tribes. After 1800
they gradually received permission from individual plantation directors
to give religious instruction on the plantations.

In 1844 missionaries received permission to teach slave children
to read in Creole. Instruction in writing was not allowed until 1856
(Hellinga 1955:13). With prohibition of the slave traffic after 1820
the condition of the slaves gradually improved. The possibility of
emancipation was debated in Holland, and this forced the Surinam
slave owners to defend their cause. In any case, written texts in Creole
got into print after 1800. The first printed Creole text (for use by
Creoles) dates from 1816 and consists of a selection from the New
Testament. The first printed and complete New Testament in Creole
(with Psalms) was published in 1829. The first Creole primer was
published in 1832. The missionaries produced a spate of religious
material and even published a Creole monthly called *Makzien vo
Kristen soema zieli* (Magazine for Christian souls) from 1852 to 1932.

(For other publications see Voorhoeve 1957(b) and Voorhoeve and
Donicie 1963(b).)

The first partly Creole poem was written by a Dutchman, Hendrik
Schouten, married to a colored woman, actually a cousin of the well-
known Nanette Samson mentioned above. He had written a beautiful
sonnet, "De geele vrouw" (the yellow woman), in Dutch in defense
of his colored wife against a prejudiced society (Lichtveld and Voorhoeve 1958:187-88). The partly Creole poem, called "Een huishoudelijke
twist" (a domestic tiff), was published in 1783. It portrays a Dutchman and his Creole concubine reviling each other in their respective
languages. (It should not be interpreted as symptomatic of his own
marriage.) The poem is given in full in appendix 3 to this volume, not
because of its literary value (though it is not without literary value),
but because it was the first Creole poem ever seen in print.

Later on, in the nineteenth century (in 1836 and 1837), but still
before emancipation, the *Njoejaari-singi voe Cesaari* (New Year songs
of Cesar) were published in loose leaflets. The song of 1837 (see
Lichtveld Voorhoeve 1958:276-83) shows great poetic skill and
cleverly exploits Creole proverbs. It was reprinted in 1843 in a Dutch
literary periodical, *Braga,* with a Dutch translation by the poet J. J. L.
ten Kate. Presumably these songs were sold in Paramaribo by a deaf-
mute named Cesaari. The clever use of Creole proverbs seems to point
in the direction of the Creole lawyer H. C. Focke as the possible
author. Focke lived from 1802 to 1856 and in 1855 published an
excellent *Neger-Engelsch woordenboek* (Negro-English dictionary),
which is still one of the best sources for the Creole language and its
proverbs. His study of Creole songs and music was published post-
humously (Focke 1858).

In 1858 a "Lofdicht na tappoe Hernhutter kerki" (Praise poem
on the Moravian church) was published. On the eve of emancipation,
in 1862, there appeared one issue of a Creole weekly, *Krioro Koranti*
(Creole paper), which contained a Creole poem on the pending
emancipation. This is about all the traceable literature in Creole. The
work of the Matuari bushnegro Johannes King was written between
1862 and 1894 and reveals a close affinity with oral traditions.
Samples of his work are produced in chapter 4.

Emancipation and Assimilation

The colony lost its economic value in the nineteenth century.
With emancipation in 1863 and the end of the subsequent ten-year

period of state supervision over the former slaves in 1873, the cultural situation in Surinam changed radically and became more complex. The colonial government tried to keep the plantations going by importing contract laborers from Asian countries, mostly from China, India, and Java. About 34,304 British Indians came to Surinam between 1873 and 1916 on five-year contracts. About 32,976 Javanese came on similar contracts between 1891 and 1939. Many remained after their contracts expired (Speckmann 1965:29; Waal Malefijt 1963:22). Half of the population of Surinam today is of Asian descent. Where the Asian immigrants constituted a minority in the Creole community, as happened for instance in Coronie, they were easily assimilated. More often than not, however, they preserved their own language and culture and thus added to the cultural diversity that is so characteristic of modern Surinam society.

When the slaves became free, and the old distinction between masters and slaves ceased to exist, the slaves were expected to acquire the culture linked with their newfound status, i.e. of their former masters. Thus they were expected to become Christians, learn Dutch, get instruction, and behave like Europeans—in short, become assimilated.

The assimilation policy of the colonial government was especially noticeable in education. Before emancipation all instruction of slave children had been in Creole. In 1856 the governor of Surinam protested against the fact that the medium of instruction in a Dutch colony was a foreign, non-Dutch, language, to wit, Creole. His remarks anticipated the emancipation. The mission schools, however, had difficulty changing to Dutch. Their instructional material had been printed in Creole, and their teachers were often not familiar with Dutch. Pressure from the government, which stipulated Dutch as the medium of instruction from 1877 onward, and no doubt also the wish of parents who desired instruction in the official language for their children forced the schools to capitulate. Only in the mission schools in bushnegro communities was Creole the medium of instruction for a long time.

The general change in attitude is reflected in the Creole grammar, *Wan spraakkunst vo taki en skrifi da tongo vo Sranan* (A grammar to talk and write the language of Surinam) published in Creole by J. N. Helstone in 1903. The author had to defend himself in the introduction against those who criticized his work as hampering the cause of the Dutch language in Surinam. He explicitly stated that his purpose was primarily to teach Dutch to illiterates.

In the early twentieth century the educational authorities were
confident that they would be able to eradicate the Creole language
from Surinam in only one generation. Their campaign was based on
the strong conviction that Creole prevented the children from
acquiring a good command of Dutch. Some educators were aware
that the campaign was contrary to new ideas about the value of a
mother tongue as a medium of instruction but rejected this for the
West Indian colonies because, as one of them said, Creole languages
are mutilated languages that could survive only because of unnatural
conditions in the past (Kesler 1927).

Creole children were severely punished if they used Creole in
school, and the cooperation of the parents was sought to prevent
them from using it at home. The result was that today most Creoles
in town have a fairly reasonable command of Dutch. The old slave
language, however, did not cease to exist. A new situation emerged
in which Creoles learned to deal with two cultures simultaneously.
According to the pressure of the situation, they could act in one way
or another. A Creole may participate actively in the Christian religion,
but this does not mean that he may not also become possessed by
non-Christian gods. He is quite capable of expressing himself in Dutch
and may even take part in a Dutch literary movement, but this does
not mean that he will shy away from any form of expression in
Creole. In fact he has become bicultural. For this special type of
cultural situation Herskovits coined the term *socialized ambivalence*
(Herskovits 1937:292-99).

The old slave language and culture continued to exist, but they
were regarded as a mark of low social status and a sign of lack of
proper schooling. Creoles may still be offended when addressed in
Creole, as if the addresser underestimates their social status and
educational level. The same holds true for other types of social behavior. In a colonial society the cultural norms are set by the colonial
elite, which in this case consisted almost completely of Dutch people.
Thus Dutch culture and language were normative in the society,
all other cultural expressions betraying a lower social status. This
situation influenced the way Creoles thought about their own socially
stigmatized language and culture. The psychological effect led in
many cases to a complete lack of self-respect and a waste of creative
talents.

How Creole Became Respectable

Almost everywhere a Creole language is regarded as a mongrel

product unworthy of attention. It is therefore important to describe
the special conditions in which one of the Creole languages, Surinam
Creole, reached a stage of respectability.

During the Second World War the Creole teacher J. G. A. Koenders,
a man of great intellectual integrity, started a one-man campaign
against the lack of self-respect that threatened his pupils as a result
of the then existing educational policy. He had always been a rather un-
orthodox teacher, refusing to mutilate the self-esteem of his pupils,
but now he decided to remedy the damages of the educational system
on a wider scale. For a period of ten years (1946-56), he issued a
monthly paper, *Foetoe-boi* (Servant), in Creole and Dutch, illustrating
on almost every page his ardent wish to bolster the self-esteem of the
Creole part of the population. Some of his articles are reproduced in
chapter 5 of this book. With deadly irony he attacked every official
statement that tried to minimize the value of the Creole culture and
language and unmasked the absence of sound intellectual arguments
behind it.

Koenders was a rather lonely man. Amidst the jubilations accompany-
ing partial independence in 1954, he had to sell his basic idea that self-
respect was the only way to freedom. The Department of Education
was firmly opposed to his ideas. Political independence did not change
their policy. His fellow countrymen thought him rather crazy and
were even sometimes offended by his ironic reactions. He had a much
more willing ear in the younger generation.

The young intellectuals had been raised under colonial conditions.
They had adapted themselves so well to Dutch culture that they were
invariably sent to Holland to complete their studies at Dutch universities.
They had done brilliantly and were much applauded at home. In
Holland, however, they discovered that their fellow students did not
quite appreciate their adaptive talents but on the contrary expected
from them a new and original contribution to the students' cultural
life. A man who could sing Creole ballads was most applauded, although
he was despised back home for his interest in the culture of the uneducated.

In this way many Creole students in Holland became conscious of
their different, non-European culture, which was not inferior at all,
as was suggested under colonial conditions. This realization came to
some individuals in a dramatic way and to others as simply a confirmation of deep-rooted beliefs. In both cases, the ideas were strengthened
by the writings of Koenders in *Foetoe-boi,* which had a wide distribution among Creole students in Holland.

They soon started to question the old cultural hierarchy in a more
systematic way. Why should Dutch be considered a superior language?
Why should a knowledge of Creole retard their progress? Why should
European marriage practices be preferred to lower-class concubinage?
Why should Christianity be more respectable than the voodoo-like religion of lower-class Creoles? How did one arrive at a true Surinam culture that united all racial groups in Surinam? The students in Holland
founded a new cultural movement, Wie Eegie Sanie (Our own things),
in which intellectuals and laborers for the first time met on an equal
basis. At the same time, they tried to unite the different racial groups
in Surinam. Their aim was to give Surinam its own cultural identity,
in which all people could identify themselves. Clear political aims
were absent, but the basic ideas were social dynamite. They could
blow up the existing social hierarchy.

The greatest achievement of the group has been in the realm of
language. Once the students had decided that there were no sensible
arguments for the inferiority of the Creole language, they trained
themselves to use it under all circumstances, even in their writing. It
was quite clear that Creole was and still is the most widely used
language in Surinam. A population survey undertaken in 1950
showed the distribution of knowledge of the main languages of
Surinam to be the following (taken from an unpublished book by
Douglas McRae Taylor): Creole, 85-90 percent; Dutch, 50-55 percent;
Hindi, 30-35 percent; Javanese, 15-20 percent. This shows clearly
that the students' choice was a very sensible one from the point
of view of reaching the greatest number of people. It was, however,
rather differently motivated: for them, Creole was best suited to
become the national language because it was the only language spoken
in Surinam that had indigenous roots.

It has been said that Creole might be a nice language to tell jokes
in or to boss your maid around in but that it could not possibly be
used as a vehicle for more refined speech and that Dutch should
therefore be preferred. Could one ever imagine the beautiful sonnets
of the famous Dutch poet Willem Kloos (the Shelley of Holland) in
Creole? When this point was raised in a public speech, Koenders
translated one of the most beautiful poems of Kloos into Creole in
a completely convincing way. He just wanted to prove that the arguments were false. In his typical way he stated: If Surinam people
with creative talents are not able to produce poems in Creole, *they*
must be blamed, not the language.

The Surinam students in Holland started to write original poems

in Creole and to explore the poetic possibilities of their language.
Not surprisingly, support came from Friesland, an area that has also
steadfastly campaigned for its own Frisian language and literature.
In 1952 the Frisian cultural magazine *De Tsjerne* (The churning tub)
devoted an issue to the new Creole literature, publishing Creole poems
and one Creole short story in Frisian translation. At that time only
a few poems existed in Creole. The oldest one must have been
written in 1949, as far as can be ascertained, and was published for
the first time in 1951. These poems of the first hour have been
reproduced in chapter 6.

There are reasons for singling out two poets for separate treatment
in chapters 7 and 8. Eddy Bruma has had the greatest political and
theoretical impact of any Surinam poet. In a way he shaped the
cultural ideals of Wie Eegie Sanie and can be regarded as the leader
of this cultural movement and the natural successor of Koenders.
He has written poems, short stories, and dramas in Creole. During
several successive years he produced in conjunction with the drama
association of Wie Eegie Sanie new original dramas, based mostly on
the history of Surinam. The period of slavery is the main source of
inspiration for popular drama in Paramaribo, which is often based
on a fixed theme but performed without a written text. Bruma
brought the drama to a higher level by writing out the texts and by
perfecting the technical side of production. He often did not have
enough time to write a well-balanced play. The production
time was often extemely short, a few weeks only, including the
writing.

Henny F. de Ziel, writing under the pseudonym Trefossa, should
be regarded as the most important poet, who proved for the first
time that poetry of very high quality was possible in Creole. He is
the author of a very small number of poems, each one, however,
being a perfect jewel. His first poem, "Bro," was published in a
teachers' periodical and immediately reprinted by Koenders in
Foetoe-boi. (It is reproduced here in chapter 7.) The poet arrived in
Holland in 1953. He agreed with the general ideas of Wie Eegie Sanie
but never took an active part in the organization. In the following
years more of his poems were published in *Foetoe-boi.* In 1957 he
published a small collection of Creole poems under the title *Trotji.*
This collection showed such consistently high quality that it really
dealt a major blow to all those who were still convinced that Creole
could never become a sophisticated language. The educational
authorities were caught off guard by this publication. How could

they go on preventing their pupils from speaking Creole if the language lent itself to expressions of such unadulterated beauty?

While Creole was at that moment still regarded as vulgar, it was not excluded from use in more elevated circles, such as the church. Creole had survived in church as a respectable language used in Bible reading, in devotional literature, and in the pulpit. It could survive there only by developing a specific pronunciation, as far removed as possible from the everyday language of the street. Thus there really existed two different varieties of Creole: the vulgar variety used by uneducated people and the church variety, which apparently was purged of all vulgarities. The church variety was characterized to a great extent by a foreign accent (no doubt originally in imitation of the speech of foreign missionaries) and by the absence of vowel elision (Voorhoeve 1971(a)). The rules of vowel elision give the language a natural rhythmic flow but make it difficult for foreigners to speak and understand it. Church Creole avoids all vowel elisions and therefore gives the impression of a very emphatic and stilted pulpit language.

All early attempts at Creole poetry were (naturally) based on this stilted literary language. The great value of Trefossa as a poet is that he succeeded for the first time in breaking away from the literary tradition by using the common language of the street, as if he were not bothered at all by its so-called vulgarity. By doing this he could convey subtle shades of meaning and use more complicated rhythmic patterns. It seemed as if he had freed the language from unnatural chains and had given free reign to all the possibilities locked up in it. Today one cannot very well imagine what a major cultural achievement this was, but in his time such a bold step was stupendous. It was as if he confirmed for a great many people things they had always subconsciously known. He was enthusiastically followed by others, who also exploited the new possibilities of the common Creole. Today there is a regular flow of literature produced in Creole. This new generation of poets is treated in chapter 9.

A remarkable side effect should not be left unmentioned. The policy of assimilation had created a type of personality that regarded imitation as the highest possible accomplishment. The literature produced and sometimes published in local periodicals consisted of cheap imitations of nineteenth-century Dutch models. The new literary movement in Creole seems to have freed creative possibilities altogether. The young generation did not feel frustrated any longer by foreign models when using Dutch. They started to use local varieties of Dutch and really tried to go their own way.

Literary achievements in Creole have undoubtedly raised the
social status of the language rather dramatically. Creole has become
a cultural language in a very short period of time. It has gained acceptance in the broadcasting system, on the stage, in society, and
even in school, although not as a medium of instruction. Part of the
national anthem has even been rendered into Creole. The birth of a
new Creole literature has made Surinam Creole one of the very few
Creole languages in the world that has gained social status and
respectability. While the multiracial setting of Surinam will perhaps
prevent the language from becoming the national language, its influence
is still comparable to that of any other national language. Its speakers
have gained the proud confidence that through this medium they
have been able to contribute to and enrich world literature.

CHAPTER 1

Folksongs (*Banya*, *Du*, *Laku*, and *Lobinsingi*)

In Creole society songs can be tender or humorous, but they can also
be used as deadly weapons. Street concerts in Surinam's capital,
Paramaribo, have been responsible for bitter fights in the past, and
Surinam is possibly one of the few places in the world where concerts
have been repeatedly forbidden by law. In a government proclamation
of 19 November 1828 the so-called Du societies (for dance and song)
were forbidden in Paramaribo and other parts of the country. Free
people who were caught at a performance were subject to a fine of
200 florins. Slaves received a hundred strokes and a fine that their
masters were expected to pay. This proclamation was repeated on
21 May 1833 (*Encyclopaedie*, s.v. Dansen). Around 1900 the police
temporarily stopped all *lobisingi* ("love song") performances in
Paramaribo (Comvalius 1939:358), and one still has to ask for police
permission for a performance of this type.[1] In an excellent description of the *lobisingi*, Herskovits characterized it as "an established
form of social criticism by ridicule [bearing] particularly on the
reprehensible conduct of women" (Herskovits 1936:23).

Songs provided almost the only outlets for interpersonal tension.
The social hierarchy on the plantation did not permit direct criticism
of superiors (especially whites), and the plantation slaves constituted
such an isolated, close community that open rivalry was well-nigh
impossible. Indirect, symbolic criticism may also be reflected in the
material culture of the Creoles. The choice of a kerchief and the way
it is bound around the head may convey a message (Herskovits 1936:
3-9). Market women continue to give to newly imported kerchiefs
names that may reflect political or social issues in the community.[2]

1. Focke 1858 (p. 100) states that bitter criticism of the songs forced the government to take action: "Light-hearted jests soon turned into scornful jeers, and
the attacks back and forth became so sharp, so bitter, that the government
considered it necessary to ban these singing and dancing societies. Later the
Du societies were permitted to function again, under the general name of
Baljaar (in Spanish *bailar*, "to dance"), or singing parties, on the condition
that they took care to obtain written permission." (Translated from Dutch).
2. A certain kerchief was dubbed *Tangi fu dri pikin moysmoysi Anansi go na
ini Koro bere* ("Thanks to three little mice, spider Anansi got into the belly

Songs, however, are more powerful and can really hurt someone, as
we have witnessed on several occasions.

During the time of slavery, New Year's Day and the first of July
were fixed occasions of celebration, when the rations were brought
in from town and distributed among the slaves. It was possible to
create other special occasions, for example at the end of harvest time,
and by some unwritten law or agreement slaves were then allowed to
dance.[3] Cancellation of one of these occasions was regarded as one
of the heaviest punishments.

White observers were apparently not sufficiently interested to give
accurate descriptions of this type of slave festivity. The earliest account
in print is found in the *Essai historique sur la colonie de Surinam* of
1788. The best description was by H. C. Focke, a colored lawyer
(Focke 1858). Drawings also provide some information.

The dances and songs were often composed, rehearsed, and executed
in special societies called Du, a name no longer in existence. It was
mentioned for the first time in the *Essai historique.* Comvalius ven-
tures the hypothesis that there is a relation between the terms *banya*
and *du* (Comvalius 1935/36). *Banya* designates a special type of song
and dance, which in the *du* form has been organized and dramatized.[4]
There are indications that the term *du* was used for every cultural
group, even a church choir, and was not exclusively associated with
banya.

Free colored people and slaves mixed in these societies, which
might have been the main reason why the government opposed them,
since the slave colony is essentially a two-caste society with a sharp
distinction between slaves and free people. Comvalius mentions that

---

of Cabbage"). The general meaning is that Anansi revenged himself on Cabbage.
Triplets were born in the hospital of the Creole doctor Nassy (here identified
with Anansi). A rivalry existed between him and the Dutch doctor Kool
(creolized to *koro,* "cabbage"), the director of the government hospital.
Doctor Kool ordered the triplets to be brought to his hospital, because it
was better equipped to take care of them. Doctor Nassy refused to let them go.

3. This kind of "play," as it was called in Creole, took three days. During
the first two days the slaves danced from the afternoon until the early morning.
On the third day they could rest. (Focke 1858:99).

4. Du societies carried proverbial names like Bunati gi ondrofeni (Mercy gives
experience), Paroewa prenspari (Plantation Pieterszorg is the most important),
Hati tya hebi (The heart carries a load), Pori nen no de puru geluk (A bad
name does not spoil happiness), Ondrofeni fu lobi no abi kaba (There is no end
to love's experience), Lobi Konkroe (Love's gossip). Such names are still used
for different kinds of Creole societies, and songs may refer to the name of the
society (Focke 1858:99).

after slavery the societies were sometimes hired by whites to ridicule their enemies (Comvalius 1935/36).

The dramatized *banya* is based on a simple story with fixed characters: Afrankeri, who defends high morals; Asringri, singing in honor of the band; Abenitanta or Momoi, criticising persons or events; Temeku, explaining the hidden allusions in the song; Aflaw, so shocked by the revelations that she faints; and Datra, the doctor who treats the fainting woman. The last two characters are the main actors, to whom a nurse is sometimes added. The former are primarily singers.

The complete performance easily develops into a sort of musical comedy. One of the pivots of the performance is a beautifully carved and decorated cupboard, called *kwakwa,* into which spectators are required to put their contributions.[5] In the literature, two special types of *banya* performances have been mentioned: *Bakafutu-banya* (literally "back-foot *banya*"), which has been forbidden because of pagan rituals associated with it; and *yorka-banya* (literally "ghost *banya*"), which might be executed in honor of the ancestors. It has in fact been observed that until the present time most *banya* performances have been given in honor of the ancestors. It can be said generally that the ancestor cult preserves old cultural institutions in Creole society, because the ancestors must be placated with festivities they liked most during their lives.

The *laku* has essentially the same pattern as the *banya,* but the drama is more elaborate and executed by many costumed actors, both men and women. In all probability the *laku* play is a fairly recent adaptation of a general *banya* theme; the use of the European kettle drum in the orchestra points to a recent origin. The play was performed on a number of plantations before emancipation, but the only remaining group, as far as we know, is found in Paramaribo. The songs are rendered exclusively by a solo singer and a choir of plantation women. Several characters from the *banya* also appear here, including Afrankeri, Aflaw, and Datra. The number of actors, however, is increased to include two nurses, a doctor's assistant, a lawyer, a judge, a high administrator, the crew of a ship, and a variety of Asian immigrants recently arrived on it. The activities are centered on a

5. *Banya* and *laku* dances are accompanied on a small wooden bench played with sticks, in addition to other percussion instruments. This bench is called kwakwabangi and beats out the main rhythm. The player is especially honored and referred to in these songs as *kwakwa mayoro* ("kwakwa major"). It may well be that the carved *kwakwa* derives from this musical instrument. We have seen one of the old carved *kwakwa* but never one used in a performance.

carved and decorated boat into which spectators are requested to put their contributions. Aflaw's fainting and her recovery with the help of Datra begin this drama. Aflaw faints because she is pregnant. She is examined by a nurse, who advises her to call a doctor. The plantation people try to find out who is responsible for her pregnancy, and this finally brings them to court. We find many historical details in a careful description of a recent performance in Van Renselaar 1959.

Finally, the *lobisingi* ("love songs") are a completely feminine affair. They originated after the time of slavery. The descriptions of Herskovits 1936 and Comvalius 1939 are fairly accurate. Comvalius stresses the point that the theme is often jealousy in a lesbian love affair. Lesbian love (*mati*) is more or less institutionalized in Creole society. It is quite clear, however, that heterosexual relations are also dealt with in the *lobisingi*. The wronged woman and her friends take revenge by organizing a *lobisingi* performance in the presence of the rival or in front of her house. Aflaw and Datra are again the principal actors. Songs are accompanied by a modern orchestra with brass instruments, and the melodies have become more European. There is an alternation between *langa singi* "long songs") and *koti singi* ("interrupting songs"). The two types of songs have totally different melodies and tempos. The *langa singi* show a partiality for the slow waltz rhythm and offer possibilities for improvisation. The *koti singi* are livelier and seem to have a more fixed text.

Songs 1-23 are examples of *banya*. A public performance is preceded by a private musical rehearsal (*komparsi*) and a more or less religious preparation called *opo dron* ("to start with drumming"). After this ceremony, held at the home of one of the participants, the men are asked to keep themselves *kaseri* ("ritually clean"), which means primarily that they should refrain from sexual intercourse until after the performance. Song 1 refers to this religious ceremony held at home.

All plays, and even secular dances, start with one or more songs in honor of the earth mother, called Aysa, Maysa, Wanaysa, Gronmama, and Tobosi, as in song 2. In these songs the participants ask her permission to play. In the *banya* performance this part of the play is also called *nyanfaro* (cf. song 2). The songs are not accompanied by drums. Songs 4 and 5 ask the *kwakwa mayoro,* the player of the *kwakwabangi,* a wooden bench beaten with wooden sticks, to start the drums. Song 5 refers to stories among the slaves that should now be brought into the open.

This sets into motion the next part of the performance, the *krioro*

dron, or "Creole drum," in which everyone gets the opportunity to
venture his criticism in songs of his own making. Although new
banya songs are no longer composed, one still observes a tendency
to relate songs to social events. Several examples of this type of
song are presented in this chapter. Song 6, for instance, refers to
the fact that a slave has been sent to town with the boat, so that
another man, perhaps the black overseer or *basya,* could court the
man's wife. Many of the songs treat relations between men and
women. Song 10, for example, ridicules a man who had promised
his girl friend nice presents in return for her favors but when the
traveling peddler arrived pretended to be busy catching crabs at the
mangrove forest. The allusions are often veiled, which makes interpretation extremely difficult. Not all the songs refer to special
events: songs 18, 19, and 20 apparently cover more general complaints.

Songs 21, 22, and 23 are of a special type having a long, improvised
recitativo preamble. This introduction makes it possible to adapt old
songs to new events.

Songs 24-34 are examples of *laku* songs. The *laku* group presented
here originated on the De Resolutie plantation which existed until
1886. This plantation was also called Akademi, or "Academy," because it was regarded as a model sugar plantation. The group carries
the name Pori Nem ("bad reputation"), which explains the many
allusions to bad reputation in the songs, e.g. songs 28, 30, and 31.
Allusions to bad reputation are popular in the names of other cultural
societies as well (cf. note 2). The performance opens, as in *banya,*
with a song in honor of the earth mother (song 24). *Laku* songs often
have a very abstract meaning, which again may adversely affect the
possibility of interpretation. Song 25, for instance, seems to suggest
that a human being cannot be deprived of his human dignity. Song 33
compares the lives of a white master and a slave to a boat and a
corncob floating on the water.

Song 32 gives an example of the kind of song that is associated
with the drama. Amekisani, one of the plantation women, is asked
to call on the British high commissioner (*kuli konsro,* or "Indian
consul"), who in this play helps the blacks to pay their fines. Song
34 is about the pending departure of the carved boat: it indicates that
the spectators should now offer their contributions.

Songs 35-52 are specimens of *lobisingi* but with no distinction
made between *langa singi* and *koti singi.* Songs 35 and 36 are typical
of opening songs in which all the participants and spectators are
greeted. Song 36 starts to reveal the subject of the special occasion

for the song. We have left out the many repetitions sung by the
chorus. Song 38 contains many pseudo-Dutch words with special
sexual connotations. We have tried to give as accurate an English
rendering as possible, but many of the allusions are only vaguely
known to us.

Song 51 was composed by Christina Loloba, a famous *lobisingi*
singer. She sings about her former husband, Sander, who inquired
about her present state (Comvalius 1939). Song 52 has the same kind
of slow waltz rhythm but is possibly not a real *lobisingi*. It may be
one of the songs of the famous street singer Sonde Prodo, a nickname
meaning "[dressed up in] Sunday best," who composed many songs
that are still popular. In a way, he perpetuated the *lobisingi* tradition.

Most of the songs were recorded between 1957 and 1961 by
H. C. van Renselaar and J. Voorhoeve. Songs 41, 44, and 48 are
taken from Herskovits 1936. Songs 42 and 51 are taken from Comvalius 1939. Songs 39, 40, and 42 can with slight variations also be
found in Herskovits 1936.

"Surinam dance party," by G. W. C. Voorduin.
Courtesy of the Surinam Museum, Paramaribo, Surinam.

1. Mama Aysa fu goron,
   di u kon, u no kon a yu tapu nanga tranga.
   Un burr mama,
   di u kon, u no kon a yu tapu nanga tranga.
   U seti begi na oso,
   bifo un kon dya.

2. Nyanfaro-o, Aysa, ma tide un kon begi
   mama fu gron.
   Tobosi, tide u kon begi
   goronmama.
   Ay, nanga na mama di seti u na heri Sranan.
   Na yu-o, na yu-o, u e begi-o
   mi mama, na yu mu hori en gi u-e.

3. Fosi sani mi nene leri mi, Aysa.
   Fosi sani mi nene leri mi, Aysa.
   A taki: kowru watra na krabasi,
   kindi na goron.
   A fosi sani mi nene leri mi, Aysa.

4. Mi begi a mayoro,
   hari na udu gi mi.
   Mi moy mayoro,
   Yu mu hari na udu gi mi.
   Bika mayoro,
   yu srefi sabi, te a dey opo,
   yu nen mu opo,
   di fu mi mu opo tu.
   Mi moy mayoro,
   hari na udu gi mi.

5. Kwakwamayoro, hari na udu gi mi-e.
   Kwakwamayoro, hari na udu gi mi-o.
   Bika wan taki de a nengre-oso
   disi no abi kaba.
   Mi e begi mayoro,
   hari na udu gi mi-o.

6. Sani ben abi dyendyen, a ben sa loy.
   Sani ben abi dyendyen, a ben sa loy.

1. Mama Aysa of the earth,
   in coming here we come not unannounced to you.
   Oh good mother,
   in coming here we come not unannounced to you.
   We've been in prayer at home,
   before we came to you.

2. Nyanfaro, Oh Aysa, today we come to you in prayer,
   the mother of the earth.
   Tobosi, today we come to pray to you,
   the mother of the earth.
   Yea, the mother has settled us in all Surinam.
   Thou, thou we plead,
   mother, thou must be our shield.

3. The first thing I was taught by her
      who nursed me, Aysa.
   The first thing I was taught by her
      who nursed me, Aysa.
   She said: with cool water in a calabash
   go down with your knees on the ground.
   The first thing I was taught by her
      who nursed me, Aysa.

4. I plead with you, major,
   beat the wood for me.
   Oh handsome major of mine,
   beat the wood for me.
   For as you know, my friend,
   when the day shall dawn,
   so must your name dawn too,
   and also that of mine.
   Oh handsome major of mine,
   beat the wood for me.

5. Kwakwa major, let the wood resound.
   Kwakwa major, let the wood resound.
   There's a whisper in each nigger house,
   one without an end.
   I pray with thee, Oh major mine,
   beat the wood for me.

6. Were it a bell, it would have clanged out loud.
   Were it a bell, it would have clanged out loud.

Basya seni mi na pondo,
trawan de a mi oso.
Sani ben abi dyendyen, a ben sa loy!

7. Sani de na ala presi-o, sani de a masra kamra.
Ay, ma u kon yere fa tu sisa e feti
fu wan botrobari ede.
Noya sani kon a masra kamra.
Ay, ma u kon yere fa tu meti e feti
fu wan botrobari ede.
A sani di moni bay.
Ay, ma u kon yere fa tu sisa e feti
fu wan botrobari ede.
Ay, ma kruyara de a liba tapu
di e go na wan tata yana.
A de mi mama: wani e go moro wani.

8. Sari-o, sari, u no abi fu sari.
Sari-o, sari, u no abi fu sari.
Weti bakra kon na ini pranasi,
teki lobi fu nengre.
Sari-o, sari, u no abi fu sari.

9. Te na boto sa kon,
nomo u e way anu, fu dya u de.
Te pori nen boto sa kon,
u e way anu, fu dya u de-o.
Moy Asadu sa go a foto,
go bay lafendri gi prodo uma.
U e way anu, fu dya u, de-o.

> To the pontoon[6] I'm sent by my overseer,
> another's usurped my house.
> Were it a bell, it would have clanged out loud![7]

7. What's known to everyone is also in the master's house.
   Yes, but listen how two sisters squabble
   over a butter tub.
   Now the thing has found its way
       into the master's house.
   Yes, but listen how co-wives squabble
   over a butter tub.
   A thing that money can buy.
   Come hear two sisters fighting
   over a butter tub.
   Yes, but there's a canoe on the river
   off to a cunning man.[8]
   So be it, Oh my mother: greed shall eat up greed.

8. Grief, grief, there is no need for grief.
   Grief, grief, there is no need for grief.
   To the plantation a white man came,
   conceived a love for blacks.
   Grief, grief, there is no need for grief.

9. When the boat is coming in
   we wave with our hands
       for we are here.
   When the boat of ill repute
       is coming in
   we wave with our hands
       for we are here.
   When smart Asadu goes to town
   to buy sweet smelling perfumes
       for philandering girls,
   we wave with our hands
       for we are here.

6. A pontoon is a boat used to take products from the plantation to town.
7. The general theme is also treated in an old song presented in Focke 1858:
103: "Mienéri senni mi na koemando mi libi mi hoso gi oeman. Sikápoe de
njam na ini, krabita de njam na ini, ké! Soema froedien dà hoso, meki a holi-o!"
("The master sent me to the army. I left my house to my woman. Sheep graze
there; goats graze there. Whoever got the house, let him keep it.").
8. To get some charm, to hurt the enemy.

10. A kori mi-o. Baya Kwami kori mi.
     A kori mi. Fa mi baya Yaw kori mi.
     A taki: Pagara kon,
     a e go bay koto.
     Pagara kon,
     a e go bay yaki.
     Pagara kon,
     a e go bay krara.
     Noya di pagara kon,
     mi baya go a mangro.
     —A go a mangro,
     —a go a mangro.
     —Pagara kon,
     —mi baya go a mangro.

11. Madyo mi mama, Madyo, meki a tori tan.
     Efu u taki a tori anga leti,
     a e go tyari feanti kon na ini.

12. Tetey-o, na mi e weri tetey.
     Tetey-o, na mi e weri tetey.
     Ala den trawan, den go na waka,
     den abi den koto, den abi den linga,
     den abi den krara, den abi den pangi,
     den abi den angisa, den abi den yaki.
     Tetey-o, na mi e weri tetey.
     Pe mi baya de?
     Na mi e weri tetey.

13. Baya go a foto,
     ma a adyosi a tyari kon.
     Baya Kwami go a foto,
     ma a adyosi a tyari kon.
     Tu eren, soso tu eren baya bay kon.
     —Tu eren, soso tu eren baya bay kon.

10. He's deceived me. Friend Kwami has deceived me.
    He's deceived me. God, how friend Yaw's[9] deceived me.
    He said: When the peddler comes
    a koto you will get.[10]
    When the peddler comes
    a yaki you will have.
    When the peddler comes
    some beads will be yours.
    But now that the peddler's here,
    my friend's gone off to the mangrove bush.
    To the mangrove bush he's gone.
    Off to the mangrove bush he is.
    Now that the peddler's here,
    he's off to the mangrove bush.

11. Madyo, my mother, let's not talk about it anymore.
    For if we scratch too deep,
    We'll only bring in enmity.

12. Tatters, I'm clad in tatters.[11]
    Tatters, I'm clad in tatters.
    The others go and parade,
    they have their koto, they have their rings,
    they have their chains of beads, their wraparounds,
    they have their kerchiefs and their yaki.
    Tatters, I'm clad in tatters.
    Where is my boy friend?
    I'm clad in tatters.

13. My friend has gone to town,
    returned with mere goodbyes.
    Friend Kwami's gone to town,
    came back with mere goodbyes.
    Herrings two, mere herrings two
        my friend has brought for me.
    Herrings two, mere herrings two
        my friend has brought for me.

9. Kwami and Yaw are names for men born on Saturday and Thursday, respectively.

10. *Koto* and *yaki* are parts of the traditional costume of Creole women. For a description see Herskovits 1936:3-9.

11. *Tetey* (literally "rope") is translated here as "tatters"; it could also refer to a rope around the waist, that is, to a semi-nude state.

14. Baya taki mi no mu go a doro.
    San ede mi no mu go na doro?
    Koto kon, a mi srefi bay.
    Yaki kon, a mi srefi bay.
    Pangi kon, a mi srefi bay.
    San ede mi no mu go a doro?

15. Puru mi a yu bere, moy baya,
    puru mi a yu bere.
    Puru mi a yu bere, moy baya,
    puru mi a yu bere.
    Mi go a firi kaba,
    puru mi a yu bere.
    Mi no e tyari sroto moro.
    Puru mi a yu bere, moy baya,
    puru mi a yu bere.

16. Mi mama, sortu ay na a ay disi e luku mi-e.
    Ay mi mama, sortu ay na a ay, mama, disi e waki mi.
    Kande na munkenki ana?
    Sonten na deystari ana?
    Ay mi nene, sortu ay na a ay di e waki mi-e.

17. Hura, na un ten noya.
    Hura, na un ten noya.
    Efu un wani, u e meki a bori,
    ma efu u no wani,
    u e puru en lala gi nengre.

18. O bigi mi sa meki tide.
    Bika mi tron parwa.
    Springiwatra nyan ala mi lutu kaba.
    So mi no kan meki bigi moro na grontapu.

19. Te mi masra dede, nowan yobo wani bay mi.
    Te mi masra dede, nowan masra wani bay mi.
    Na bakabaka, tanbun masra kon bay mi.
    Now dede wanwan kan bay mi.

14. My friend decreed I can't go out
    Why can't I go?
    The koto was bought by me
    The yaki was bought by me
    So was the wraparound.
    Why can't I go?

15. Be no longer mad at me, my handsome friend.
    Be no longer mad at me.
    Be no longer mad at me, my handsome friend.
    Be no longer mad at me.
    I've already been to the fields.
    Be no longer mad at me.
    I do not wear the keys any more.[12]
    Be no longer mad at me, my handsome friend.
    Be no longer mad at me.

16. Mother, what eye is it that eyes me?
    Oh mother, what eye is it
        that stares at me?
    Is it perhaps the moon?
    Perhaps the morning star?
    Oh mother, what eye is it that eyes me?

17. Hurrah, now it is our turn.
    Hurrah, now it is our turn.
    If we so wish, we'll have it cooked.
    But if we do not wish,
    We'll dish it to the negroes crude.

18. How can I still enlarge myself
    now I'm a parwa tree?[13]
    Springtides have sucked my roots.
    Foresooth I can't project myself
        as big on this world.

19. When my master passed away, no white man wanted me.
    When my master passed away, no master wanted me.
    A bad one later did.
    Now death alone wants me.

---

12. That is, "I do not wear the keys of the master's house," perhaps referring
to a sexual relation between her and the master.
13. A kind of tree, *avicennia nitida,* found at the coast.

20. A boro gron, watra lon na mi ay,
    a fadon a mi ati, a boro gron.
    A boro gron, watra lon na mi ay,
    a fadon a mi ati, a boro gron.

21. Wan dey mi go a busi,
    tyari pori nen go poti-e.
    Wan dey mi go a busi,
    tyari lagi nen go poti-e.
    Nomo mi si wan papa.
    Nomo a taki:
    Mi pikin, pe ju e go-e?
    Nomo mi piki na papa,
    taki mi e tyari pori nen go a busi-e.
    Nomo a papa taki:
    Dray baka, dray baka, mi pikin,
    tyari pori nen go na oso-o.
    Ma yu mu teki a wiwiri disi
    te yu go, fu yu wasi yu sikin.
    Ma yu sabi ofa a wiwiri nen?
    Ke mi pikin, ke ma yu sabi ofa a wiwiri nen?
    Adamakamani
    damakamani
    damakamani.
    —Na yu pori nen ini yu koroku de.

22. Te den bigi boto kon a sey broki,
    dan mi e tanapu poti mi anu a mi baka,
    dan mi e luku son-opo anga son-dongo.
    Dan mi e tanapu luku den man a tapu broki:
    someni lay den e puru nanga someni lay den e poti.
    Dan te mi kaba luku ala den tori dati,
    dan mi e denki wan libisma anga wan sipi.
    Bika wan sipi, a watra tapu a e waka, a kan sungu.

20. It has caused the earth to tremble.
    Tears streamed from my eyes.
It has caused my heart to rend,
    caused the earth to trill.
It has caused the earth to tremble.
    Tears streamed from my eyes.
It has caused my heart to rend,
    caused the earth to trill.

21. One day I went to bush
to leave a rotten name.
One day I went to bush
to leave a lowly name.
No sooner there, an old man
appeared to me and said:
Where do you go, my child?
I answered him and said:
Taking a rotten name
    to throw away in bush.
The old man then replied:
Turn back, turn back, my child.
Take home the rotten name.
But when you go, take then
this weed, and with it bathe.
But do you know its name,
child, what the weed is called?
Adamakamani,
Damakamani,
Damakamani.
Within your rotten name
    there lies your luck

22. When the big ships are moored to the quay,
there I stand, hands on my hips,
from sunup till sundown.
There I stand, scanning all the men
    busy on the quay.
They hauled in such a load,
    discharged, discharged so much.
And when I'm finished seeing all,
I see in such a ship a man.
For sink can a ship which sails,
    on the water it can sink.

Ke, wan libisma e waka a doti tapu, a kan dede.
Ma toku a lay di wan sipi e tyari-oy,
a lay di wan sipi e tyari-e,
a lay di wan sipi e tyari,
a moro furu moro di fu wan libisma.
Ma toku na di fu wan libisma moro ebi.
Ma toku a di fu libisma moro ebi-oy.
Toku a di fu libisma moro ebi.
Bika na lay fu den sipi, na soso isri nanga siton.
Ma ke, di fu mi mama anga di fu mi tata,
dati na nowtu anga sari fu grontapu libi.
—A puru lay-o, a puru lay-e.
—A puru lay-o, a puru lay-o.
—Wan boto kon a sey broki,
—A puru lay, te a puru lay kaba.
—Ma san ati e tyari, dati no abi kaba-e.

23. A di masra Gado ben meki grontapu-o,
a ben meki kaw nanga sikapu
poti na ini grontapu.
A ben kari kaw, a taki:
Kaw, yu kan teki san yu wani.
Kaw luku lontu na ini ala den sani
di masra Gado poti.
A feni lobi fu ay.
A teki ay, moro bigi ay,
poti na en fesi.
Ma kaba di masra Gado kari sikapu, a taki:
Sikapu, yu na moro pikinwan moro kaw,
ma yu kan teki san yu wani toku,
di kaw kaba teki ala bigi san a lobi.
Nomo skapu teki barba,
a poti en na en kakumbe ondro.
Dan a poti barba na en kakumbe ondro.
Dan ala suma kon teri skapu
fu a moro hey meti di de a grontapu.

Oh man dwells on this solid earth,
 but die, but die he can.
 For he is but a man.
Yet the load a ship conveys
Yet the load a ship conveys
Yet the load a ship conveys
is so much more than that of man.
Yet heavier is the human load.
Yet heavier is the human load.
Yet heavier is the human load.
For iron and stone a ship conveys,
but all that of my ma and pa
are of distress and grief
 and of this earthly life.
—It has discharged its load.
—It has discharged its load.
—A boat is anchored near the quay.
—It has discharged its load.
 It has no more a load.
—But Oh the loads of hearts
 go on without an end.

23. When Lord the God the earth did make,
 he made a cow, a goat,
 then put them on this earth.
 To him the cow he called and said:
 Take that which you want here.
 Cow looked around
 all things on earth,
 his eye fell on an eye.
 He took the eye, the biggest eye
 and placed it in his face.
 Then Lord the God the goat did call
  and said to him:
 Though you are small compared to cow,
 take that which you want here.
 Cow has already taken his,
  the thing most craved by him.
 Then took for him the goat a beard
 and placed it on his jaw.
 And placed it on his jaw.
 Then honored all the men the goat
 the highest thing on earth.

Dan kaw ati bron.
We ma di kaw ati bron,
skapu ben tagi en, a taki:
Leki fa yu bigi, yu gersi pikin fu asaw,
yu a wan bigi man efu wan bigi uma.
Ma toku a pikin fasi
di masra Gado poti mi,
dan mi srefi abi mi bigi,
na mi fasi.
Ma o o, meki mi tagi yu, masra kaw,
taki yu abi yu bigi memre
na yu fasi,
ma mi pikin skapu a no yu boy.
—San mi wani mi kan du-e.
—San mi wani mi kan du.
—San mi wani mi kan du.
—Mi wan bigi uma de a mi oso.
—San mi wani mi kan du-e.

24. Kowru watra na krabasi, mi mama-o,
    nanga kindi na goron, Maysa.
    So u e begi na doti dya,
    dan u e begi
    u mama na ini Akademi-o.

25. Mi na kakafowru, kron de a mi ede.
    Mi na kakafowru, mi kron de a mi ede.
    Kaba wansi nefi de a mi neki,
    mi kron de a mi ede.

26. Ma malengri poti mi-o fu oloysi-o.
    Tide malengri poti mi-o fu oloysi.
    Te gusonteit go a waka, mi e go teri na yuru
    taki na yuru-o.

This roused the ire of the cow.
And when the goat saw this,
he spoke to cow and said:
You've always been so big to me,
    you're an elephant's baby, I'm sure,
a portentous one to me.
Yet within the small confines
which God has granted me,
I chose my greatness too
in manner known to me.
But Oh, but Oh, Lord Cow,
    take this from me, my friend:
You lust for power too
in manner known to you.
I am a little goat,
    no boy to you I am.
—That which I want I can.
—That which I want I can.
—That which I want I can.
—Know you that in my house
    I am a grownup too.
—That which I want I can.

24. Cold water in a calabash, my mother.
    Knees on the earth, Maysa.
    Thus we pray to the earth,
    pray to our mother
    on Academy.

25. I am a cock
        with a crown on my head.
    I am a cock
        my crown is on my head.
    Though a knife be on my throat,
    my crown is on my head.

26. This incapacity of mine
        has drawn my mind to concentrate on time.
    Today this sickness of mine
        has drawn my mind to concentrate on time.
    When good health departs from me,
        the hours I count
    become an hour.

27. Na dungru oso ini wani no dape.
    Na ini dungru oso ini wani no dape.
    Sisa Elena,
    ma efi yu meki wani,
    den e buy yu a yu futu.

28. Waka libi go, waka leri kon kaba-o.
    Waka libi go, waka leri kon kaba.
    Na ini Pori Nen ini ondrofeni
    gi mi wan bangi, mi sidon.

29. Mi naw frenti-o na mi tollenaar.
    Mi beste kompe dati na mi moordenaar-o.
    Kaba mi eygi bere famiri ala de na ini-o.

30. Ke ma mi iti mi neti-o a liba-o.
    Tide mi iti mi srepi-o na watra.
    Kaba mi kisi tu fisi: wan na koroku,
    wan na pori nen.

31. Lagi nen fu kondre na mi gowtu keti-o.
    Pori nen fu kondre na mi fingalinga,
    na mi gowtu keti-o di mi e weri na neki-o.

32. Amekisani-o, go teki mi konsro gi mi-o.
    Boketi Tanta, go piki konsro gi mi-o,
    taki mi yuru kon kaba,
    nomo mi wani si mi boto, pe a de.

33. Watra lolo sipi-o, san a kartiki-o.

27. In the jail you cannot voice your wish.
    In the jail you cannot voice your wish,
    Sister Helena.
    But if you voice your wish,
    your feet they cast in chains.

28. Living just so has now ended,
        knowledge has arrived.
    Living just so has now ended,
        knowledge has arrived.
    In Pori Nen[14] knowledge gave me
    a bench on which to sit.

29. My close friend is a traitor,
    My best pal a murderer.
    My family from my own womb
        they're party to it all.

30. Oh I cast my net in the river.
    My net in the water I cast.
    And lo behold two fishes:
        of happiness
    and ill repute.

31. A base name in this world
        to me is a golden chain.
    A rotten name in this world
        to me is a signet ring,
    a chain of gold round my neck.

32. Amekisani-o, go fetch my Konsro.[15]
    Boketi Tanta, go tell my Konsro
    that the hour has come.
    And I will see my boat,
        see where it is now.

33. If waters cause a ship to undulate,
        what then with you, Oh mealiecob.

14. Pori Nem(Spoiled name) is the name of the *laku* group in which the song
has been recorded.
15. Amekisani, meaning "She made things," and Konsro, or "consul," are two
characters in the *laku* play. See the introduction to this chapter. Amekisani is also
called Boketi Tanta ("She who takes care of the flowers"), or Tanta (see song 34).

Watra lolo sipi-o, san a kartiki-o.
Kaba libi hebi gi weti yobo, ma mi nengre.

34. Poti faya, man, poti un faya.
Un sutu faya, man, un sutu un faya.
Tanta, boto de na sey now,
ma un boto wani gowe.

35. Odi-odi, odi-odi, ala frankeri misi,
ma dan sosrefi mi bari mi bakaman wan odi.
Ma dan sosrefi mi bari mi bakaman wan odi,
ma dan sosrefi mi de bari ala den heer odi,
Ma dan sosrefi mi de bari ala den heer odi,
ma dan sosrefi mi de bari mi moy datra odi.
Ma na sosrefi mi de bari mi moy datra odi,
ma dan sosrefi mi de bari mi Afraw odi, misi.

36. Odi-odi, odi-odi, mi fariasi bakaman,
so wi e bari wan odi, mi fariasi bakaman.
So mi e bari wan odi gi mi beweygi bakaman,
so mi e bari wan odi gi ala den kompe na lontu.
Mi fariasi bakaman, mi moymoy fu lobi,
so mi tyari wan moy tori, mi fariasi bakaman.
So mi tyari wan moy tori, mi beweygi bakaman,
ma na tori e go dini fu mi eygi srefi.
So na tori e go dini fu mi eygi srefi,
sosrefi a tori e go dini fu mi anga wan seyker lobi.
Wan dey mi sidon na mofo mi doro, mi beweygi bakaman,
nomo wan doyfi frey pasa, a iti wan brifi gi mi.

If waters cause a ship to undulate,
    what then with you, Oh mealiecob.
If life presses the white man down,
    what then for me, a negro boy.

34. Light the fire, man, light your fire.
    Let it blaze, man, let it blaze.
    Tanta, the boat is at the quay
    and shortly it will go.

35. Howdy, howdy, howdy, howdy, my pretty ladies.
    But also you I greet my bakaman.[16]
    But also you I greet my bakaman.
    To all the men, I greetings call.
    To all the men, I greetings call.
    But also you I greet, my handsome doctor.
    But also you I greet, my handsome doctor.
    To you, my Aflaw greetings do I call.

36. Howdy, howdy, howdy, howdy,
    my variable bakaman.
Thus do we call greetings
    my variable bakaman.
Thus do I call a greeting
    to my versatile bakaman.
Thus I call a greeting
    to all friends around.
My variable bakaman,
    sugarpie of love.
Thus I come with a nice tale
    my variable bakaman.
Thus I come with a nice tale
    my variable bakaman.
But I'm the theme of this tale.
But I'm the theme of this tale,
and a certain loved one too.
On a day I sat in the door,
    my versatile bakaman.
Just then a dove came by.
    A letter he dropped to me.

---

16. *Bakaman* ("standby") is the principal helper of the singer in the play.

So mi teki na brifi, mi broko leysi,
ma na brifi ben skrifi nanga Hebrewse letter,
so mi bari wan lafu, dan mi leysi a brifi.
Dan na brifi warskow mi, mi beweygi bakaman,
a taki: na lobi di yu abi, dan yu mu koni anga a lobi,
bika a wani poti yu a sodro, a puru trapu na ondro.

37. Mi e go pakti wan gron, ala misi,
fu mi kan prani mi aleysi na ini,
fu mi fowru kan feni bun nyanyan.
Bakaman,
yere san tyagotyakon-man de haksi mi:
te mi gi den fowru na nyanyan,
dan san mi e libi den fu soso?
Dan yu mu yere san mi e go piki den,
taki: opo go wroko, un lesiman,
dan un sa weri bigi koto leki mi,
dan un fowru tu sa feni bun nyanyan.

38. Mi yere wan apskraps e kosi mi,
ma a no frede mi frede fu piki den,
ma mi no sta gelijke nanga den,
bika en na tigri, mi a tamanua,
dan mi e go si o-letiwan kan gi abra.
Baka so kronkron leki di mi de,
ma dan tussen fu lobi mi abi.
So wayway leki di mi de,
ma gemaakte fu a libi mi abi.
Dan fosi a masra fasi mi,
dan mi sabi a tussen di mi mu du.

I picked the letter up,
 opened it, and read.
Alas, in Hebrew it was.
In laughter I burst out,
 then read this letter of mine.
A warning it had for me,
 my versatile bakaman.
It said: that love of yours,
 beware, beware of it.
He'll put you in a loft
 and scuttle the ladder away.

37. I shall rent a farm, all my madames,
 plant it full with rice,
 have good grain for my chickens.
 Bakaman!
 Listen, what the loafers ask me!
 When I've fed the birds,
 what will be left for them?
 Listen, friend, to what I answer then:
 Sluggards, go and work.
 Then you'll also wear a koto
  just like that of mine,
 Then you'll also give some good food
  to your birds around.

38. I heard an apskraps[17] revile me.
 But I'm not scared to answer,
 for I'm not on the same par with her.
 She is a tiger,
  an anteater am I.
 Let's see who succumbs first.
 For crooked though I am,
 I'm sated with love in between.
 Lightweight that I am,
 but the pleasures of life are in me.
 And before his hands touched me
 I knew I was to yield
  the in between to him.

---

17. *Apskraps* possibly refers to leftovers in a pot that are thrown away and is a derogatory term (cf. Dutch *afkrapsel*). The poem is loaded with Dutch words used in a very abnormal way.

Dan wansi a meid e kosi mi,
dan tussen fu lobi mi abi,
gemaakte fu lobi mi abi.
Dan mi no abi nèks te make anga misi.
So kronkron leki di mi di,
so wayway leki di mi de,
dan tussen fu lobi mi abi.

39. Fa yu kan taki mi no moy?
    Na tu bromki meki mi.
    Rosekunop na mi mama,
    Stanfaste na mi papa.
    Fa yu kan taki mi no moy?
    Na tu bromki meki mi.

40. Mi gudu, tranga lobi sondro noti,
    a de gi fruferi.
    Ma a kon gersi wan roos
    di no abi smeri.

41. Mi lobi libi mi.
    —Libi en, meki a go.
    —Bika yu na banketi,
    —yu de na batra.
    —Trawan sa bay yu.
    —Libi en, meki a go.
    —Trawan sa bay yu.

42. Efi wan lobi ben lobi mi,
    a no lobi mi moro,
    mi no kan kiri mi srefi
    fu dati ede.

43. Efu mi lasi mi moy lobi,
    mi no lasi noti.

Tho' the wench reviles me now,
I'm sated with love in between,
and know all the tricks in the trade.
No truck with that woman I have.
For crooked as I am,
for lightweight as I am,
I'm sated with love in between.

39. How can you say I am not fair?
Two flowers gave birth to me.
My mother is a rosebud.
Everlasting is my pa.
How can you say I am not fair?
Two flowers gave birth to me.

40. My love, tempestuous love
with nothing more to do,
will but provide inertia.
It is but like a rose
which has no smell.

41. My love has flown away.
—Let him be, let him be.
—For you are
—a cookie in a jar.[18]
—Some other will you buy.
—Let him be, let him be.
—Some other will you buy.

42. If my love
who loved me
loves me no more,
I cannot die
for this alone.

43. If I forgo my pretty love,
I have not lost a thing.

---

18. This is a reference to cookies in a jar, which are highly prized and placed out of reach of the common visitor. Cf. Herskovits 1936:28. The song is based on a proverb: *Mi na banketi na batra: wan no wani mi, trawan sa bay mi* ("I am a cookie in a jar: one does not want me, the other will buy me"). Some people add a second strophe with the following lines: *Mi lasi wan apra, ma mi feni wan figa* ("I lost an apple, but I found a fig").

Ma efu mi lasi mi gusontu,
mi no warti moro.
Efu mi lasi mi moy gudu,
mi no abi trobi.
Ma efu mi lasi mi gusontu,
mi no warti moro.

44. Yu moy moro mi,
yu fatu moro mi,
ma mi switi moro yu.
Dati ede meki
gudu-gudu no kan ferdwal
fu libi switi roos
fu kon na krabu Dinki oso.

45. Eri grontapu de bari ondrufeni fu lobi,
ma mi dati mi de bari ondrufeni fu libi.
Ondrufeni ondrufeni fu den akwabutuman:
den de nyan nanga mi, den abi mi sani fu taki.

46. Mi ben sweri fu Gado, mi no o lobi moro,
ma mi go agen.
Dan mi weri patapata, dan mi e trapu taki,
ma mi go agen.
Mi donke nebermind ba, mi no frede noti,
ma mi go agen.
Ma mi weri braka susu, dan mi e trapu taki,
dan mi go agen.

But if I lose my health anon,
I have lost all that's dear.
If I forgo my pretty dove,
I do not miss a thing.
But if I lose my health anon,
I have lost all that's dear.

44. Thou art more lovely than I am,
and fuller than I am.
But I am sweeter than thou art.
Therefore my sweetheart
will not stray,
abandon his sweet rose,
and go to crab Dinki.[19]

45. The whole world cries out
for experience in love.
But I, in contrast, ask
for experience in life.
Experience! Experience!
and with the thankless ones
who profit and betray
while supping with me
and talk behind my back.

46. By God, I swore,
I will not love again.
Alas, I fell into the trap anew.
I wear my patapata,[20]
trample on all rumors.
Alas, I fell into the trap anew.
I cast all caution to the wind.
Alas, I fell into the trap anew.
I put on black shoes,
trample on all rumors.
Alas, I fell into the trap anew.

---

19. Herskovits 1936 (p. 26) remarks: "Our informant states that the girl's name was Dina, hence Dinki is a play on her name; while for 'crab' any animal may be substituted, the choice being left to the fancy of the singer." The choice of this animal recalls the expression *law krabu* ("crazy crab"), which is also used for a girl who cannot control her sexual desires.

20. *Patapata* is a kind of cheap cotton shoe.

47. Na eri dey a e bari fa en lobi switi,
    dan mi no e piki en.
    Ma di mi meki a frigiti,
    dan mi go tesi lobi,
    dan mi no e libi en.
    A no fu gowtu moni, a no fu sorfru moni,
    dan mi no e libi en.

48. Moy misi, fa mi mu libi?
    Gowtu keti na yu neki
    a de meki kamalama.
    Tranga lobi na wan sani . . .
    waka go, na wan dey blaw bromki.
    A no langa, a no langa.
    Switi lobi na wan sani.

49. Pikin uma, fyofyo seni kon tagi yu,
    taki wan nyun yari opo
    fu yu mu tyari yu deken go wasi.
    Ma dan so efu yu no kan wasi en,
    wakti te doti wagi e kon pasa,
    ma dan yu saka yu deken na ini,
    dan u e bari ipipi-ure.
    Bigi deken e go na Branspen.
    Bari ipipi-ure.

50. Broyn misi, wan seyker dey mi e kon pasa,
    nomo tu doti pikin uma e kosi mi.
    Dan mi no dray me fesi fu mi luku den.
    Gudu, mi sabi san de a mi ede.

47. The whole day long he brags to me,
    his love is so sweet,
but I speak not a word to him.
    No answer does he get.
But just when it had slipped his mind,
then tasted I his love,
won't ever let it go.
No matter how much gold or coins,
I'll never let it go.

48. Oh lovely one, how will I live?
The golden chain
kamalamas round your pretty neck.[21]
Strong love is something . . .
transient
    like unto a small flower
    blue on a day.
It is ephemeral. It is ephemeral.
Sweet love is something else.

49. Woman of no significance,
fleas for you the new year herald:
go and wash your filthy blanket.
But if this prove not possible,
then you should wait for the garbage truck
and chuck your blanket there.
And we will shout, hip, hip, hoorah,
big blanket is off to the dumping hole.
Yell hip, hip, hoorah.

50. Oh bronze maiden,
    on a day I came along,
Lo and behold! two filthy sluts
    reviling me at once.
I did not turn my head
    or look.
Dear bronze maiden mine,
    I know the thoughts I have.

---

21. *Kamalama* is a onomatopoeic verb describing the tinkling of the golden chain. The word is also used in song 32 of chapter 2.

Dan mi no dray mi fesi fu mi luku den.
Bika a no kisi wan wiki na baka,
luku, en pikin tatay na en anu.
Mi gudu, en pikin tatay na en anu,
leki den e seni sikiman go a Syatrion.
En pikin tatay na en anu.

51. Wan lage karakter meki ondrosuku
pe mi de, fa mi tan,
pe mi de, fa mi tan.
A no yere mi nen, a no de si mi persoon,
ofa mi tan.
Nanga mi broko koto en mi doti yaki,
so mi de, so mi de, so mi tan.
Mi no kon moro hey, mi no kon moro lage:
so mi de, so mi tan.

52. San yu e luku mi?
San yu e waki mi?
Mi a no paarderij,
mi a no payasiman.
San yu e luku mi?
San yu e waki mi?
Mi a no paarderij, payasiman.
Mi no e nyan fu yu.
Mi no e dringi fu yu.
San yu e luku mi?
San yu e waki mi?
Mi no e nyan fu yu.
Mi no e dringi fu yu.
Mi a no paarderij, payasiman.

I did not turn my head
 or look.
For lo! a week from thence,
behold there in her hand
 her earthly goods I see.
Behold there in her hand
 her earthly goods I see.
Like afflicted off to Chatillon,[22]
carting a bundle small
 clutched in their hands.

51. A vile one let out feelers
how I'm faring now,
how I'm faring now.
He has not heard my name,
 seen me not alive,
knows not how I fare.
With my tattered koto dress,
 with my unwashed yaki dress,
So fare I now, so fare I now.
I haven't become any higher,
I haven't become any lower.
So fare I now, so fare I now.

52. Why do you look at me?
Why do you stare at me?
I am no circus to you.
I am no clown to you.
Why do you look at me?
Why do you stare at me?
I am no circus clown.
I do not eat your food.
I do not drink your wine.
Why do you look at me?
Why do you stare at me?
I do not eat your food.
I do not drink your wine.
I am no circus clown.

22. Châtillon is a former plantation on the Surinam River, which since 1897
has become an institution for lepers.

CHAPTER 2

Folksongs (Religious Songs, Play Songs, Dance Tunes)

A sharp distinction between the different genres of songs cannot be drawn, due mainly to the fact that children's songs, if old enough, can be used in the ancestor cult to please the *yorka* ("ancestral spirits")[1] and that dance bands use all kinds of materials, including Christian and non-Christian religious songs that may even be featured on the local hit parade. This use of old religious songs for modern dancing usually entails drastic changes in the rhythmic and even the melodic patterns of the original songs.

The non-Christian, or so-called "pagan" religion of Surinam has not yet been described in full, although Herskovits 1936 gives some useful indications of it. Marked African and Amerindian influences are present. Most river deities are of Amerindian descent and their worshippers even use Indian languages for cultic purposes. Many other gods can be traced back to African rituals and African words are used in their cult language. There are striking resemblances to religious cults in Haiti and Brazil, which were formed under approximately the same conditions. However, unlike the latter, they show no clear signs of syncretism. The Christian and non-Christian religions seem to coexist rather peacefully, although practised by the same people. Important officials of the non-Christian religion may even occupy key posts in the Christian church. There is no general feeling that the two religions exclude one another, although the official view of the church is different.[2]

The present system in Surinam must be the product of fairly recent developments. In nineteenth-century accounts, the dancing of *watra mama* ("the water mother") is described as violent and even dangerous, whereas in present-day local folklore *watra mama* seems to be a rather harmless creature. The *gronmama,* or "earth mother," and *kromanti* (a group of African gods) are much more

1. See chapter 1 for comments on the ancestor cult.
2. Herskovits 1937 (pp. 292-99) had similar facts in mind when he coined the term *socialized ambivalence.* Not only in religion but also in marriage customs, linguistic behavior, and other spheres of daily life, a Creole seems to have a quasi-free choice between two totally different sets of human behavior patterns. Cf. Introduction.

important in contemporary religion. In former times there was some specialization on different plantations. The local priest achieved some fame for curing specific illnesses or organizing specific cults. Fairly recent urbanization has nearly destroyed this geographic diversity. Successful specialists tend to go to town to earn more money. Town rituals therefore have acquired a rather baroque appearance and may extend over several days.

Religious diversity may even become a matter of personal taste. The younger generation in Paramaribo shows a marked preference for the *kromanti* gods and does not seem interested in other rituals. Boys and girls, mostly teenagers, arrive very late at the ceremony, after midnight, when the *kromanti* gods are about to put in an appearance. They at once take over control from the older people, who gradually retire. The violent *kromanti* dances seem to offer a useful outlet for repressed aggression.

The non-Christian religion centers on two basic concepts: *winti* literally "wind" but indicating the gods, and *kra,* or "soul." The high god or creator is called Anana and is not regarded as a *winti.* He reigns over the whole creation, including the *winti.* Anana is always mentioned in prayers, especially in the final formula *na nen fu Anana* ("in the name of Anana"). There exist no songs in his honor,[3] nor will anyone become possessed by him. Human beings can reach him only through the intervention of the *winti.*

There are a great many *winti,* and they are grouped in several distinct pantheons. It is not entirely clear, however, how many separate pantheons there are and which gods belong to which. During a *winti* ceremony, the *winti* may take possession of a human being and completely change his personality. They are, however, invoked in a certain fixed order. First, the earth deities, headed by Aysa or Wanaysa, the earth mother, are called upon, then Loko, Leba, and others. The snake god Fodu, also called Dagwe or Papawinti, comes last in this group; it is not quite clear whether he heads a separate pantheon or should be included in the range of earth deities. After a short pause follow the river deities, especially the Indian gods. They are also invoked in a certain fixed order, starting with the deities of the Commewijne River. Finally, in the very early morning, come the *kromanti,* who seem to consist of African gods

3. Some informants stated that church hymns must be regarded as songs in honor of Anana. This may indicate that a certain degree of syncretism is found at the very base of the system. I once heard a 'pagan' priest cite the Bible as *a buku fu Anana* ("the book of Anana").

only.[4] This is the general outline of a *winti* dance in Paramaribo, as far as I could distinguish. The only exception is that sometimes a special dance is organized for the so-called *tapu kromanti*, or "sky *kromanti*," on Saturday afternoon. I am, however, fully aware of the possibility that I could have missed some distinctions.[5]

Winti performances are prohibited by law. Adherents therefore perform their rituals in special places off the main roads around the capital. The prohibition has also given rise to performances in disguise, sometimes as a costume ball (*bar maske*), to which participants wear costumes of their *winti*. Even more disguised are apparently ordinary dance parties where the brass band plays exclusively *winti* songs in the given order, allowing the dancers to become possessed in a discreet manner. It must be said, however, that the law against pagan rituals is no longer enforced. Performances have increasingly moved back into town. The people have also become aware of the cultural value of the *winti* songs and dances. Choirs include them in their repertories, and *winti* dances are even shown on stage. In general, people no longer feel the need to hide the "pagan" background.

The other main concept in the non-Christian religion is the *kra*, a more or less personified soul concept.[6] The *kra* can be consulted when its bearer does not feel well. There are special divination rituals used to arrive at the right diagnosis and the right treatment. The dividing line between non-Christian and Christian religions is much thinner here. The *kra* often asks for a church service and seems to love church hymns in general.

We have excluded official church hymns from this anthology, although they are very popular among Creoles. The hymns are mostly translated from German, Dutch, or English sources. There are, how-

4. Fodu, the Indian gods, and the *kromanti* gods each have a different cult language in which certain key words in common Creole are replaced by secret words of Amerindian or African descent (Voorhoeve 1969).

5. Herskovits 1936 made a distinction between sky gods (including Anana and the *tapu kromanti*), earth deities, river gods (mainly Indians), *kromanti*, and bush gods. He is partly followed by Wooding 1970, who makes a distinction between sky gods (*tapu kromanti*, but this category in fact includes all *kromanti*), earth deities, river gods, and bush gods. In a private discussion Wooding suggested that I might have missed the transition in the ritual order between *kromanti* and bush gods, which would be difficult to observe.

6. Herskovits 1936 (p. 44): "Of all supernatural forces which govern the destiny of the individual, none surpasses the role of the *akra*, —the soul—in determining that destiny." In the following pages Herskovits presents a rather complete and accurate description of soul ceremonies. Most Creoles regard other terms like *dyodyo* and *se* as alternative words for the same concept. Specialists, however, make a distinction.

ever, a few unofficial Christian songs that are not sung during church services and seem to have a genuine Creole origin. They are often performed at birthday parties or other informal gatherings, for instance at the weekly meeting of the so-called *begi,* a local prayer group.

Play songs are of a different nature. The *susa* is a play for adult men in which the players face each other. One person has to imitate the steps of the other. When he has been tricked into making a wrong step, his place is taken by another.[7] The songs often treat relations between men and women, just as in the *banya,* but from the male point of view. *Kangga* songs are children's play songs (Comvalius 1946).

The *kawna* was originally danced in a counterclockwise circle. The songs are accompanied by a special kind of drum, beaten with a stick and hand, and by a quatro (a small guitar). A voice sings the melody. *Kawna* songs are also performed by modern bands with brass instruments, in which case the dance is executed in pairs and called *kaseko.*

Songs 1-11 are *winti* songs evoking the different *winti* in the right order: Loko, an earth deity, in song 1; Fodu, the snake god, in songs 2-5; different Indian gods (river deities) in songs 6-10; *kromanti* in song 11. Song 12 is also of a religious nature and generally called a *Soko psalm* ("Soko hymn"). It may have a Moslem background. We were unable to obtain many examples of this type of song, which is executed without drums. Its words are largely unfamiliar to the singers. The line *mi na Kabre* ("I am a *Kabre*") could indicate a tribe in northern Togo or a very old *yorka* ("ancestor spirit"), sometimes called *kabra yorka.* A Chokosi informant from northern Togo translated the line *santre fa nyuma* as "Santre has got me today." He suggested that the song might be the complaint of a Cabrais slave (Cabrais refers to a tribe in northern Togo). Song 13 is in honor of the ancestors. Song 14 is the only recorded example of a song in honor of the *kra.*

Songs 15-20 are Christian songs of the sort not tolerated in church. Those reproduced here are almost all the songs of this type that we were able to find. Song 20 shows by its opening lines that this kind of song is used at birthday parties, even if the content does not seem to fit. Songs 21-25 are *susa* songs. Songs 26-30 are children's play songs, of which 29 and 30 are generally called *kangga.* Song 26 is used by children as a means of counting before they start to play.

7. A description of the *susa* play can be found in Comvalius 1922. I have seen *susa* only when played in honor of the ancestors. The play does not seem popular in town any more.

The interpretation of song 26 presents serious difficulties, as is so often the case in children's songs. Comvalius 1938 has given a historical explanation based mainly on the identification of Perun with the historical figure Peronne, commander of the fortress dominating the Surinam and Commewijne rivers. However, one must stretch too many details to fit this conception. A general weakness of this kind of historical explanation is that one has to assume that the colonial wars of the European nations made a big impression on the slaves, which does not often seem to have been the case. One of the biggest difficulties is the interpretation of the first line. Comvalius interprets the first occurrence of *sin* as a variant of *sibi,* a term of address between slaves who were transported on the same ship or worked on the same plantation, and the second occurrence of *sin* as a variant form of *se* ("sea"). The Englishmen in the fourth line would in that case be English invaders. Clearly related children's play songs have been found on Curaçao, though they might best be regarded as corruptions of this Surinam song, because their interpretation in terms of Papiamentu (the local Spanish-based creole of Curaçao) presents even more problems. As the word *sin* does not mean anything in Creole, it is probably a name. A great many alternative interpretations offer themselves in that case. We will mention only two. *Sin* could be regarded as a creolization of the Indian name *Singh,* in which case the song deals with early racial tensions between British Indians and Creoles. *Sin* could also be the name of a ship; around 1825 there was an English steamer bearing the name *Seine,* actually pronounced "sin," that regularly visited the Caribbean.

Songs 27 and 28 are sung while a stone is passed around. Song 27 recalls the times of slavery: a child is flogged by the overseer because he has failed to fill his basket. Songs 31-34 are short dance tunes. Songs 35 and 36 are ballads of the gold diggers and balata bleeders. Song 37 is a ballad that goes back to the days of slavery.

Most of the songs were recorded by H. C. van Renselaar and J. Voorhoeve between 1957 and 1961. Song 36 was recorded by U. M. Lichtveld in 1970. Song 37 was found in Hoëvell 1854, 2:54-56.

1. Loko, mi kanti.
   Wanaysa, kari a boy
   kon opo mi.

2. Mi a no legwana,
   mi a no legwana,
   mi na papa gado.
   Mi a no legwana,
   mi na papa winti.
   Mi a no legwana.

3. Someni langa mi wani kon dya,
   ma agida no ben de.
   Aye, ayo,
   agida no ben de.

4. Fodu dede, ma a de.
   Yu kapu en nanga howru,
   ma a de.
   Yu naki en nanga tiki,
   ma a de.
   Fodu dede, ma a de.

5. Dagwe peni weti-o.
   Fa a moy te.
   Peni weti-o.
   Fa a moy te.

6. Ala den ingi, kon na dan.
   Ala den mati, kon na dan.
   Kon na dan, kon na dan.
   Ala den ingi, kon masi agida.

7. Mi no e trobi den, ba,
   mi no e meri den.

1. Loko, I am sagging,
    Wanaysa, summon your aide
    ro raise me anew.

2. No iguana am I,
    no iguana am I,
    the snake god I am.
    No iguana am I,
    the snake's spirit I am.
    No iguana am I.

3. For all too long I yearned to come,
    agida[8] was not there.
    Aye, ayo,
    agida was not there.

4. Voodoo snake god is now dead,
        dead and yet alive.
    Chop him down with a machete.
    He will still remain.
    Beat him with a stick.
    He'll remain alive.
    Snake god is now dead,
        dead and yet alive.

5. Dagwe is spotted white.
    How very pretty is he.
    He is a spotted white.
    How very pretty is he.

6. All ye Indian gods,
        haste thee to the place.
    All ye Indian friends,
        haste thee to the place.
    To the place, to the place,
        haste thee.
    All ye Indian gods,
        come, beat the drum.

7. I do not disturb them, friend,
    I do not touch them at all.

---

8. *Winti* dances are performed to the basic rhythm beaten on the *agida* drum
and the *kwakwa* bench.

Sramakaliba mi de,
Hamborgu mofo mi de.
Mi no e meri den, ba,
na den e trobi mi.

8. Mi na broko kurkuru,
mi de go nanga frudu,
mi de kon nanga fara.
Bosugwaragwara,
bosugwara dyaruma.

9. Eru eru, ma fu sowan libi,
Eru eru, ma fu sowan libi.
Mi na eru gado, mi na Ganggaso.
Eru eru, ma fu sowan libi.

Efu a bun na yu, dan a sa bun na mi.
Efu a bun na yu, dan a sa bun na mi.
Efu goron boro, mi no de na ini.
Efu mama dede, mi no sabi.

10. Arwaka taki, a tori kaba;
ma Kribisi bari, a de ete.
Ingi-o akaya,
mi koni moro den ala.

11. San komopo a nengre kondre?
San komopo a farawe?

12. A ningi ningi ningi ningi,
mi na Kabre.
Busmu.
Mi na Kabre.

At Saramacca River am I.
I face Hamburg plantation.[9]
I do not touch them, friend,
I am disturbed by them.

8. I am a basket torn apart.
I ride on the flow,
recede with the ebb.
Bosugwaragwara,
bosugwara dyaruma.[10]

9. Sorrow! But what a life!
Sorrow! But what a life!
I am the sorrow god, I'm Ganggaso.
Sorrow, sorrow! But what a life!

If you think it's good for you, so will it be.
If you think it's good for you, so will it be.
When grounds vibrate, I am not there.
When mother is no more, I know no way.

10. The Arawak has a saying,
the story has run its course.
The Carib goes on calling,
the story is still there.
Oh Indians, ouch!
I'm cleverer than them all.

11. What has arisen
from the black man's land?
What has arisen
from afar?

12. A ningi ningi ningi ningi,
I am a Kabre.
Busmu.
I am a Kabre.

9. It is said that this special *winti* is present in a log floating on the Saramacca River in the vicinity of the Hamburg plantation.

10. Lines without special meaning are left untranslated in the text. They are quite numerous in *winti* songs and popular children's play songs. These lines may contain special cult words or corruptions of expressions in Indian or African languages.

A santre fa nyuma.
A mi na Kabre.

13. O di fu Sranan moro,
    di fu Sranan moro.
    Nowtu de na ala kondre,
    ma di fu Sranan moro,
    di fu Sranan moro.

14. Pimpana pimpa na popo-e,
    mi e begi akara.
    Pimpana pimpa na popo yanda,
    mi e begi akara.

15. Kuneti alamal,
    Kuneti, sribi bun.
    Mi poti mi ede
    na Masra futu sey
    Mi lobi en sote,
    ma en lobi moro mi.
    Kuneti,
    Kuneti, sribi bun.

16. Engelsten ben tyari
    wan nyun boskopu kon:
    te na ini baki
    wan nyun pikin didon.
    Glori haleluya, glori haleluya,
    yere san pasa.

17. Wan bun bigi feest ben de na Nazareth,
    —Nazareth—
    di na koning ben kon.
    O mi yas, mi yas,
    singi tapu kaba.

18. Di Moses teki a tiki,
    a naki a tapu a watra,
    a watra kon makandra,
    —Haleluya.
    O di tambak tambak tambak
    O di tambak tambak tambak
    O di tambak kweri so,

Santre has gotten hold of me today.
I am a Kabre.

13. Oh, that of Surinam is so much more,
that of Surinam is so much more.
Want is found in all the lands,
but that of Surinam is so much more,
that of Surinam is so much more.

14. Pimpana pimpa na popo-e
I am supplicant to kra.
Pimpana pimpa na popo yonder.
I am a supplicant to kra.

15. Goodnight to you all,
Goodnight, sleep well.
I placed my head
at the feet of God.
I love him so much,
but his love is even more.
Goodnight,
Goodnight, sleep well.

16. Voices of the angels
brought new tidings here:
Deep down in a manger
lay a newborn child.
Glory Halleluyah, Glory Halleluyah!
Hark, what's happened here.

17. A big feast was in Nazareth,
—Nazareth—
when the King arrived.
Oh my coat, Oh my coat,
the song is at an end.

18. When Moses raised his staff high,
the water he then beat,
the waters came together,
—Halleluyah.
Oh, the tambak tambak tambak
Oh, the tambak tambak tambak
Oh, the tambak swishes so.[11]

11. *Kweri* is a regular creolization of the English word *square*. It is also used

—Haleluya.

Den suma fu Egipti,
den begi na den masra,
fu feti fon srudati,
—Haleluya.
O di tambak tambak tambak
O di tambak tambak tambak
O di tambak kweri so,
—Haleluya.

19. Nowan suma
    —Husuma dati baka dan?
    Nowan suma
    —Husuma dati baka dan?
    Nowan suma no lobi mi,
    nowan suma no lobi mi
    leki Jezus, mi bun Masra.

20. Di mi yere yu feryari,
    ne mi kon fristeri yu.
    —Halelu, halelu, haleluya.
    Wan fu den tu ogri suma
    begi masra taki: Ke!
    —Halelu, halelu, haleluya.
    Ke Masra, na yu kondre yanda
    tangi tangi membre mi.
    —Halelu, halelu, haleluya.
    Jezus piki en, a taki:
    Tide srefi yu sa de . . .
    —Halelu, halelu, haleluya.
    nanga mi na paradijsi.
    Gado kondre yu sa si.
    —Halelu, halelu, haleluya.
    Yeho Yeho Yeho Yeho
    Yeho Yeho yehova.
    —Halelu, halelu, haleluya.

21. Boy, un no yere suma na mi?
    Boy, un no sabi suma na mi?

—Halleluyah.

The people out of Egypt,
they pleaded with their masters
to fight off all the soldiers.
—Halleluyah.
Oh, the tambak tambak tambak
Oh, the tambak, tambak tambak
Oh, the tambak swishes so.
—Halleluyah.

19.   Nobody,
—Whoever it may be,
Nobody,
—Whoever it may be,
Nobody loves me,
nobody loves me,
but Jesus, my good Lord.

20.   When I heard of your birthday,
I came to say hullo.
—Hallelu, Hallelu, Halleluyah.
Of the sinners on the cross,
one asked the Lord, Oh yea!
—Hallelu, Hallelu, Halleluyah.
Oh Lord in your land yonder,
please will you think of me?
—Hallelu, Hallelu, Halleluyah.
Then Jesus said to him:
This very day you'll be . . .
—Hallelu, Hallelu, Halleluyah.
with me in paradise.
God's Kingdom you'll behold.
—Hallelu, Hallelu, Halleluyah.
Jeho, Jeho, Jeho, Jeho,
Jeho, Jeho, Jehova.
—Hallelu, Hallelu, Halleluyah.

21.   Fellers, haven't you heard who I am?
Fellers, don't you know who I am?

---

for the swishing of a stick. *Tambak* must in that case be a name for Moses's
stick.

Mi na Kwaku Lamberti
fu bilo Kawna liba.
Boy, un no yere suma na mi?

22. Mi de a dorosey, mi de a dorosey.
    Mi no yere gengen,
    mi no yere tutu,
    mi de a dorosey.

23. Yu mu kari den uma 'den sani'.
    Yu mu kari den uma 'den sani'.
    Sensi manspasi kon,
    uma no e teri man moro.
    Yu mu kari den uma 'den sani'.

24. Kamra doro yu no wani sori mi.
    Kamra doro yu no wani sori mi.
    Na ini yu kamra
    mi e go lolo wan dey.

25. Mi a no peprebon fu den uma.
    Mi a no peprebon fu den uma.
    Fu den uma waka sey pasi,
    den broko wan pepre.
    Mi a no peprebon fu den uma.

26. Sin san de na mofo sin de kon.
    Perun Perun mi patron,
    san wani kon, meki a kon.
    Ingrisiman sa tyari a planga
    go na yobo pran
    Bakuba bakuba kaseri kaseri
    nimbo nimbo yaasabo,
    bosroma penki, bosroma bo.

I am Kwaku Lamberti
from the lower Commewijne.
Youths, haven't you heard who I am?

22. I am outside, I am outside,
    I don't hear the bell,
    I don't hear the horn,
    I am outside.

23. Go ahead and call the women names.
    Go ahead and call the women names.
    Ever since our freedom day
    women no longer respect the men.
    Go ahead and call the women names.

24. You refuse to show me
        where the door of your room is.
    You refuse to show me
        where the door of your room is.
    In it I'll enter still,
    come frolic with you there.

25. To women I'm no pepper tree.
    To women I'm no pepper tree,
    for which they leave the way and stray,
    to pluck from it a pepper red.
    To women I'm no pepper tree.

26. Sin? What do they say? Sin is coming?[12]
    Perun, Perun, my boss,
    let come who wants to come.
    Englishmen will carry the wood
    to the white man all at once.[13]
    Bakuba bakuba kaseri kaseri
    nimbo nimbo yaasabo,
    bosroma penki, bosroma bo.[14]

---

12. Variant lines that have been observed in Paramaribo are: *Sin, san de na mofo se de kon; go na yobo pan; nimo nimo yaasabo; den sabi a finifini wroko; fa yu don, yu don so.* We followed the recorded text.

13. The variant word *pan* might be the ideophone *pam* (cf. Focke 1855), expressing fullness. Comvalius 1938 interpreted *yobo pan* as "the big water" or "the sea." *Pran,* as recorded by us, is also an ideophone expressing suddenness.

14. The words have possibly been chosen for their rhythmic quality, without

Ala den grikibi,
den no sabi den finifini wroko.
Ma Kodyo, fa yu don so?
A don so kita kita kay koy.
—Basi Grinya, yu mofo langa tumusi,
—puru wan.

27. Mamama
    Papapa
    Kofi lepi na bon,
    tobo no furu.
    —A da mi-o pa pa a da mi-o.
    Basya e wipi mi.
    —A da mi-o pa pa a da mi-o.

28. Fayasiton no bron mi so,
    no bron mi so,
    dan yu lon gowe.
    —Agen masra Jantje e kiri suma pikin.

29. Broko futu loli e loli, ba.
    —Tyengele.
    Sika futu loli e loli, ba.
    —Tyengele.

All those common birds are ignorant
when it comes to finer points.
But Kojo! How can you be so dumb?
He is dumb as kita kita kay koy.
Boss Grinya, your mouth is too big,[15]
withdraw![16]

27.   Mamama
Papapa
The coffee is ripe on the tree.
The basket is not full.
He gives it to me
   Papa! He gives it to me.
Overseer lashes me,
He gives it to me
   Papa! He gives it to me.[17]

28.   Hot stone burn me not so,
burn me not so.
Go away, go away!
Once again Master John
   is out to kill
     somebody's child.

29.   Lame foot dangles and dangles.
Tyengele.
Foot with chigger under the nail
   dangles and dangles, friend.
Tyengele.

---

reference to a particular meaning. Therefore they are left untranslated in the text. *Bakuba* means "raw banana," *kaseri* "ritually clean," *bosro* "to brush," and *penki* was the place in Paramaribo where criminals were hanged.

15. Literally, "your mouth is too long." This might also mean "you show contempt."

16. *Puru wan,* literally "Withdraw one." The children who use this song in their game sit in a circle and one counts the legs. On *puru wan* one of the feet has to be withdrawn, and the singing starts over again until no feet are left.

17. Two interpretations are possible. If the word *da* comes from the Saramaccan verb *da* ("to give"), we have to interpret *papa* as an ideophone, indicating the beating the child gets. If, however, the word *da* comes from *de a* ("to be at"), the line means: "Father, he is after me." During the game a stone is passed around, as also in the next song.

30. Mi tay mi amaka kaba.
    Mi poti mi pikin didon.
    —Kamalamba sende,
    kon fiti yapon.

31. O mi abi wan lobi,
    fu saynde mi lobi en.
    Switi tongo na mi mofo,
    nanga kamalama na mi sribipe.

32. Mati te yu go, yu no mu tan langa.
    Gudu te yu go, yu no mu tan langa.
    Bika kaneridoyfi go a kankantri.
    Te yu go, yu no mu tan langa.

33. Mi empi priti a mi baka.
    Suma e go nay en gi mi?
    Suma e go nay en gi mi?
    Mi yayo.

34. Mati go a mati oso,
    mati teki en mati manu.
    Way angisa-e,
    way angisa gi na uma.

    Ma efu a ben de mi ankanamu,
    kondre ben sa yere.
    Way angisa-e,
    way angisa gi na uma.

35. Mi komopo na busi, mi kon na foto.
    —Sinaweren sarambabu—
    Mi go a kantoro fu go teki mi moni.
    Mi anga mi mati waka langalanga,
    Saramakastrati langalanga.
    Di un doro na Agutobo a watrasey,

30. I have unrolled my hammock.
     Laid my child to rest.
     —Kamalamba sende,
     —come try this dress for size.[18]

31. Oh, I have a love.
     Why do I love her so?
     Ah, her sweet tongue in my mouth,
     her frolicking on my bed.

32. Friend, when you go, do not stay too long.
     Dearest, when you go, do not stay too long.
     For cinnamon dove has flown to the cotton tree.[19]
     When you go, do not stay too long.

33. My shirt is torn in the back.
     Who will come sew for me?
     Who will come sew for me?
     I am a free bird still.

34. A friend went to a friend's house,
         a woman to a woman's,
     took from her her husband.
     Honor then this woman
     with waving of kerchiefs.

     But if it pleases me,
     it will be known to all.
     Honor then this woman
     with waving of kerchiefs.

35. I emerged from the bush and went to town
     —Sinaweren sarambabu—
     I went to the office for my pay.
     My friend and I strutted up and down,
     all along the Saramacca street.
     When we came to Agutobo near the shore,

---

18. According to my informant, this song was first used by a woman to signal to her lover outside that the coast was clear.

19. "Cinnamon dove" is a literal translation. According to my informant, the song refers to a man smitten with venereal disease, who was sent to the hospital for treatment. Cinnamon dove could refer to his sexual organs, which were wrapped in a cotton bandage, hence the reference to a cotton tree.

nomo mi anga mi mati dyompo na ini a wenkri.
Un kari a sneysi kon gi un wan bita.
Dan pikinmoro yu o yere na dan.
Seybi motyo ben tringi na lo.
Den taki: Pikin masra, kon yere wan tori.
Un kari den motyo kon na ini a wenkri.
Seybi motyo, seybi pisi tabaka.
Seybi motyo, seybi dosu swarfu.
Seybi motyo anga seybi pipa.
Seybi motyo, seybi grasi sopi.
Wan ben de na ini di mi ben lobi.
Mi taygi mi mati: Mi o suku a meid.
Sensi mi e taigi yu de, mi e suku a meid.
Yere san a lobi e go taygi mi:
Masra mi gudu, na pe mi e libi,
wan owru granmisi de a mi sey.
Mi taki: Mi gudu, u o waka safri.
Dan mi anga a lobi ben go na oso.
A puru en koto, mi puru mi bruku.
A puru en yaki, mi puru mi yas.
A puru en angisa, mi puru mi ati.
A teki wan koto, a trowe a gron.
Nomo kopiplanga e go krey en nowtu.
Wan pôti granmisi ben de a sey.
A taki: Pikin masra, mi gudu, meki safri.
Yu e go broko a planga kiri mi dya.

36. Zestien April. Di mi boto lay.
    Tapanahoni, na dape mi de go.

    Ma te mi doro na Ansubangi,

we dropped into a shop, my friend and I.
We summoned the Chinee man to bring us a shot.
Now you'll see some fireworks.
Seven tarts like a row of beads.
They said: Sweetheart, Sirs, come listen here.
We invited the tarts into the shop.
Seven tarts, seven tobacco strings.
Seven tarts, seven matchboxes full.
Seven tarts with seven pipes.
Seven tarts means seven shots.
One there was I fancied most.
I said to my friend:
    I'll try that one.
No sooner said,
    than I tried the bitch.
Listen what the darling tells me:
Sweetheart Sir, there where I live,
lives an old dame immediately below.[20]
I said: My sweetheart, we'll softly work.
And then I took the darling home.
She took off her dress, I my pants.
She took off her blouse, I my coat.
She took off her kerchief, I my hat.
She took a cloth and spread it on the floor.
The burden caused the boards to creak.[21]
A poor old lady below her lived.
She said: Sweet Sir, my dear,
    go slowly please!
You will cause the boards to break
    and kill me here.

36.   Sixteenth April. My boat is ready.
Tapanahoni, thither I am off.

But when I came to Ansubangi,[22]

---

20. The text says literally "next door." This creates a problem, however, in interpreting the last lines, where the old lady is clearly threatened by the boards above her head. Thus, we took the liberty of adapting the translation.

21. There is reference in the text to a certain kind of hard wood, *kopi.*

22. Ansubangi is a place just opposite Paramaribo, on the other side of the river. The general meaning is that a girl has promised her boy friend to accompany

ne mi ati ben sari fu tru.

Fingalinga na yu finga,
gowtu keti na yu neki,
Rosalina, san ede yu de krey.

Di mi memre den fotowenke,
ne mi ati ben sari fu tru.

Rosalina, Rosalina,
Rosalina, fu san ede yu de krey.

Bastian fon

37. Meneri, meneri, da piekien, pardon.
    Membrie wan tem, membrie wan tron,
    Fa joe ben lobbie mie so té,
    En fa mie lobbie joe jette.

    Bastian fon! bastian fon!
    Da oeman meekie mie hatie bron!

    Té na condré joe kon fo scrifiman,
    Mie no ben sabie san na wan man;
    Fa joe ben lobbie mie so té,
    En fa mie lobbie joe jette.

    Bastian fon! bastian fon!
    Da oeman meekie mie hatie bron!

    Mie ben dé kalli joe mooi scrifiman,
    Joe poeloe mie na mie nenne Anan;
    Fa joe ben lobbi mie so té,
    En fa mie lobbi joe jette.

then was my heart with sorrow filled.

Finger rings on your finger,
golden chains on your lovely neck,
Rosalina, why do you cry?

When I thought of the girls in town,
then was my heart with sorrow filled.

Rosalina, Rosalina,
Rosalina, why do you cry?

Bastian fon

37.   Master, master, forgiveness, the child,
think of the time, think of the time,
how you loved me then.
Oh, how I love you still.

Overseer lash out, overseer lash out,
the woman fills my heart with ire.

When you came to this land to keep the books
I had not yet been near a man,
How you loved me then.
Oh, how I love you still.

Overseer lash out, overseer lash out,
the woman fills my heart with ire.

My handsome keeper of books you were.
Didn't you snatch me from my mother's breast?[23]
How you loved me then.
Oh, how I love you still.

---

him to the bush, where he probably worked as a gold digger. But having crossed
the river, she started crying. When the man asks her what is wrong with her, she
confesses that she cannot leave her friends in town.

23. The word *Anan* in the song has been interpreted as a woman's name because
of the capital letter used in the Sranan text. This is probably not correct. The
word refers to a now almost obsolete question particle, which in Focke 1885
has been written *anáä*. The same particle may be found in song 16 of chapter
1. We did not change the orthography in which this song was originally
published.

Bastian fon! bastian fon!
Da oeman meekie mie hatie bron!

Té joe ben bossi joe JABA,
Mie ben takki: kaba! kaba!
Da falsie lobbie, joe no ké,
Ho fassi joe doe so to dé.

Bastian fon! bastian fon!
Da oeman meekie mie hatie bron!

Pardon Meneri! Pardon! pardon!
Joe ben lobbi da skien wan tron.
Mie beggi joe! mie beggi: ké!
Meneri a no noffo jette?

Bastian fon! bastian fon!
Da oeman meekie mie hatie bron!

Meneri, meneri, membrie da piekien,
Da sori joe mie lobbi krien.
Mie beggi joe, mie beggi: ké!
Bastian a no noffo jette?

Bastian fon! bastian fon!
Da oeman meekie mie hatie bron.

Hoe fassi? mie takki fon!
Da oeman meekie mie hatie bron!
Mie takki fon! fon hin so té,
Al wassi a fal don deddé.

Bastian fon! bastian fon!
Da oeman meekie mie hatie bron!

Overseer lash out, overseer lash out,
the woman fills my heart with ire.

When you kissed your Yaba,
lay off I cried.
This love is false.
    You do not care.
Why this behavior today?

Overseer lash out, overseer lash out,
this woman fills my heart with ire.

Forgiveness, my Lord, forgiveness please.
You loved this body once.
I pray, Oh I pray to thee.
Master, isn't it enough?

Overseer lash out, overseer lash out,
the woman fills my heart with ire.

Master, master, please think of the child.
It shows you that my love is pure.
I pray, Oh I pray to thee.
Overseer, isn't it enough?

Overseer lash out, overseer lash out,
the woman fills my heart with ire.

What? Lash out, I say.
The woman fills my heart with ire.
Lash out, I say, lash out so hard
till down she drops dead on the ground.

Overseer lash out, overseer lash out,
this woman fills my heart with ire.

CHAPTER 3

Folktales

Creoles have a great and long-standing tradition of storytelling dating back to the time of slavery. As in so many other countries, there are informal occasions when, on a moonlit night, the children of a compound crouch around an old woman to hear their bedtime stories. When a story is told during the day, the Creole storyteller is supposed to pluck an eyelash, which seems to suggest a more sacred origin (Penard 1917:242-43). In general, however, storytelling is not a children's affair. Most stories are told during wakes, especially on the eighth night after death but also at a later stage in mourning ceremonies. It is said that the *yorka,* the spirit of the deceased, should be entertained with stories before he leaves his relatives. Although other occasions with a more sacred character seem to exist, presumably as part of the ancestor cult, we have not had a chance to observe them, nor have they been described in the literature.

Storytelling with an adult audience is highly formalized. The narrator opens and closes his tale with certain fixed formulas in which the audience participates. The audience in fact participates actively, in a formalized way, during the entire session. One is entitled to interrupt the narrator by calling out something like *Bato, mi ben dape* (*"Bato,* I was there"). The narrator pauses, turns to the interrupter, and asks something in the vein of *San den taki?* ("What did they say?") or *San yu si?* ("What did you see?"). The interrupter may then start a song, during which he is joined by the rest of the audience. After the song is finished, he says something like *Waka anga yu tori* ("Go on with your story"). Skilled interrupters can link the song to the tale by means of a few introductory lines. It is also possible to throw in a proverb that fits the tale.

In most cases the interruptions are not related to the story or are related in only a very superficial way. We once witnessed a very intricate pattern of interruptions during a mourning feast in a Djuka village. The first story was interrupted by a second, which was interrupted by a third, and so on. The deepest embedded story must be finished first, before the less deeply embedded can go on. The main function of the interruptions seems to be to distract the audience a bit and to show appreciation for the story. An extremely lively session may so please the narrator that he himself starts inter-

spersing his tale with interruptions or praises it as very interesting.
Skilled narrators may even use the interruptions to structure their
story. If a story really warms up, a short interruption may be highly
effective. It presents an outlet for the tension created and at the same
time arouses curiosity about further developments. Consequently
some famous storytellers may have as part of their retinue skilled
interrupters who guide the audience in their interruptions. For a
description of this type of session see Herskovits 1936:138-46.

Songs that are not used as interruptions but as part of the tale
have quite a different function. In Mende folktales "songs of this
third group occur at climactic points or at crises in the narrative;
they are most often uttered by a character in a tale who is under
severe stress, either physical or mental, though perhaps rather more
frequently the latter . . . at these points the stories are raised to a
higher level of feeling than could perhaps be reached by means of
ordinary speech" (Innes 1965:60-61). Some narrators start with a
song instead of an opening formula and then present the story as an
explanation of the song, whether the explanation is plausible or not.
It is not quite clear whether in Surinam this type of storytelling is an
individual departure from Creole tradition or an established alternative
method of storytelling.

Surinam Creoles make a clear distinction between two types of
tales: *Anansitori* ("spider stories") and *Ondrofenitori* ("experience
stories"). A third type called *Laytori* contains only riddles and are
often extremely short. They can hardly be considered folktales.
Herskovits 1936 (p. 138) considered the *Ondrofenitori* a subclass of
Anansitori, but we do not think this holds true. At present the distinction between the two types may roughly coincide with our distinction
between more and less serious stories. *Anansitori* are considered to
be pure entertainment, while *Ondrofenitori* must bear a message.
The distinction between the two types is not absolute and may depend
on the attitude of the narrator or even of the audience. The same story
may be presented as pure entertainment or as moral instruction. But
this uncertainty does not make the basic distinction less real. It seems
to us more acceptable than the classification of Herskovits: "those that
have animals as their *dramatis personae,* those with human characters,
and those containing animals and humans, who appear to share the
world they inhabit on equal terms" (Herskovits 1936:139). This sort
of classification seems rather foreign to the culture in which these tales
function.

The *Anansitori* (tales presented as pure entertainment) are named
after the trickster hero of many of these tales, the spider Anansi. Of
a total of 148 stories published in Herskovits 1936, 93 are animal

stories, of which 81 centered on the spider. An earlier collection
published in Capelle 1916 and 1926 contained 39 stories, of which
29 were animal stories and 27 centered on the spider. The clear
preference for stories about Anansi may be attributed to the collectors.
Capelle and Herskovits were both very much interested in the African
background of Surinam culture. The same applies to Lichtveld, who
treated the mythical origin of the spider in Africa (Lichtveld 1930/31).
It is quite clear that the spider and the hare as Caribbean tricksters
have an African background. Their appeal, however, is much more
universal. They are the cunning creatures who succeed in outwitting
their superiors, and as such they appealed to the Creoles, who often
constituted the lower ranks of society.

Ondrofenitori are certainly as important for Creole culture as the
other stories. They may have diverse origins. Next to tales with a clear
African origin, we have encountered Andersen's tales, changed but still
quite recognizable, tales from Dutch folklore (Voorhoeve 1950), old
Italian stories, and others. A special subgroup of *Ondrofenitori* is called
Srafutentori (tales of slavery). For a long time they passed unnoticed.
The first mention of them in the literature was in a description of a
storytelling session by W. Campagne, cited in Donicie 1952/53. The
first publication of such a story can be found in Drie 1959. Here we
certainly do not have in mind nonformalized historical traditions but
formalized folktales. The historical truth is uncertain, although names
of plantations and plantation owners are frequently mentioned. The
themes are clearly derived from oral literature, but the tales have their
setting in the historical past, especially in the period of slavery. We
even recorded a story that started in Africa, in Mende country.

In this chapter we have selected three very different specimens of
Surinam folktales, leaving aside the better known spider stories. While
not denying the African background, they illustrate, we think, how
deeply rooted Creole culture is in America. The first is a *Srafutentori*
showing how the slaves outwitted their masters with the help of magic
and even succeeded in driving one of them away. This is not the only
theme nor the most important. Of great import is the moral, that reward comes to him who cares for his parents. The story starts with
a quest that came about as a result of a task set by one of the parents.
The experience gained during the quest, with the help of a mythical
creature, leads to the reward: a certain kind of magic or *juju* that gives
power to endure the hardships of slavery. The entire structure is very
symptomatic of general folklore themes but deeply embedded in the
special conditions of slavery. Numerous digressions on the slave
culture reveal that these tales are used to give historical instruction
to the audience.

The second story has been presented explicitly as an *Anansitori* by the narrator, although it is not even an animal story, let alone a spider story. This proves that tales with human characters may be regarded as *Anansitori* (pure entertainment). In this special case, the story was told to two Europeans without an audience. For this reason the narrator may have decided to present his story as fiction or entertainment. With a different audience he might have made a different decision. The story, which is not very well told, is included because it is the only one of its kind in our collection.

The third story is an animal story that does not focus on the spider. The curious thing about this story is that it describes the details of a *banya* performance (for *banya* see chapter 1). A *banya* performance is divided into three stages. Before midnight, the big drum is lightly played with the thumb and forefinger. This manner of playing is called *sabaku,* after a kind of heron. After midnight, until daybreak, the drum is played with four fingers together. Then it is associated with *owrukuku* ("owl"). After about four o'clock in the morning the palm of the hand is also employed. This manner of drumming is called *kakafowru* ("rooster"). The story is about these three birds, who visit a *banya* performance.

The stories were recorded by H. C. van Renselaar and J. Voorhoeve between 1957 and 1961. Stories 1 and 3 were told by Alex de Drie, who in our estimation has no peer in Paramaribo as a narrator. We recorded a second version of the first story, which differs in some respects. This version seemed on the whole better organized and was recorded under better conditions (with an audience). An asterisk in the text indicates an interruption by someone in the audience. For this reason, the last part of the story is repeated after the interruption. The second story was related by Jacob Babel, an old man living in the immediate surroundings of Paramaribo. He is a descendant of a small group of runaways, the so-called Broos negroes, and told us many stories about the history of his group. Possibly there are special traditions in this group. In one of his stories the hare takes the place of the spider as trickster, which is exceptional in Surinam. According to Lichtveld (1930/31:314) the trickster is a hare in North and Middle America but a spider in the southern Antilles and the mainland of South America.

Stories are often regarded as the spiritual possession of a specific narrator and as such will not easily be narrated by someone else. For this reason we insist on linking the tale with the name of its narrator.

Basya Adyuku koni

Mi kownu mi yere
yu abi wan tutu-oi.
Ma na ini yu kondre
nowan man man fu bro a tutu-oi.
Mi kownu, ma ne mi kon begi yu taki:
—Mi kownu, pruberi efu mi sa bro a tutu.
Ne mi kownu taki:
—Ay yu boy Anansi,
yu kan teki a tutu,
dan yu pruberi efu yu bro a tutu.
Ne mi teki a tutu,
mi poti a tutu,
mi bro a tutu, ba:—
Pan pan pan pan!
Ma bifosi mi doro a pranasi
na opo Kotka
di den e kari Morgudan,
ne mi nyan ala a tutu, ba:
—Fan fan fan fan!
Teri en go, ma mama un go teri en kon.
—Teri en go, ma mama un go teri en kon.

We yu si, a singi di mi singi de, hn!, na wan srafuten tori. Yu ben abi
wan pranasi na opo Kotka, den e kari Suksesi. Dan yu ben abi wan
pranasi na ini Motkriki, den e kari Dagrâti. Ma na Suksesi yu ben
abi wan man dape, den ben e kari en basya Adyuku. Ma now, te yu
kon owru na ini a pranasi te, dan granmasra no wani si yu moro.
Bika a taki yu e tan nyan nyanyan fu soso. Bika yu no man wroko
moro, dan yu no mu tan na ini a pranasi ini moro. Dan den pikin fu yu,
dan den mu go koti wan pikin busi, dan den meki maka-oso, dan den poti
yu. Ma pranasi nyanyan yu no kan nyan moro. Bika san dan? Den srafu
ben e kisi nyanyan ala wiki. Efu a pikin abi wan yari, tokoe a e bigin
kisi lansun. Pondo e kon a foto, a kon teki batyaw. O-nyanyan den

The juju of Basya Ajuku

My chief, I have heard
that you possess a trumpet,
but in that land of yours
there is no one who can blow it.
My chief, now I come to ask you:
—My chief, may I try the trumpet?
Then said my chief to me:
—Yes you, small boy Anansi,
you can take the trumpet
and try your luck with it.
Then took I the trumpet,
raised the trumpet high,
and blew the trumpet friends:
—pam, pam, pam, pam!
But before I came to the place
on the upper Cottica
which is known as Morgudan,
then swallowed I the trumpet, friends:
—fan, fan, fan, fan!
—Count on the way to, mother.
—Count on the way from, mother.

Well you see, the song I sang there was a slave-time story. For see,
there was a plantation on the upper Cottica, which they called
Success. But see, there was another plantation in Mot Creek, which
they called Dageraad.[1] But at Success, there was a man whom they
called Basja Ajuku. But now, when you grow old on the plantation,
then the master does not want you around any longer, because he
says, you only keep on eating for nothing, for you can't work any
more, and then you must not stay on the plantation any longer.
Your children must open up a piece of forest for you and build you
a house of reeds and let you live in it. But of the plantation food
you cannot taste any more. For see how it fits in? The slaves used to
get their food every week. When a child is one year old it already gets
its portion. The pontoon[2] goes to town and returns with salt fish.

1. Dageraad, meaning "Dawn," is the Dutch name of the plantation.
2. The plantation owned two kinds of boat: the so-called *pondo,* used for
transporting goods and slaves, and the *tenboto,* used for white passengers.
The *tenboto* had a canvas roof for protection from the sun.

ben e gi den. A bâna nanga batyaw. Nanga a weti maka, dati den abi
fu weri go na kerki, nanga a braka maka. Den uma e kisi tu braka
maka pangi. A fu heri yari.

Ma now yu ben abi wan mama den ben e kari mama Amba. Dan
en man ben nen Kwami. Dan a ben abi wan manpikin, den ben e
kari Akampe. Dati na en fosi manpikin. Tu manpikin a ben abi.
Dan a wan a ben gi en nen Adyuku.

Ma te Akampe komopo a baka gron—dati a ben e wroko—, ma
efu a kon na oso—a mama no man wroko moro, a papa no man
wroko moro—kaba mama Amba kari en, a e piki: —San yu e kari
mi? Yu grani kaba, yu no kan dede? Anga moeilijkheid a mi tapu!

Te Adyuku kon, a kari en, a taki: —Adyuku?

A taki: —Ya mi mama?

—Kon dya mi boy.

Adyuku e go. A taki: —Mi mama, yu nyan kaba dan?

A taki: —N'n!

—Mi mama, san yu wani nyan?

A taki: —We a no wan pikin tonton yu mu bori gi mi?

Adyuku e go a gotro, a kisi srika, a srepi fisi, a kon,
a fon en mama anga en papa tonton gi den. Sonten a e puru
sika gi den. Satra bakadina, te a komopo a wroko, dan a kon
puru sika, krin den futu gi den. Sonde mamanten a e teki a makapangi
fu a mama, a gowe go wasi. A e teki a pikin krio fu a papa, a go a
liba, a wasi, a drey. Ma a papa ben abi wan koni. Dan a luku
duun.

We yu si a tori di mi e gi yu de, dan a tata luku Adyuku, dan a
kari mama Amba, a taki: —Amba, kon.

> Amba lelele, kari mama Amba kon.
> Amba lelele, srafûma, kari mama Amba kon.
> Amba lelele, srafûma, kari mama Amba kon.

Now see what sort of food they gave them. Plantains and salt fish. And also with it came white cotton cloth which they wore when they went to church, and also black cotton cloth. Women received two wraparounds of black cotton. That was supposed to last the whole year.

But see, there was a woman whom they called Mama Amba. Her husband was called Kwami. They had a son. They called him Akampe. That is the first son. Two sons they had. The other, that is the second one, they named Ajuku.

Now when Akampe returned from the bakagron[3] behind the plantation—here it was that he worked—now when he came home his mother could not work any more, his father could not work any more. Then Mama Amba called him. And he answered (this oldest child): "Why do you call me? You're old already. Can't you kick the damn bucket? You and your infernal botheration!"

Now when Ajuku came, she called him and said: "Ajuku?"

He said: "Yes mother?"

"Come here, my boy."

Ajuku went to her and said: "Mother, have you eaten already?" She said: "No."

"Mother, what do you want to eat?"

She replied: "Well, isn't there a little bit of pounded plantain that you could perhaps cook for me?"

Ajuku went to the ditches. He caught land crabs. He caught fishes in a net. He returned. He pounded the plaintains for his mother and father. Sometimes he took out the chiggers from under their nails. On Saturdays, when he returned from work, he took out the chiggers and cleaned their feet. On Sundays, he took his mother's cotton wraparound and went to wash it. He took his father's small loincloth, went to the river, washed it and dried it. But see now, the father owned a juju. He looked and stared attentively, the father.

Well, do you see, this tale that I here tell you—now the father he looked at Ajuku and then he called Mama Amba and said: "Amba, come!"

> Amba lelele, call Mama Amba here.
> Amba lelele, slave girls, call Mama Amba here.
> Amba lelele, slave girls, call Mama Amba here.

---

3. The director's house was always built on the river bank. The area farthest removed from the river and the director's house was called *bakagron*.

We na mama Amba a e kari so. A taki: —Amba lelele, kari na
mama gi mi. Amba lelele, srafûma, kari na uma gi mi.

Hn! Bika mama Amba, Adyuku na en pikin. Ma a yuru di a
papa si fa Adyuku e libi anga en, dan a e kari mama Amba, fu den
taki makandra fu den gi Adyuku a koni. Ne mama Amba e gowe,
teki pasi e go anga en tiki. Ne a papa bari gi en taki: —Mama
Amba lelele, kari na uma gi mi. Mama Amba lelele, srafûma,
kari na uma kon.

Dan mama Amba dray kon. Nomo a taki: —Mi uma, we luku,
u abi tu boy dya. Tata Gado leni un tu boy. Ma a wan bigiwan,
yu no si, a e si un leki noti. Ma Adyuku, te a kon, a e puru sika
gi unu, a e kisi watra gi un fu wasi un skin. A e go a gotro, a e
go srepi fisi kon, a e kisi srika, a e kisi krabu, a e bori brafu gi
unu. We luku, mi abi wan koni dya di mi tata ben leri mi. Ma
mi no pruberi fu mi srefi. Ma meki un pruberi en gi Adyuku.

A mama no piki. Twarfu dey langa a papa e begi en. Mama,
den abi swaki ati so. Ma na mama dati ben abi a tranga ati, a papa
ben abi a swaki ati. Di fu tinadri dey, nomo a papa kari Adyuku a
wan sey, a taki: —Adyuku!

Adyuku taki: —Ya mi papa.

A taki: —Kon dya boy. Efu un gi yu wan wroko, yu sa du en?
Adyuku taki: —San mi papa wani. Bika mi papa wroko te yu kon
grani. Now granmasra taki: nowan enkri suma no mu tan na ini
pranasi. Hala den trawan mesandel den bigisma, den houders fu
den, te den dede. Ma tog mi tyari yu kon dya a mindri busi. Mi
meki wan oso fu yu anga mi mama. Mi e tyari nyanyan kon gi unu.
Dùs te yu si un tapu bro, mi poti un na ondro doti, dan mi sa
kaba anga unu.

A papa taki: —So mi boy. A taki: —We yu sabi san mi o seni
yu? Yu mu go na busi. Dan yu mu suku a mira di den e kari
wrokoman. Dan yu puru na ati tya kon gi mi.

Adyuku teki prakseri. Nomo a mama sidon a wan sey. Di Adyuku
e prakseri de, ne a mama bari, a taki: —

Yu sabi na odo di mi e bari de-i?
Hay, mi pikin wani sabi na odo
di mi e koti de.
Go na mindri busi,

Well see, in this way he called Mama Amba and said! "Amba lelele, call the woman for me. Amba lelele, slave girls, call the woman for me."

Well, Hmm! For see, because for Mama Amba, Ajuku is her child. Now when the father saw how Ajuku behaved toward him, then he called to him Mama Amba, to arrange with her that they should give the juju to Ajuku.

Then Mama Amba walked away, and took to the path with her stick. Then the father called after her: "Mama Amba lelele, call the woman for me. Mama Amba lelele, slave girls, call the woman here."

Then Mama Amba turned back. Then he said: "Wife, look here, we have two boys. The Lord God has given us two sons in custody. But the eldest, you see, we do not count with him. But as for Ajuku, when he comes, then he takes chiggers out of our feet. He fetches water for us to wash with. He goes off to the ditches to catch fish in his net. He catches land crabs, cooks soup for us. Well, you see, I have here a juju which my father has taught me. But I myself have never put it to a test. But now let us try it out on Ajuku's behalf.

But the mother answered not. Twelve days long the father begged her. Mothers, their hearts are so soft. But this mother had a strong heart. The father however had a soft heart. On the thirteenth day the father called Ajuku aside and said: "Ajuku."

Ajuku answered: "Father."

He said: "Come here, my boy. If we ask you to do something, will you do it?" Ajuku answered: "Whatever my father wishes. For see, my father slaved until he was old. And now the owner has said no one like that can stay on the plantation. All the others treat their parents badly until they die. But still, I have brought you here to the bush. I have made a house for you and mother. I bring food to you. For see, when you two give up the ghost, and I have put you in the earth, then only will I be finished with you."

The father said: "So my boy." He said: "Do you know where I am going to send you? You must go into the bush and then you must look for the ant which they call the Worker. Then you must take out the heart of the Worker and bring it to me."

Ajuku pondered a while. The mother, as for her, she sat a little aside. When the boy pondered, the mother started to intone:

> Do you know the proverb which I here intone?
> Yes, my child wants to know the proverb
> which I throw out here.
> Go into the bush,

go teki na ati fu na mira den e kari wrokoman.
Dan yu sa sabi na odo di mi e bari de.

Adyuku teki prakseri te. Adyuku go, a sribi. Tamara mamanten
a go a busi. A waka, a waka, a waka, a waka, a waka, a waka, a
waka, te a doro twarfu yuru. A no man miti noti. A go na ondro
wan bon. A dokun di a ben tyari, a koti wan pisi, a nyan.
Ma a yuru di a nyan a dokun, nomo a si wan krabdagu kon
na en fesi. A ten dati den meti ben e taki. Nomo a krabdagu
taki anga en. A taki: —We mi yonkuman, fa yu tan?
Adyuku taki: —Mi krabdagu, fa yu tan?
A krabdagu taki: —Angri e kiri mi ba. A di mi si yu e nyan, ne mi
kon.
Adyuku taki: —We san mi e nyan, mi no sabi efu yu sa nyan en.
Na kasaba dokun mi tyari. Efu yu sa nyan en, dan mi sa gi yu.
A krabdagu taki: —We, di yu nyan en, a no kiri yu, a no kan kiri
mi.
A opo en katasú, a teki a afu dokun, gi a krabdagu. A krabdagu
nyan. A krabdagu sidon na en sey, a bigin prey anga a krabdagu. A
yuru di a prey te wan pisi anga a krabdagu—un ben de tranga dreyten
nanga tranga son—, dan fa a feni a kowrupe, dan a winti kon bigin
way, dan a sribi bigin kiri en, dan a dyonko. Ma a yuru di a dyonko,
a fadon a wan pikin sribi. A krabdagu sidon na en sey. Te a sribi te
wan pisi ten, a krabdagu si a no e wiki, a krabdagu krabu en anga en
finga, a wiki. Ne a krabdagu tagi en taki: —We mi yonkuman, yu
fadon a wan pikin sribi, ma mi tan dya, mi waki te yu sribi, fu noti
no du yu.
A taki: —Ay mi krabdagu, mi e taki yu tangi.
A krabdagu aksi en taki: —Ma pe yu e go dan?
A taki: —We luku dya, na ini mi pranasi ini, pe mi de, sodra yu
si yu wroko gi granmasra te yu kon grani, dan yu no e kisi lansun
moro. We so hala den trawan, den bigisma fu den, di den no e kisi
lansun moro, den ferferi anga den, den mesandel den te hala dede.
Ma mi dati, mi kon meki wan oso na busi. San mi man prani, mi prani.

go fetch the heart of the ant they call the Worker.
Then you'll know the proverb which I here intone.

Ajuku pondered on this for a long time. Then he went home, he
slept. The next morning he went to the bush. He walked and walked
and walked and walked and walked and walked and walked until it
was twelve o'clock. He did not come upon a thing. He went to sit
under a tree. He took the sweetmeat he had with him, cut off a
piece and started to eat it.

But see, now, when he was busy eating the sweetmeat he saw
Krabdagu[4] coming toward him. At that time the animals could still
speak. Krabdagu said to him: "Well, young man, how are you faring?"

Ajuku asked: "Krabdagu, how are you faring?"

Krabdagu replied: "I am hungry, my friend. Because I saw you
eating, I decided to come."

Ajuku said: "I don't know whether you will like what I am eating.
I have sweetmeat made of cassave with me. If you will eat that, I
will give it to you."

Krabdagu replied: "Well, since you eat it and it does not kill you,
then it cannot kill me either."

He opened his hunting bag, took half of the sweetmeat and gave
it to Krabdagu. Krabdagu ate it and went to sit next to him. He
started playing with Krabdagu. After he had played with Krabdagu
for a little while—it was the dry season, the heat beat down on them—
he found a shady place, and since the wind was starting to blow a
little, he got sleepy and he began to doze off. And from dozing he
fell into a small sleep. The Krabdagu sat beside him. When he had
slept for some time, and the Krabdagu saw that he did not wake up,
the Krabdagu scratched him with his finger, and he woke up. Then
the Krabdagu said to him: "Well, look here, young man, you've have
fallen asleep a little bit, but I have remained with you. I have kept
watch here while you slept, so that nothing should happen to you."

He said: "Yes Krabdagu, thank you very much."

The Krabdagu asked: "But where are you off to?"

He said: "Well see, it is like this. On my plantation where I live,
when you have slaved for the owner until you are old, see, then
you don't receive your ration anymore. Well now, as for all the
others, when their parents do not receive their rations anymore,
they detest them and treat them badly until they die. But as for me,
I have built them a hut in the bush. I have planted what I could.

4. *Krabdagu* is a kind of raccoon, *Procyon cancrivorus.*

Dan mi tyari mi mama—a no man wroko moro, a nen mama Amba—
go poti a busi nanga mi papa. A lansun di mi e kisi, a dati mi anga
den e prati, nanga san mi e wroko nengregron.
    A krabdagu taki: —O! A taki: —Ma pe yu e go dan?
    A taki: —We a no mi papa seni mi taki, meki mi kon a mindri busi,
meki mi go suku na ati fu a mira den e kari wrokoman gi en. We
yu si, a dati mi e go suku.
    A krabdagu taki: —O! We mi yonkuman, efu mi ben sabi en, mi ben
sa sori yu. Ma di yu e go de, waka, masra Gado sa de anga yu.
    Adyuku teki pasi, a waka, a waka, a waka, a waka, te a kon
doro wan pikin kriki. Ma a yuru a doro a kriki, a koti wan tiki,
a wani go abra a kriki, a firfiri a tiki, ma a si wan bun bigi pisi . . .

                                    *

    Adyuku koti wan tiki, a firi. Ma pe a e firi so, nomo a si wan
bigi pisi udu didon so. Ma na udu ben didon leki fa a kriki didon
so. Ma na udu dray en srefi. Ma ala dati, san na a udu? Na wan
bigi kayman. Te yu wan go abra a kriki dati, dan na a kayman baka
yu mu waka.
    Nèt Adyuku wani poti en futu fu go abra na udu, a krabdagu dape
de. A krabdagu kon, a taki: —Mi yonkuman, mi miti yu baka. A
fu yu ede meki mi kon dya.
    Adyuku taki: —So?
    Krabdagu taki: —We, yu no feni na ati fu a mira den e kari
wrokoman ete?
    A taki: —Nono! We, mi doro a kriki, dan now mi wani go abra.
    Krabdagu taki: —We, yu no mu go abra, bika yu si, na bigi udu
di yu si yu wani abra dape de, nowan libisma e kan abra dya. Na
wan bigi kayman. Èn ala den tra pispisi udu di seti de, sodra yu
si yu sa poti yu futu, na soso kayman. Fa yu si yu e miti a watra,
so den o nyan yu. Dùsu dray baka, meki mi tyari yu go.
    Adyuku waka. A krabdagu teki fesi. A yuru di a waka, a waka
te wan pisi, nomo a go, a miti wan bigi bon, a gersi na sibi sibi
a bon ondro. Ma fosi a doro, dan a krabdagu tagi en taki: —We
luku, yu si yu e go miti wan bigi bon dape de. Ma te yu go na
ondro a bon—a bon sibi leki suma e go sibi en—ma te yu go dape
na ondro a bon, no tan nowan henkri yuru. Bika te yu go na ondro

Then I brought my mother—she can't work any more, she is known
as Mama Amba—and put her in the forest with my father. The ration
that I receive, I share with them, also that which I cultivate on the
piece of land set aside for the niggers.

Krabdagu said: "Oh." He said: "But where are you off to?"

Ajuku replied: "Well, did not my father send me into the bush to
find for him the heart of the ant they call the Worker? That is what
I am after."

The Krabdagu said: "Oh. Well, young man, if I knew it, I would
have pointed it out to you. But see, now that you're going there,
the Lord God will be with you."

Ajuku went on his way. He walked and walked and walked and
walked, until he came to a small creek. Now when he came to the
creek, he cut off a stick. He wanted to cross the creek. He felt about
in the creek with his stick, but just then he saw a big log of wood. . .

*

Ajuku cut off a branch and felt. But there where he is feeling he
sees a log of wood lying. The log of wood does not lie in the direction
of the creek. No, it has turned itself. What type of log is it? It is a big
alligator. If you want to cross that creek you must step on the back of
the alligator.

Ajuku wanted to do just this, when the Krabdagu appeared. The
Krabdagu came and said: "Young man, we see each other again. For
your sake I have come here."

Ajuku said: "So?"

Krabdagu said: "Well, have you not yet found the heart of the
ant which they call Worker?"

He replied: "No. I have come to the creek and want to get across."

Krabdagu said: "Well you mustn't cross it for you see, that big
piece of wood on which you want to cross, no human being can
cross here. It is a big alligator. And all the other pieces of wood that
you see adrift here, as soon as you set your foot on them, they turn
into nothing but alligators. As soon as you get into the water, they
will eat you up. Turn back, let me guide you."

Ajuku walked. The Krabdagu was in the lead. When he had walked
for some distance, he stumbled on a big tree. It looked as if a broom
had swept underneath the tree. But before he came there, Krabdagu
said to him: "Well see, you will come across a big tree over there.
But now, when you go under the tree, it is swept clean as if there a
person had swept it—do not spend a minute under it. For see, when

a bon, a o gi yu fu yu sidon, a o gi yu fu yu kanti didon srefi. Ma
no prefuru, waka so tranga leki yu kan.

A yuru di Adyuku waka te a go doro na ondro a bon so, wan
switi winti way na ondro a bon sote—hn! Adyuku wani tanapu.
A prakseri san a krabdagu ben tagi en. A waka tu futu, a tanapu.
A prakseri san a krabdagu ben tagi en. A winti e komopo ala sey fu
en. A yuru di a pasa a skadu te, nomo a yere wan sten na en baka:
—Hn! Disi a fosiwan! Na a sten piki so. We dati, a sten di piki dape
de, dati na pe hala den busimama fu a busi e libi. Ma libilibi sma
no e kon pasa dape de.

A yuru di Adyuku pasa dape, a kon miti wan kanti udu, a mu
go abra na udu dati. A krabdagu ben dape wantron. A krabdagu
tagi en, a taki: —No abra na udu, mi yonkuman, bika na udu di yu
e si de . . .

*

We, a yuru di a krabdagu doro na en, a taki: —We i si, na udu
di yu wani abra de, na a Grandagwe, na a gran heygron aboma di
den kon pina dyaso, di granmasra ben meki sweri anga en fu a
pranasi taki: hala yari a sa gi en dri nengre fu a nyan. Bika hala
yari granmasra ben mara sukru moro leki den tra pranasi di de.
Ma di en ati ben e kaba den nengre, ne yu si—yu ben abi den bigi
suma dati fu pranasi—ne den kon tyari en kon pina dya. Dan toku
ete granmasra, di den suma dati kon grani, toku a yagi den
puru na ini pranasi, taki den pikin mu tyari den gowe. Dosu mi
yonkuman, no go habra en srefsrefi. Dosu fa yu e si a tan seybi
yari langa di a no nyan, nyan a e nyan yu de. Ma dray baka go na
oso. Te yu go, dan yu tagi yu bigisuma, taki yu feni na mira di
den e kari wrokoman, na ati fu en.

Adyuku dray. A ten di Adyuku teki fu waka go, a no a ten
dati a teki. A waka kon ben waka langzaam, ma a waka go hesi.
Bika a feni a mira di den e kari wrokoman, te a puru na ati fu
en. A yuru di a go, en papa kari en taki: —Adyuku mi boi, yu
doro?

A taki: —Ya mi papa, mi doro.

you go under the tree, then it would invite you to sit down, it will
even lure you into lying down. But do not dare to do it. Run away
as fast as you can."

When Ajuku went on until he came to the tree, a nice wind fanned
him under the tree: "Ha!" Ajuku wants to stop. He thought of what
Krabdagu had told him. He took two paces, he stopped. He thought
of what Krabdagu had told him. A wind fanned all around him. When
he passed the shadow, he heard a voice behind him: "Ha! This is the
first!" So spoke the voice. Well see, there where the voice spoke,
there is the place where all mothers of the bush live. But as for
living beings, they never pass this place whole.

Now when Ajuku has passed this place, he stumbled on a block
of wood. He was forced to go over that piece of wood. All at once
the Krabdagu was there. The Krabdagu said to him: "Do not go
across this piece of wood, young man, for the wood that you see
there . . .

*

Well, when the Krabdagu came to him, he said: "Well see, the
piece of wood over which you want to cross is Grandagwe. It is the
biggest Aboma of the land, which people have succeeded in cornering
here, and with whom the plantation owner has sworn an oath on
behalf of the plantation, that he would give him three negroes to
eat every year if he could harvest each year more sugar than the
other plantations. So his heart caused the negroes to diminish in
numbers. But then, see, on the plantations there were men of
cunning. Then they came and cornered him here. And yet, when
these men of cunning had become old, then the owner still chased
them away from the plantation, saying that the children should
take them away. Therefore, young man, please, don't step over it.
For, as you see, he has been without food for seven years long, and
for sure he'll gobble you up. But return home. And when you get
there, then see, tell your parents that you have found the ant that
they call Worker, and that you found its heart also.

Ajuku turned back. The time he took over his journey back was
shorter than the time to this point. On his outward journey he
walked very slowly, but on his homeward journey he walked fast.
For see, he had found the ant that they call Worker, and he had
taken out its heart. When he was back, his father called him and
said: "Ajuku, my boy, are you back?"

He said: "Yes, father, I am back."

A taki: —Pe na mira di yu tya kon de, pe na ati fu en de?

A taki: —Mi papa, mi tya en kon.

A taki: —Pe a de? Kisi en gi mi.

A taki: —Mi papa, wakti. Mi o kisi en gi yu. Di mi e go, so mi si, so mi si. Mi waka, so mi si, so mi si. Mi waka, so mi si, so mi si. A laste presi mi go miti wan bigi pori udu. A bigi te, yu no sa abra en srefi, a kren yu ben o kren abra en. Ne wan krabdagu kon tagi mi taki: na a Grandagwe di granmasra ben meki sweri nanga en fu en pranasi, taki hala yari a sa gi en dri nengre fu a nyan, fu a mara moro sukru leki den tra pranasi di de krosbey. Granmasra ben meki sweri anga en fu dri nengre, ma son yari a ben nyan twenti te a ben nyan twenti na feyfi, te a ben kaba ala nengre fu Suksesi. Ne yu si, den bigisuma kon pina en poti dyaso seybi yari kaba. We, efu mi kren na en tapu, a e go nyan mi, bika angri e kiri en.

A papa taki: —Hay mi pikin, dan yu waka! We, yu sabi san na a krabdagu di yu si?

A taki: —Nono.

A taki: —We, a krabdagu dati na a mama fu a pranasi, a gronwinti fu en. A gronwinti fu en na Luangu. Na hen tyari yu.

A taki: —We mi pikin, fa yu tagi mi de, dan yu waka ay. Ma luku, mi o gi yu wan koni. Ma yu sa ori yu brede. Yu brada yu no mu tagi.

A taki: —Kwetkweti mi papa.

A taki: —We luku, mi abi wan bigi drifutu patu. Dan te musudey mamanten, dan mi o tjari yu gowe go wasi. Ma te mi wasi yu tin dey langa, dan yu sa si sortu bun mi du yu. Ma di fu erfu dey, te yu go a firi, te basya gi yu wan marki, yu no mu wroko en. Yu mu koyri fu yu.

So. A papa teki Adyuku, a tyari en go pe a obiagodo ben de, wasi Adyuku. Ma a tra brada a no wasi. A wasi en tin dey langa. Di fu erfu dey den go a firi. Basya marki wroko gi Adyuku. Adyuku teki en pipa, a e smoko fu en. Basya lontlontu ala sma wroko, a si en wroko, a taki: —Adyuku!

A taki: —Ya basya?

A taki: —Yu no e wroko?

A taki: —Nono basya, mi no e wroko.

A so Adyuku prey a sani a heri wiki, munde te doro satra. Satra

He said: "Where is the ant you bring with you, where is its heart?"
He replied: "Father, I have brought it with me."
He said: "Where is it? Bring it to me."
He replied: "Father wait. I shall bring it to you. For see, when I
left, I saw this, I saw that. I walked, I saw this, I saw that. I walked, I
saw this, I saw that. At last I stumbled on a big piece of rotten wood.
It was so big, one could not even step over it. One had to climb over
it. Then a Krabdagu said to me: It is the Grandagwe with which the
owner has sworn an oath on behalf of the plantation that he would
give him three negroes each year to eat, so that he, the owner, could
grind more sugar than the other plantations in the area. The owner
had sworn an oath for three negroes, but see, sometimes he gobbled
up twenty to twenty-five until he had devoured all the negroes on
Success. But see, then the elders—it was seven years ago—came here
and cornered him. Now if I had climbed onto him, he would have
eaten me up, because he is hungry."
The father said: "Yes, my child, then you've certainly walked far!
Well, do you know who the Krabdagu is that you saw?"
He answered: "No."
He replied: "Well, see, that Krabdagu is the mother of the plantation, its earth goddess. And that is a Luangu. She has guided you."
He said: "Well, my child, you see, as I've heard it from you, you've
certainly walked far. But see now, I shall give you a juju. But be sparing
with it. Do not tell your brother about it."
He said: "Certainly not, father."
He said: "Well see, I have a big tripod pan. Tomorrow morning
very early, I will take you there to wash. But see now, when I have
washed you for ten days on end, then you will find out how good I
have been to you. But then, on the eleventh day, when you go to the
field and the overseer asks you to do something, see now, then you
must refuse to do it. You must go and walk a little."
Then the father took Ajuku and brought him to the sacred tripod
pan. He washed Ajuku. But the other brother, as for him he did not
wash him. He washed Ajuku for ten days long. The eleventh day they
went to the field. The overseer entrusted Ajuku with his task. Ajuku
took his pipe and started to smoke. The overseer controls the work
of everyone. He saw Ajuku's work and said: "Ajuku!"
He replied: "Yes, overseer?"
He said: "Aren't you working?"
He replied: "No, overseer, I am not working."
In this way Ajuku played the game the whole week long from

bakadina basya kon na Adyuku, a taki: —Adyuku!

A taki: —Ya basya?

A taki: —We tamara mamanten. . . . Yu no wroko a heri wiki, yu no kan kisi lansun.

Adyuku taki: —Mi no abi bisi.

A taki: —We ma u o fon yu. Granmasra gi mi order fu fon yu.

Adyuku aksi, a taki: —Basya, omeni tetey yu o naki mi?

Basya taki: —We, u o naki yu wan ondro tetey.

We, wan ondro tetey di yu e yere de, na tu ondro tetey. A dati ede tamalen di nengresuma, blaka suma, Afrikan lutu, e teki meki stroop e dringi, efu den abi frustan, den no sa dringi en. Bika den suma di ben abi pranasi, den tya tamalen komopo te a tra kondre kon prani dya. Nanga dati den ben e fon katibo, fon srafu, den ben e losi en. We, efu yu sabi dati, dan tamalen mu de yu trefu.

Ya. We, a ten dati, te den tagi yu taki den o naki yu wan tetey, dan a tu tetey. Bika tu basya e de. Dan den e losi den tamalenwipi, dan den e brey en, dan den e broko batra, dan den tai den. Efu basya naki yu wan so a yu pipa, kaba brudu komopo, dan granmasra e lafu: —Basya, yu abi moi anu!

Dùsu tu basya, te den tu naki yu tu tetey, dan a e teri fu wan. Dan basya tagi Adyuku, a taki: —We Adyuku, u e go naki yu wan ondro tetey. (Dati wani taki a kon tu ondro). Bika fosi ten yu ben e wroko, ma now yu kon lesi, yu kon vrijpostuku. Mi tya go taigi granmasra. Dùsu yu e go kisi seybi-uku pansboko.

Adyuku taki: —Mi no abi trobi. Tu ondro tetey . . . We basya, a prey yu o prey anga mi. Efi yu ben gi mi wan seybi ondro ete, dan a kan de a ben sa betbeti mi skin. Ma tu ondro . . . Na soso yu e kon trobi mi skin basya.

Basya luku Adyuku so duun. A hari rapport, a tya en go gi granmasra. Granmasra taki: —Hn! Takel na kel, a vrijpostek.

Monday till Saturday. On Saturday evening the overseer came to
Ajuku and said: "Ajuku!"

He replied: "Yes, overseer?"

He said: "Well, tomorrow morning . . . you have not done a stitch
of work the whole week. You can't get any ration."

Ajuku replied: "I can't be bothered."

He said: "Well now, we shall trounce you. The owner has ordered
me to flog you."

Ajuku asked: "Overseer, how many strokes will you give me?"

Overseer replied: "Well, let's see now, we'll give you a hundred
strokes."

Well see, the hundred strokes which you hear now, they are
actually two hundred strokes. Therefore, the tamarind which negroes,
black people of African origin, use to make syrup which they drink,
if they had any brains, they would not drink it. For see, the people
who started the plantations, they brought the tamarind from other
parts of the world to plant here. With this they beat their chattels,
their slaves, they warmed the tamarind. Well now, when you know
this, the tamarind must be taboo to you.

Well see, at that time, when they said that they would give you
one stroke, it meant two. Because there were always two overseers
who did it. Then they warmed the tamarind whip, they braided it,
then they broke bottles and had glass woven in between. Now when
the overseer gives you a blow with it and the blood streams out, then
the owner laughs: "Overseer, you have golden hands."

Thus, you see, two overseers, when they give you two strokes,
then it counts for one. Then the overseer said to Ajuku: "Well Ajuku,
we are going to give you a hundred strokes (which means two
hundred), because formerly you used to work, but now you've become lazy, you've become cheeky. I shall tell it to the owner. Thus
you shall receive a flogging on the seven-cornered Spanish buck."[5]

Ajuku said: "It's all the same to me. Two hundred strokes . . .
well, overseer, that is child's play. Now if you were to give me seven
hundred strokes, then it might dent my body. But two hundred . . .
you disturb me for nothing."

The overseer looked fixedly at Ajuku. He reported to the owner.

---

5. The so-called *Spaanse bok* ("Spanish buck") was one of the cruelest punishments used in Surinam. The slave was tied in a bent-over position and flogged.
His wounds were rubbed afterward with lemon and gunpowder.

Na soso a e go dede, want a sa man teki seybi ondro tetey?

Sonde kon. Fosi den go kari Adyuku, Adyuku fosi doro kaba.
Adyuku taki: —Hodi mi granmasra! Nanga en pipa na en mofo. Granmasra
no e piki.

—Daki mi granmasra!
Daki mi sisi!
Daki mi bigi misi!
Den e luku Adyuku so duun.
Dan basya kon. Adyuku tanapu. Adyuku kren go. A yuru di Adyuku
go, a taki: —Mi basya, mi e haksi yu ete wan tron, taki omen tetey yu o
gi mi.

Basya taki: —Tu ondro.

A taki: —Basya, prey yu o prey anga mi. Mi denki a wan seybi
ondro yu ben o gi mi. Dati a fu mi krasi mi skin srefsrefi.

Dan granmasra tanapu anga en bigi pipa na barkon. A yuru
di basya naki a wan tetey so "taw!" a tra tetey fadon "tyaw!", sisi
bari: —Mi gado, mi baka! Bika a tetey di fadon na Adyuku skin, dan
sisi firi en. A yuru di sisi dray so, luku so, a bigi yáki di a weri sidon a
tapu a dyarususturu, a priti opo. Ala en baka priti opo.

Adyuku bari gi basya, a taki: —Basya, kanti tetey gi mi. Dati mi abi
fanowdu. Saka tetey gi mi! Basya kanti baka. Sisi flaw. Granmasra lon,
a taki: —No naki moro! No naki moro! Sisi e dede!

Adyuku dray, a taki: —Basya, saka tetey gi mi! Tetey mi mu abi!

Dan basya ook no e ferstan a sani. Den bigin naki Adyuku
bruyabruya tetey. Ala tetey di e fadon, granmasra bari te a lolo
na a balkon. Ala pipa komopo na en mofo. Ala en mindri baka priti.
Granmasra flaw, sisi flaw, pranasi trubu. Dan basya no sá san fu
du. Den libi Adyuku.

Adyuku e kari den taki: —U kon fon mi no?

Basya srefi trowe ala tetey. Adyuku gowe fu en na oso. A yuru di
a go, en papa aksi en taki: —Mi boy, fa a pasa?

A taki: —We mi papa, noyti mi si so.

A saka, a brasa en papa, a go a gotro, a go kisi fisi, a kon bori

The owner said: "Beat the hell out of him, cheeky nigger. He will only die, for who can stand seven hundred strokes?"

Sunday came. Before they even came to call Ajuku, he was there. Ajuku said (still with his pipe in his mouth): "Howdy, owner." The owner answered him not.

"Howdy, owner!"

"Howdy, Sisi!"[6]

"Howdy, Madame!"

They looked at Ajuku fixedly.

Then the overseer arrived. Ajuku stood. Ajuku climbed up. Now see, when Ajuku climbed up, he said: "Overseer, I ask you once again, how many strokes will you give me?"

Overseer replied: "Two hundred."

He said: "Overseer, child's play. I thought you would give me seven hundred. Then at least you'd scratch my body."

The owner stood with his big pipe on the balcony. Now see, when the overseer gave one stroke "whack!" and the other also came down "whack!" then Sisi yelled out: "My God, my back!" For see, the stroke which fell on the back of Ajuku was felt by Sisi. Now see, when Sisi turned round then she saw, sitting on the jealousy chair, that the yaki she had on was torn open. Her whole back was torn open.

Ajuku called to the overseer: "Overseer, pour out your strokes on me! That I have need of. Let the strokes rain on me." Basja let it stream forth again. Sisi fainted. The owner came running and said: "Don't hit any more, don't hit any more. Sisi is dying.

Ajuku turned his head and said: "Overseer, let the strokes fall on me. Strokes I must have."

As for the overseer, now, he did not understand anything of this. They started to beat Ajuku in a rather confused manner. But see, for all the strokes which came down, the owner shouted until he was rolling across the balcony. His pipe fell out of his mouth. His entire back was torn. The owner fainted, Sisi fainted, the plantation was in confusion. Then the overseer did not know what to do. They left Ajuku there.

Ajuku called: "Aren't you coming to beat me?"

The overseer threw down his whip. Ajuku returned home. When he came back, his father asked him: "My boy, how did you fare?"

He replied: "Well see, father, I've never seen such a thing."

He crouched down, embraced his father, he went to the ditch, he

6. The more or less official mistress or housekeeper of the owner, herself a slave, was called *sisi*. She occupied an important position between masters and slaves.

tonton gi en papa. Adyuku, a so a e waka na ini a pranasi.

Ma now, yu ben abi wan man na ini Motkriki di abi wan
pranasi den e kari Dagrâti. Den ben e kari en masra Müringen.
Dan a yuru di granmasra kon betre, dan granmasra komopo anga
en boto. Den tentiboto dati, a fositen den ben e kari den
tenboto. Dan den e poti den srafu e lo. Na a tenboto u waka now:

> A Sinamari di e beni,
> Sinamari di e prodo,
> Sinamari-o.
> —A-e!
> A Sinamari di e beni,
> Sinamari di e prodo,
> Sinamari-o.
> —A-e!
> —Mi weri-o, mi weri-o.
> —Timan, timan, pa . . . ruu!

A boto e lon go a Motkriki. Nanga dyentiwatra den e waka.
A yuru di a masra fu Suksesi doro a Motkriki, a masra Müringen,
a go, den sidon, den taki tori. A tagi en taki: —Luku, mi abi wan vent
dape na ini mi pranasi, geen land te bezeilen anga a vent. A vent no
wani wroko. Efi yu go fu fon a vent, ala den tetey, na mi skin a e fadon,
na sisi skin a e fadon. Voor wan dri maanden geleden den fon a vent.
Ala mi mindri baka priti, dati bijna mi dede srefi. Mi no sabi fa fu du
anga a vent. Man, yu no kan gi mi wan raad, fa mi sa ruim a vent op?

Müringen taki: —A wan lawlaw sani. Wel kijk, mi e go sori yu
wan sani. Sonde mi e kon a yu. Mi e teki ala den tra mati fu mi.
Dan u e poti den kel, meki den go puru kokronto. Dan u e sutu
den trowe.

A masra e kisi wan troostwoord. A dray en boto gowe baka.
Den lon go na oso.

> A Sinamari di e beni,
> Sinamari di e prodo,
> Sinamari-o.
> —A-e!
> A sinamari di e beni,

caught some fish, he came back to cook the plaintains for his father.
For see, in this way Ajuku went about his business on the plantation.

Now there was a man in Mot Creek who had a plantation called
Dageraad. They called him Mr. Mühringen. When the owner was a bit
better, then he went out in his boat. Formerly they called these boats
tenboto. Then they ordered the slaves to row. In this tenboto we are
now sailing:

> It is Sinamari which makes its curtsy here,
> It is Sinamari which gives a show.
> Sinamari-o
> Hey-ho.
> It is Sinamari which makes its curtsy here,
> It is Sinamari which gives a show.
> Sinamari-o
> Hey-ho.
> I am weary, I am weary,
> Timan, timan, pa . . . ruu.[7]

The boat is off to Mot Creek. The boat goes with speed against the
tide. When the owner of Success came to Mot Creek, to Mr. Mühringen,
they sat down and chatted. He said to him: "See, I have a Johnny on
my plantation, but as for him, he is absolutely beyond control.
The guy does not want to work. When you proceed to beat him up,
then all the blows descend on my body, on Sisi's body. Three months
ago they thrashed the fellow. My whole back was torn so that I nearly
died. I am at my wit's end with the chap. Can't you suggest a plan to
get rid of the fellow?"

Mühringen said: "Oh well, this is nothing. Well see, I shall show
you something. On Sunday I will visit you. I'll take all my friends
along. Then we will instruct the chap to go and pluck coconuts. And
then we take potshots at them, blast them out of the tree."

The man was consoled. He turned his boat and returned. He sailed
home swiftly.

> It is Sinamari which makes its curtsy here,
> It is Sinamari which gives a show.
> Sinamari-o
> Hey-ho.
> It is Sinamari which makes its curtsy here,

7. The *ruu* refers to the swishing of the boat through the waters, which, in
the song, is represented by the dropping of the voice to an almost sibilant
whisper.

Sinamari di e prodo,
Sinamari-o.
—A-e!
—Mi weri-o, mi weri-o.
—Timan, timan, pa . . . ruu!

A yuru di a doro oso, den botoman tay boto, a dyompo go na
inisey. Sisi aksi en taki:—Granmasra fa a pasa?

A taki: —Wel, mi go na mi mati Müringen na Dageraad na ini
Motkriki. Dan dati gi mi wan troostwoord. U e go opruim a vent
dalig!

Ma a yuru di a taki so, dan sensi di a teki en boto e go,
dan Adyuku sabi. Adyuku go na en papa. En papa taki: —We mi
boy, yu sabi san o pasa? Granmasra e go na ini Motkriki, a masra
Müringen. Ma arki. A o kari yu te sonde mamanten fu go puru
kokronto. Dan den o sutu yu. Ma a no yu wanwan. Den o kari negyi
fu unu. Dan den o sidon nanga den gon na bakra oso.
A taki: —Go kari sowan yonkuman kon, kari sowan yonkuman kon.
Bika na neygi fu unu den de, di den o kari. Dan den o seni un
go puru kokronto. Ma yu na a fosiwan den o sutu.

So Adyuku go kari hala den trawan. A papa tyari den go,
a wasi den te a doro. Di a kaba wasi den, —satraneti na a laste
wasi di a wasi den—deybroko fu sonde musudey mamanten feyfi yuru,
wan sani leki arfu siksi so kon a siksi yuru tapu, granbasya doro na
Adyuku oso.
—Adyuku.
—Ya basya?
—Granmasra e kari yu.

A go na den trawan oso. Adyuku, a waka go a fesisey. A so a
karikari den, te den doro neygi. A yuru di den kon a fesisey, den
seni Adyuku: —Yu e go na a bon disi, yu mu go puru kokronto.
Yu e go na a disi, yu mu go puru kokronto. Bika den kokrontobon
ben prani anga langa rij.

A yuru di den bigin kren go a tapu a kokrontobon—un mu
reken taki granmasra abi wraak a tapu Adyuku—a lay ala en tu
dobluloop gon, a naki "kraw!" Hn! A yuru di a skot komopo,
presi fu Adyuku fadon a tapu a bon, Adyuku dray, a luku

It is Sinamari which gives a show.
Sinamari-o
Hey-ho.
I am weary, I am weary,
Timan, timan, pa . . . ruu.

When they came home and the rowers had moored the boat, the
owner alighted and went inside. Sisi asked the owner how he had
fared.

He replied: "Well, I went to my friend Mühringen at Dageraad,
which is in Mot Creek. He gave me some consolation. Soon we are
going to mop up the man."

But see now, no sooner had the boat left than Ajuku knew it.
Ajuku went to his father. His father said: "My boy, do you know
what's in store for you? The owner is on his way to Mot Creek to
Mr. Mühringen. But listen carefully. He will call you on Sunday
morning to go and pluck coconuts. Then they will take potshots at
you. But not only at you. They are going to summon nine of you.
Then they will sit down in the house of the white man with their
guns." He said: "Go and call such a boy. Go and call so and so.
Summon them, because they will call nine of you. Then they will
send you to pluck coconuts. But see, you are the first one they will
take a shot at."

Thus Ajuku went to summon the others. The father took them
with him, washed them until he was finished. When he had finished
washing them—on Saturday night he washed them for the last time—
then in the early hours of Sunday, round about five o'clock, that is,
between half-past five and six o'clock, the chief overseer came to
the house of Ajuku.

"Ajuku."

"Yes, overseer?"

"The owner calls you."

The overseer went to the house of the others. Ajuku walked to the
mansion. In this way the overseer called the others until there were
nine. When they came to the mansion, they said to Ajuku: "Ajuku,
you get into this tree. You must go and pluck coconuts. As for you,
you go to this tree, for you too must pluck coconuts. For the palms
were planted in a long row."

Then when they started to climb the palms—bear in mind that the
owner was out to have his revenge on Ajuku—then he loaded both his
double-barreled guns. He let fly. Wham! Oh! Now when the shot went
off, Ajuku, instead of falling out of the tree, turned, looked at the

granmasra, a taki: —Granmasra, teki den kugru fu yu dya baka.

Granmasra skreki te a gon komopo na en anu fadon. A Müringen di ben dya, a lay wasi gi a trawan. En gon puru watra. A so den sutu sote. Trawan gon e broko, trawan skot no e piki. Masra Müringen kon beyfi. A heri sopi di den ben poti fu dringi, den no man dringi en. A saka ini en tenboto, a gowe fu en a Motkriki. Dan den yonkuman anga Adyuku, den go a den oso.

A yuru di masra Müringen go na en pranasi, na Dagráti pranasi, dan Adyuku meki wan pikin faya na wan ipi so, a e poti wanwan pisi udu gi en. We a wanwan pisi udu di a e poti gi en, masra Müringen no man sribi. Fa yu si a faya e bron, na so en heri skin e bron. Ne a kon, a kon tagi a masra fu Suksesi taki: —Yu sabi san? Yu poti mi na ini wan sani ini. Yu tyari mi kon dya nanga den nengre fu Suksesi dya, dati heri neti mi no man sribi. Mi musu e waka lontu. Mi skin e faja, dati mi skin e bron, ala mi buba. Mi no dede ete, mi skin e bron. Ma mi sa libi a pranasi disi, mi sa gowe. Yu Woiski, yu kon poti mi, tyari mi kon na ini a verdoem dya, meki den nengre di yu abi dyaso, mi no dede ete, den e bronbron mi skin.

Ne masra Müringen komopo ini Motkriki. A libi Dagráti pranasi, a e kon a Parasey. Ne den nengre fu Suksesi, di a ben de mofoyari, a yuru di den prey den susa, ne den e bari:

> Yu e yere wan bari a Parasey
> —dyendyen.
> —Yu e yere wan bari a Parasey
> —dyendyen.
> Masra Müringen go na Para
> —dyendyen.
> —Yu e yere wan bari a Parasey
> —dyendyen.

We ne masra Müringen, a no man tan a Motkriki. Ne yu si, a feroysi kon bay pranasi a Paraliba. Na Suksesinengre lon masra Müringen komopo na opo Kotka. Bika a ben go fu go yepi en mati, masra Woiski, di ben abi Suksesi.

We kondreman, dan un musu hori den tori disi na ede. Mi srefi no ben de a srafuten, ma san den bigisma fu mi kon tagi mi, a so den ben e du anga nengre a fositen. So a tori kon kaba.

owner and said: "Owner, take these bullets of yours back."

The owner had such a fright that the gun fell out of his hands. Müh-ringen, who was present, loaded his gun and let fly at one of the others. Water gushed forth. Thus they shot. One person's gun broke. The other's shells did not go off. Mr. Mühringen started shivering. All the drinks which they had standing ready for drinking, they found impossible to drink. Mr. Mühringen went to his tenboto and rushed off to Mot Creek. The young men and Ajuku returned home.

Now when Mr Mühringen was on his way to the plantation, that is, Dageraad, then Ajuku made a small fire on a heap. He placed a few pieces of wood on it. Well see, because of the pieces of wood he placed on it, Mr. Mühringen couldn't bat an eyelid. As the fire glows, so his whole body glows. Then he came to say to the owner of Success: "Do not you realize that you are responsible for my plight? You have brought me here with the niggers of Success, so that I could not sleep a wink all night. I am forced to run around. My skin is afire, my whole body. I am not yet dead, and my whole body is already afire. But I shall leave this plantation. You, Woiski, you've brought me to this sorry plight, with the result that the niggers whom you have here— I am not even dead and they are burning my body."

Then Mr. Mühringen departed from Mot Creek. He left Dageraad plantation and went to the Para River. And the negroes of Success, when the new year arrived, the time when they play the Susa game, then they sang:

> One hears a yell on the Para,
> —Tingaling.
> —One hears a yell on the Para,
> —Tingaling.
> Mr. Mühringen left for the Para,
> —Tingaling.
> —One hears a yell on the Para,
> —Tingaling.

Well then, as for Mr. Mühringen, he could not stay in Mot Creek. Well, you see, he moved his house and bought a plantation on the Para. The niggers of Success forced Mr. Mühringen to leave the upper Cottica at a trot. For he had come to help his friend, Mr. Woiski, who owned Success.

Well, countrymen, keep these stories in your head. I myself was not there during the time of slavery. But according to what the old people told me, that is the way they used to treat negroes in the old days. Thus the story is at an end.

Baya Afrenkuma

Moy baya Afrenkuma-oi,
kon teki nyanyan-o, mi baya-o.
Moy baya Afrenkuma-o,
kon teki nyanyan-o, mi baya.
Mi delima, mi delima,
mi sisa, a no yu mi wani.

Na Anansitori. We na Afrenkuma na wan yonkuman. We, wan
mama ben abi dri umapikin, nanga Afrenkuma, wan manpikin. Dùsu
meki u taki, dati Afrenkuma ben de bigiwan fu den sisa, den dri
sisa.

We ma now di Afrenkuma tan te, dan a ben abi ay na en pikin
sisa tapu. Dati wani taki a laste pikin fu a mama. En nanga a pikin
na wan mama, wan papa. Ma now a ben abi ay na en tapu. Dan
Afrenkuma tan te, a no sá san a mu du. Dan a mandi libi oso,
a no e kon na oso kwetkweti. Dan a ben abi wan pikin boto, dan
a e sidon na ini a pikin boto, du leki a e drifi uku a liba.

Ma now dan a mama wakti en, a papa wakti en.
A taki: —Tan! Ma a boi Afrenkuma. San? A no e kon na oso.
Seni den sisa fu en gowe go kari en.

—Kwetkweti, a no kan kon. A taki, en no e kon na oso moro.
—Mi Gado. Luku wán manpikin mi abi. Dan san du en?

A mama taki: —Ma luku, angri sa e kiri en. A bun. A taki, en
no e kon. Ma te mi bori, mi sa seni en nyanyan gi en.

Dan te a mama bori, dan a puru nyanyan, meki u taki: gi a
bigi sisa. Dan a taki: —De, go gi yu baya Afrenkuma! Kari en.
A no e kon a sey. Ma te yu kari en, a si taki a nyanyan, a sa kon
teki en.

Dan a sisa teki a nyanyan, dan a go leti a sey liba so. Dan
Afrenkuma de na mindri, a e pari en pikin boto, We na pikin
wenke e go singi, Afrenkuma sisa, dan na en e go singi gi en.

Baya Afrenkuma-oi,
kon teki yu nyanyan-e, mi baya-o.
Moi baya Afrenkuma-e,
kon teki yu nyanyan-e, mi baya-e.

Friend Afrenkuma

> Handsome friend Afrenkuma,
> come fetch your food, my friend.
> Handsome friend Afrenkuma,
> come fetch your food, my friend.
> My delima, my delima,
> my sister, it is not you I want.

This is an Anansitori. Well, this Afrenkuma is a young man. See, his mother had three daughters and, in addition, Afrenkuma. Therefore, let us say, Afrenkuma was older than his sisters.

Now when Afrenkuma was a little older, that is to say, later on, then he had an eye on his youngest sister. That is to say, the last child of his mother. He and the girl are of one mother and father. But yet now he fancied her. Afrenkuma was stumped for a while. He did not know what to do. Then he became angry and left the house, he did not come home any more. He had a very small canoe; he went and sat in it and pretended he was angling.

His mother waited for him. His father waited for him. The mother said: "Oh, so. But the boy is not coming home. His sisters will have to go and fetch him."

"Not a chance, he will not come. He says that he won't come home again."

"My God! Look, I have got only one son. What's the matter with him?"

The mother said: "But just wait and see; he will get hungry. Okay. He says that he won't come. But when I cook, I shall send some food to him."

When the mother had finished cooking, she dished up some food and gave it to the eldest sister. And then she said: "Here have it. Give it to your brother, Afrenkuma. Call him. He does not come to the land. But when you call him and he sees the food, he will come and fetch it."

The sister took the food and went directly to the river bank. Afrenkuma was in the middle of the river, paddling his boat. Well now, the young girl sings, she, the sister of Afrenkuma, sings for him.

> Handsome friend Afrenkuma,
> come fetch your food, my friend.
> Handsome friend Afrenkuma,
> come fetch your food, my friend.

A yonkuman dray, a luku en. Dan Afrenkuma e go piki en baka: —

> Mi delima, mi delima,
> mi sisa a no yu mi wani.
> Mi delima, mi delima,
> mi sisa a no yu mi wani.

A wenke dray nanga en nyanyan go baka. Di a go, mama taki:
—Tan! Fa? Yu kon nanga a nyanyan baka?
A taki: —Mi mama, mi brada Afrenkuma taki, a no mi en wani.
A mama taki: —We a bun, tamara mi sa seni yu tra sisa.
Tamara a seni a tweyde go.

> Moi baya Afrenkuma-e,
> kon teki yu nyanyan-e, mi man de.
> Moi baya Afrenkuma-o,
> kon teki yu nyanyan-o, man de.

> Mi delima, mi delima,
> mi sisa a no yu mi wani.
> Delima-o, delima-o,
> sisa a no yu mi wani.

A dati dray baka, a go. A bun. A tra dey a mama bori a nyanyan
baka, dan a tapu en gi na lastewan. A taki: —Tyari gi.
A yuru ten a doro, a bari en baka: —

> Moi baya Afrenkuma-o,
> kon teki yu nyanyan-e, man de.
> Mi moy baya Afrenkuma,
> kon teki yu nyanyan-o, mi baya-e.

A yuru ten a dray, a si a pikin sisa, a bari: —

> Mi delima, mi delima,
> mi sisa na yu mi wani.
> Mi delima, mi delima,
> mi sisa, na yu mi wani.

A yuru ten a sutu a boto, a teki a nyanyan poti a boto, a teki
a pikin sisa kon na en boto . . . srr!
Mama de na oso, a e luku pikin fu kon. Pikin no sa kon.
A taki: —Ma tan! Pe a boy e tan so?

The young man turned, looked at her and then he answered her:

> My delima, my delima,
> my sister, it is not you I want.
> My delima, my delima,
> my sister, it is not you I want.

The girl returned with the food. When she came home, the mother said: "So! How now? Are you back with the food?"

She replied: "Mother, my brother, Afrenkuma, says it is not me that he wants."

The mother said: "Okay, tomorrow I shall send your other sister." The next day she sent the second sister.

> Handsome friend Afrenkuma,
> come fetch your food, my friend.
> Handsome friend Afrenkuma,
> come fetch your food, my friend.

> My delima, my delima,
> my sister, it is not you I want.
> My delima, my delima,
> my sister, it is not you I want.

She also returned. Good. The following day the mother once more cooked food. She dished it up and gave it to the last one. She said: "Take it and give it to him."

When she approached, she also called:

> Handsome friend Afrenkuma,
> come fetch your food, my friend.
> Handsome friend Afrenkuma,
> come fetch your food, my friend.

He turned, saw his little sister, and shouted:

> My delima, my delima,
> my sister, it is you I want.
> My delima, my delima,
> my sister, it is you I want.

Then he caused the boat to shoot forward and came quickly to the bank. He took the food and placed it in the boat. He took his little sister in the boat with him and was off.

Mother sits at home and waits for her child. Her child does not come home. She says: "What's the matter? Where is that boy?"

Ne a komopo, ne a go a watrasey. A kari en pikin uma. Afrenkuma
taki: —O mama, mi no kan tyari en kon moro.
—Afrenkuma, fa?
A taki: —We mama, disi a mi frow!
—Yu pikin sisa, na en na yu frow?
A taki: —Ya!
En mama broko wan apra. Umasuma no ben abi borsu. Dan
nèleki mi anga yu de, so a ben de. Ne a broko na apra. A frrr! Pap!
A kisi bobi. A taki: —Yu Afrenkuma, tapu yu sa frey. Yu sa e saka
a gron, ma yu sa e frey a tapu.
We Afrenkuma, san na en? A nen di den e kari Afrenkuma?
Na doyfi. Doyfi di den e kweki na oso. Na en na Afrenkuma . . .
Dùsu dati wani taki: a kon leki a yonkuman tron doyfi. Dati
wani taki: en nanga en sisa tron wan pari doyfi, uma nanga man.

Mati e nyan anga mati, ma mati e kiri mati

> Makukukuku,
> ten de,
> —No meki den uma kori yu.
> —Ten de,
> —no meki den uma kori yu.

We yu si, a singi disi di singi de taki "Makukukuku, ten de,
no meki den uma kori yu," a tori disi nen taki "Mati e nyan anga
mati, ma mati e kiri mati."
We, na mati Owrukuku nanga Kakafowru ben de bigi mati.
Ala presi den tu e waka. Ma wan dey mati Kakafowru komopo, a
go a mati Owrukuku, a taki: —Mati Owrukuku, luku, ala presi
mi anga yu nomo e waka. Ma nomo den kari mi a wan prisiri na
oposey. Dosu, ne mi kon kari yu fu yu kon anga mi.
A taki: —Tru mi mati? We, san na a prisiri dan?
A taki: —We, wan bigi banya e go prey dape de. We, mi Kakafowru, di mi sabi dansi so, a dati ede den kon kari mi. We,
yu a mi mati. Den taki mi kan tyari suma mi wani. We, mi no
a tra suma e tyari, yu nomo. Ne mi kon kari yu fu go anga mi.
Mati Owrukuku taki: —We mati, a no wan sani? Dan yu
wakti, meki mi weri mi krosi. Dan un sa teki waka.
So Owrukuku dyompo, a weri en krosi. Den tu teki waka.
Den waka, den waka, den waka. A yuru den waka leti mindri

She went to the side of the water. She called her daughter. Afrenkuma answered: "Oh mother, I can't return her."

"Afrenkuma, what's the matter?"

He said: "Well see, mother, she is my wife."

"Your youngest sister is your wife?"

He said: "Yes."

Then his mother broke an apple in half. See, at that time women didn't have breasts. They were just like you and me. Then she broke the apple. She took aim and let fly, and—whizz! . . . bang!—she had breasts! She said: "You, Afrenkuma, you shall fly in the sky. You will regularly come to earth, but will inhabit the sky."

Well now, Afrenkuma—what is it really? The name Afrenkuma, it is a dove, a homing pigeon. That is Afrenkuma . . . that is to say, the young man became a dove. That is to say, he and his sister became a pair of doves, male and female.

Never trust a friend

> Makukukuku,
> It is time,
> —Don't let the women fool you.
> It is time,
> —Don't let the women fool you.

Well, you see, this song that I sing here—"Makukukuku, It is time, don't let the women fool you—this story is called "Never trust a friend."

Well, friend Owl and Rooster were good friends. They went together everywhere. Now one day friend Rooster went outside, came across friend Owl and said: "Friend Owl, look here, we're seen together everywhere. But now I've been invited to a feast upstream. Therefore, I'm coming to fetch you to go with me."

He said: "Really, friend? Well, what sort of a feast?"

He replied: "Well, there's going to be a big banya. As for me, Rooster, because I dance so well they've invited me. But see, you are my friend. They've told me to bring along whomever I wish, and I have no one else to bring along, except you. Therefore I've come to fetch you to go along."

Friend Owl said: "Well, friend, you don't say. Wait a minute so that I can put on my clothes and then we can be off."

Owl jumped up and put on his clothes. They went on their way together. They walked and walked and walked. When they were half-

fu a pasi, suma den si e kon? Mati Sabaku. Mati Sabaku taki:
— Mati Kakafowru, fa yu de?
A taki: —Baya, fa yu de?
— Mati Owrukuku, fa yu de?
A taki: —Baya, fa yu de?
— Baya, pe u e go so dan?
A taki: —We, a no wan gran banya o prey dape de? Ne den seni
kari mi. Ne mi e go.
A taki: —We mati, dan meki u waka makandra. Bika mi srefi
den kari tu. A dape mi e go.
A so ala den dri mati, den waka, den go. A yuru di den
go so, umasma leki pesi.
We, te banya e prey, mofoneti, dan a mandron e prey sabaku.
Mindrineti a e prey owrukuku, èn te musudey mamanten dan a e
prey kakafowru di e broko dey.
We fa yu si den doro na a prey ini, mati Kakafowru bigin dansi.
Mati Owrukuku sidon fu en a wan sey pii. A e luku mati
Kakafowru dansi, te a doro wan pisi. Nomo a kon mindrineti. Dan
mati Sabaku, na en ben de a tapu a dron, en e prey a langa dron.
Nomo mati Owrukuku go na en, taki: —Mi mati.
A taki: —En?
A taki: —Gi mi afu dya, gi mi wan anu dron, mi prey.
A taki: —Baya, teki.
Owrukuku dyompo a tapu a dron. A bigin prey. We fa yu si
Owrukuku bigin prey, we ala den suma di ben sidon a sey,
ala dyompo so, den kon bigin e dansi, den way angisa gi en e
figi en fesi. Ne mati Kakafowru luku duun, ne a bari a singi disi
taki: —

> Makukukuku,
> ten de,
> —No meki den uma kori yu.
> —Ten de,
> —no meki den uma kori yu.

Ma mati Owrukuku no e ferstan, leki a e prey a dron nomo.
Ma di Owrukuku sidon a wan sey, te a a e prey dron so, nomo mati
Sabaku kon, a taki: —Grantangi-oi! Ala suma dya na a prisiri, mi e
begi un meki mi kan bari wan mofo singi anga un prisiri.
Ala suma piki taki: —Ya, masra Sabaku, yu kan singi, bika yu ben
e prey dron. Ibri sma e komopo anga wan singi na en oso.

way, who do they see coming on? None other than friend Heron.

Friend Heron said: "Friend Owl, how are you?"

He answered: "Well, and you?"

"Friend Rooster, how are you?"

He replied: "Man, how are you?"

"Gentlemen, where are you off to?"

Rooster replied: "Well, isn't there a big banya being held? They have invited me. Thither I am going."

He said: "Well, friends, let us then go together for they have also called me. I too am going there."

In this way the three friends went on their way. When they arrived there, ho, women galore.

Well now, when a banya is being performed at the beginning of the evening, then the long drum plays heron fashion. At midnight it plays owl fashion. And in the early morning it plays rooster fashion, because the rooster announces the day.

Well, as soon as they arrived at the performance, friend Rooster started to dance. Friend Owl sat quietly aloof. He peered for a time at Rooster dancing. Then it was midnight. Friend Heron was sitting on the drum, beating the long drum.

Then friend Owl went to him and said: "Friend?"

He answered: "What?"

He said: "Let me too have a go at the drum."

He said: "Take over."

Owl jumped on the drum. He started to play. No sooner did Owl start to play than all the women who were sitting aside jumped up in unison and started to dance. They honored him by fanning him with their kerchiefs, and wiped the sweat off his face. Then friend Rooster looked fixedly at him, and sang this song:

> Makukukuku
> It is time,
> —Don't let the women fool you.
> It is time,
> —Don't let the women fool you.

But friend Owl did not understand, because he was so carried away by the drum.

And while he was sitting aside and playing, friend Heron stepped forward and said: "Please. All of you here, I beg permission to sing a song at your feast."

All the people answered and said: "Yes, Mr. Heron, you may sing, for you have finished playing the drum. Everyone leaves his home

We dan a de fu yu taki nomo, u e harki meki un piki.
  Nomo Sabaku bari, a taki: —

> Kolon kolon kolon,
> san koniman.
> Te na dey kon,
> un sa si den moyman.

  Ala suma piki. A dron bigin prey, den e dansi. Ma en, mati Owrukuku
di sidon a tapu a dron e prey, a no frustan, taki na en Sabaku taki
taki: te a dey opo, den sa si a moyman di den e way angisa gi, di
den e figi en fesi. Bika Owrukuku fesi no switi. Dati ede a no e waka
a dey, a soso neti a e waka. Ma en mati Kakafowru frustan, a dray
baka, a luku mati Owrukuku, a bari baka: —

> Makukukukuku,
> ten de.
> —No meki den uma kori yu.
> Ten de,
> —no meki den uma kori yu.

  We yu si, a yuru di mati Owrukuku e prey a dron so, nomo a haksi
mati Sabaku, a taki: —Mati, olati u de? Dan u de dri yuru mamanten
kaba.
  Sabaku piki: —Mati, yu no abi fu frede, fa yu e prey a dron so
moy. U no de lati, a dyonsnode twarfu yuru naki. Owrukuku e prey
nomo.
  We, a taki: —Mati, olati u de?
  Sabaku piki: —Mati, yu no abi fu frede, prey fu yu doro, a
dyonsno twarfu yuru naki. Dan u de fo yuru kaba.
  Owrukuku de a tapu a langa dron nomo: akankan gringrin,
kankan gringrin. Kakafowru e dansi. Sabaku e luku en nomo.
  Owrukuku taki baka, a taki: —Mati, olati u de? Dan u de arfu
feyfi mamanten. Sabaku piki: —We mati, a dyonsnode twey yuru naki.
  Dan Owrukuku seri ede a tapu a langa dron. We, so a Owrukuku
e prey a langa dron so, hala suma, nowan sribi no e kon na ay, leki
a dansi nomo. Owrukuku saka en ede so, a kanti ede gi a langa
dron. Nomo Sabaku luku baka, a bari baka taki:

with a song. You have only to sing and we'll listen so that we can
join you."

Then the Heron sang:

> Kolon kolon kolon,
> Oh, what clever ones
> when the day dawns,
> you will see the pretty ones.

All the people joined in. The drum started to play. They danced.
But friend Owl who sat on the drum did not understand that Heron
referred to him when he said: "When the day dawns you'll see the
pretty boy whom they now fan and whose face they wipe." For the
face of the Owl is a sight to give you sore eyes. For this reason he does
not walk around during the day, only at night. But friend Rooster
understood. He turned around, looked at friend Owl and once more
sang:

> Makukukuku
> It is time
> —Don't let the women fool you.
> It is time
> —Don't let the women fool you.

Well see, while friend Owl was sitting thus and playing, then he
asked friend Heron what the time was. It was already three o'clock
in the morning.

But the Heron answered: "Friend, don't be afraid, you are playing
very well. It is not late. The clock has only struck twelve." Owl continued playing.

Well, he said: "Friend, what time is it?"

Heron answered: "Friend, don't be afraid. Play on. The clock has
only struck twelve." But then it was already four o'clock.

The Owl sat on the long drum: akankan-gringrin, kankan gringrin.
The Rooster danced. The Heron only looked at him.

Again the Owl said: "Friend, what time is it?" By then it was already
half-past four in the morning.

The Heron answered: "Well, friend, the clock has just struck two."

Then Owl spent himself completely on the drum. Well, so hard did
Owl beat the drum that all the people thought only of dancing and
not of sleeping. The Owl bent his head, tipped his head to the side of
the long drum. Then the Heron looked again and sang:

Kolon kolon,
san koniman,
te na dey kon,
u sa si den moyman-oy.

Mati Kakafowru dray en ay baka, a luku, bari baka taki:

Makukukuku,
ten de,
—No meki den uma kori yu.
Ten de,
—no meki den uma kori yu.

We yu si, a yuru di Owrukuku prey a dron, a saka en ede, a e
prey. Sabaku srefi hopo, a e dansi.

Yu sabi fa dey e tan so, fa a broko so wantron so. A dey broko
so wantron so. A yuru di mati Owrukuku hopo ede, a si dey
fresfres kon ala presi. Hm! Now den suma si so takru fesi
sani di den ben abi dape de. A yuru di Owrukuku wani gowe,
ne den grabu tiki, ne den fon Owrukuku kiri.

We, na a tori disi: Mati e nyan anga mati, mati e kiri mati. A
tori kaba.

> Kolon kolon,
> Oh, what clever ones
> when the day dawns,
> you will see the pretty ones.

Friend Rooster turned his eyes again, looked and sang:

> Makukukuku
> It is time,
> —Don't let the women fool you.
> It is time,
> —Don't let the women fool you.

Well, you see, when the Owl was playing the drum, he dropped his head and beat it so that even the Heron got up and danced.

You know how it is at dawn; how it breaks out so suddenly. The day dawned all at once. When Owl lifted up his head, he saw that the dawn had come freshly all over the place. Oh! Look now. The people saw how ugly he really was. When Owl tried to steal away, they pounced on him with sticks and beat him to death.

Well see, that is this story, "Never trust a friend." My story is over.

CHAPTER 4

Johannes King

Johannes King was a Matuari bushnegro. The Surinam bushnegroes are descendants of former runaway slaves organized in several tribes in the interior. The principal tribes are Matuari, Saramacca, and Djuka. The first two speak a special Creole language heavily spiced with Portuguese elements. The third speaks an English-based Creole more reminiscent of the Creole spoken in town and on the coast. The bushnegro tribes lived in complete isolation and carried on continuous warfare with the colonial government until peace treaties were concluded with the main tribes in 1760 (Groot 1970) and in 1762 and 1767 (Groot 1969). They continued, however, to live inland in splendid isolation. They could visit the town only by permission of the government. The government, however, paid them a regular tribute, mainly provisions of food, iron implements, and gunpowder.

King's mother, Adensi, was a daughter of the Matuari chief, Kodyo, also called Boyo in the reproduced fragments of King's diary. A serious illness, presumably caused by evil magic, made her leave her first Matuari husband in search of treatment in town. There she married successively two husbands from the Djuka tribe. The first one was the father of Noah Adrai, King's elder brother, who became chief of the Matuari in 1870.[1] Adensi had eight children by her second husband, one of whom was Johannes King.

After the death of her last husband the large family of Adensi was in trouble. There was no responsible male to support the family, and all the responsibilities devolved on Noah Adrai, who was still very young. For some unknown reason the family was no longer accepted in the traditional Matuari society, but at the same time it did not

---

1. Matrilineal descent is customary in the bushnegro tribes. Therefore Noah Adrai and Johannes King were both eligible to be Matuari chief as members of the chief's family, although they had Djuka fathers. This does not mean that patrilineal descent does not count in other respects. In the conflict between Djuka and Matuari, described in the text, King could very well side with his father's tribe. In concluding a peace treaty with the Djuka, the Matuari chief purposely selected as his personal messengers two members of his family with strong paternal ties in the Djuka tribe.

receive permission from the government to stay in town without
proper means of subsistence. In 1852 Noah founded the village
Maripaston on the Saramacca River, on the periphery of the Matuari
territory. About that time King must have taken his first wife. By
1855 he had already divorced her and taken a second wife, Magdalena
Akuba, from the Saramacca tribe. He was at that time very ill and
had his first visions.

In these first visions a strange god ordered him to go to town and
be baptized. The head of the Moravian Mission reported Johannes
King's first visit to his office in 1857. King could not stay long enough
to get the necessary religious instruction for baptism, so he returned
to Maripaston, taking with him a primer and a hymnbook. His second
visit to the Moravian Mission took place in 1860, again for a short
period. Still directed by visions, he started to build a church in
Maripaston. He also consulted the Matuari chief before he was baptized in 1861. A year later, eight other members of his family were
baptized. It is said that they were instructed by King. In his visions
King was directed to preach the gospel to the bushnegro tribes. The
Moravian Mission gladly accepted his cooperation and later even paid
for his services. Thus he became a self-styled missionary. He was regarded as a prophet in his own tribe and even in Europe.[2] What is
generally called King's diary contains writings of very different kinds.
In it are found reports on his missionary visits to the different bushnegro tribes and to the negroes living in the Para district. But it also
contains some individual books. About 1868 King wrote a small
book on bushnegro religion and customs. Sometime in 1886 he wrote
his *skrekibuku* ("book of terror"), mainly describing his visions, with
some illustrations. An account of the difficulties in Maripaston
between him and his brother, the newly appointed chief of the
Matuari, culminating in 1892 in his expulsion from his home village,
must have been written around 1893. A fourth book, called *dresibuku*
("medical book") is a compilation of medical treatments used among
the bushnegroes. This book is kept away from foreign eyes. We
managed to see one of its pages purely by chance.[3]

2. A biography of Johannes King by Gottfried A. Freytag was given the title:
*Johannes King der Buschland-Prophet. Ein Lebensbild aus der Brüdergemeine
in Surinam. Nach seinem eigener Aufzeichnungen dargestellt* (Herrnhut,
1927). Cf. also Voorhoeve 1964(a).

3. A complete bibliographic description of King's manuscripts is to be
found in Voorhoeve and Donicie 1963(b). See for indications about unrecovered
manuscripts Voorhoeve 1958. Parts of King's manuscripts have been published
in *Vox Guyanae* 3, 1 (1958):41-45 (the first vision), and in Lichtveld and

In his writings King used not his own bushnegro Creole but the town language, and especially the church version of this language. He was born and bred in town and must have been fluent in that language. It is assumed that King taught himself to read and write.[4] The only examples of writing he ever saw were the Bible and other religious works translated into the church language. It is quite clear that King often wavered between a somewhat awkward speaking style, with all the marks of the not always well-organized performance that are characteristic of undisciplined speech, and the stilted literary language of the Bible. In our English translation we did not try to imitate the awkward constructions of the Creole, although we did try to keep the flavor of the spoken language with its sudden, unexpected interruptions in the flow of thought.

The great cultural achievement of Johannes King should not be underestimated. Born and raised in a completely illiterate society, he discovered on his own the main function of writing: the use of written signs to reach people not present, especially future generations. His last book, from 1893, had just this purpose. It was written in a period of crisis in his life. His own people had deserted him. The chief of the Matuari, his own brother, had expelled him from their country and prevented other Matuari from having contact with him. The Moravian church criticized his stubborn character, deprecating in particular the fact that, after the death of his brother, he claimed the chieftaincy. His candidacy was fiercely opposed by Noah Adrai's son, Samuel Koloku. Shortly afterward King resigned the chieftaincy. Around 1893 he must have been undergoing a great spiritual crisis and mental dilemma. He wrote this book explicitly in defense of himself for future generations.

In this book King wrote down the story of his first missionary visit to the Djuka in 1864. He went there with his brother Noah Adrai on a double mission. In the first place they came to conclude a peace treaty between the Matuari and the Djuka, acting on behalf of the Matuari chief. In the second place they came to preach the gospel. King may have inserted the report of his mission in this book written in 1893 to prove that close cooperation always existed between Noah Adrai and himself. The report of this more or less official mission to his father's tribe contains many interesting historical and anthropological details.

Voorhoeve 1959 (fragments on the history of the bushnegroes). See also some small scattered fragments in Voorhoeve 1964. Cf. King 1973.

4. It is possible that he had some schooling in a mission school near town, but we could find no confirmation of this.

The text has been taken from an edition of the work by H. F. de Ziel. Parentheses and slant lines indicate parts of the text that should be omitted or added, respectively, to facilitate comprehension of the text. King's rather personal and ad hoc orthography has been adapted by the editor to the standard orthography (*Woordenlijst* 1961). The punctuation is entirely by the editor.[5]

Tori foe go na granman Beiman
pranasi na Dritabiki
Den 21. Augustus 1865

Wi komopo na Krementi foe go na granman pranasi noja, bikasi
di wi ben doro na Djoeka (èn) den hedeman foe den pranasi, disi
de na bilosé, ben hori wi wan pisi ten, (èn) wan wiki langa, foe
den kan seni mofo gi granman, foe a sabi taki, wakaman de kon
na hen. (Èn hen) dan fosi granman seni mofo kari ala den edeman,
a taki: wi nanga den moese waka kon na hen. Èn a dé, di wi komoto
na Krementi, wi tan pikinso, meki den seni boskopoe gi granman
taki wi de krosibé kaba. Èn granman Beiman taki: a boen, meki wi
alamala kon. Wi ala go na granman, (èn)/ma a ben de/ wan toe
joeroe na baka, fosi wi go doro na sjoro. We, den tjari wi go taki
granman odi, nanga ala den tra soema toe. 22 / augustus/. Dati
ben de toedewroko na mindri dé.

Tori /foe/ granman Beiman

(Ma) soema ben foeroe na granman pranasi foe kon jere na
njoensoe di wi tjari. Ma di wi tan wan joeroe langa taki soso
tori solanga, nomo granman Beiman taki: we, wi de taki soso
tori troe, ma meki wi jere sortoe njoensoe den soema tjari kon
na wi. Èn hen, granman, haksi Noah, a taki: hoefasi, pikin,
hoesortoe njoensoe oen tjari kon na mi? Èn Noah ferteri den
na tori, a taki: wi kon foe meki fri nanga oen, (èn) na so mi
granman Josua seni mi. Oenoe no si, granman Josua gi mi soema
foe tjari mi kon na oen. Èn den alamala hopo go pikinso na sé
go taki makandra. Dan fosi den kon piki Noah, den taki: a
prisiri gi wi. (Èn) na tori foe granman Josua, a prisiri na wi
alamala foe wi meki na fri èn foe na fri moese de, meki wi

The story of his journey to Chief Beiman's
village at Dritabiki[6]

21 August 1865

We came from Clementi to travel to the village of the chief. But when we arrived among the Djuka, the heads of the villages which are situated downstream detained us for a whole week in order to send a message to the chief, so that he would know that there were travelers on their way to him. Only then did the chief send a message summoning all the village heads. He said that we should travel with the village heads to him. Before we departed from Clementi we tarried awhile, so that they could dispatch a message to the chief that we were already nearby. And Chief Beiman said: "It is well, let us all come forward to the chief." We all went to him, but it was only a few hours later that we came ashore. Well, they brought us to greet the chief and his retinue. 22 August. That was on a Tuesday at noon.

Story of Chief Beiman

There were many people in the village of the chief to hear the message that we had brought. But when we continued to regale ourselves with small talk for about an hour, then Chief Beiman said: "Well, we have spoken nicely about all sorts of things, but let us now hear what the message is that these people have brought.[7] And the chief asked and said to Noah: "Well my son, what message have you brought to me?" And Noah told them the story and said: "We have come to conclude a peace with you. To this end has Chief Joshua sent me. Do you not see that Chief Joshua sent people to accompany me and bring me hither?" Then they all got up and went aside to speak with one another. Only then did they return to answer Noah. They said: "It pleases us. That story of Chief Joshua is pleasing to us all, that we conclude peace, and in order that there be peace let us

6. The Djuka live on the Tapanahoni River. The Matuari mission passed different Djuka villages, like Clementi, before arriving at Dritabiki, the chief's village.

7. Bushnegro etiquette demands that the purpose of one's visit should not be disclosed immediately. One bides one's time patiently until the chief gives permission to introduce the subject.

alamala tron wan makandra. We, tamara mamanten wi sa dringi
sweri. Èn granman Beiman taki: joe si, na fositen maniri foe den
gransoema foe wi, te wan tra kondre soema kon na wi foe kon
/meki/ fri, dan a moe gi wi ala gon nanga den owroe, meki den
tan (na so) solanga; te wi dringi sweri kaba, dan fosi wi sa gi den
baka. We, te wi si den gi den feti sani, dan wi sabi taki, den wani fri
nanga wi troe. Èn so Noah meki den soema foe wi go teki ala den
owroe, den gon, tjari kon gi granman Beiman. Èn granman Beiman
meki na manpikin foe hen, a nen Baja Zando, teki ala den sani
tjari go poti na ini wan hoso. Dati kaba, (èn) dan granman Beiman
haksi wi agen, a taki: efi wan tra taki de agen foe taki, meki wi
taki wanten, bikasi te wi dringi sweri kaba, dan wi no moe taki
wan tra taki moro. We, di granman Beiman taki so, nomo Johannes
King taki gi Noah taki: mi de hopo pikinso. Èn mi hopo pikinso,
nomo mi kon sidon baka. We, di mi ben hopo, Noah nanga den
tra gransoema sidon dape, nomo granman Beiman taki: ibriwan
boskopoe oen tjari mi wani jere, ma kerki taki mi no wani jere.
Èn di a taki so, nomo mi Johannes King kon sidon baka, èn granman
Beiman hori doro foe taki: mi no wani, mi no wani jere kerki tori
na mi jesi kweti-kweti. Bikasi bakra ben kon na mi, mi taki gi
den taki: mi habi mi obia, èn efi mi jere kerki tori na mi jesi,
wanten mi sa dede. (Èn) den dede soema foe mi nanga den gado
foe mi sa kiri mi. Mi no wani kerki na mi pranasi. Ma mi no tapoe
wan soema foe a no go na kerki. Ibriwan kapiten wani, meki
a teki kerki na hen pranasi, mi no tapoe hen foe dati. (Èn) ma
foe mi pranasi, mi tapoe; oen no moe taki kerki tori na ini hoso,
èn mi no gi oen pasi foe oenoe taki kerki tori na ini mi hoso.
Ma di granman Beiman taki so, nomo ala den tra soema mandi
nanga granman Beiman, èn den kapiten mandi toe, foe disi
granman Beiman no wani jere Gado tori, èn na boskopoe foe
Gado. Foeroe foe den hopo go na sé, den go taki nanga makandra.
Èn dan den kon kari granman, den taki: meki granman jere den

all become one. Well, tomorrow morning we shall drink an oath."[8]
And Chief Beiman said: "See, it is an old custom of our ancestors
that when someone from a different country comes to us to conclude
peace, he has to hand over all his guns and machetes to us, so that
they can be put in safekeeping for the time being. Once we have drunk
an oath, we shall return them. Well, when we see that they have
handed over their weapons, then we know that they truly desire peace
with us." Thus Noah asked all our people to fetch their machetes and
guns and lay them down before Chief Beiman. And the chief let his
son, Baya Zando, lock up all the arms in a house. After this Chief
Beiman once again asked us and said: "If there is anything else to be
discussed, let us talk about that now, for once we have drunk the
oath, then we must not talk about other things any more." Well,
when Chief Beiman spoke thus, then Johannes King said to Noah:
"I'll remove myself for awhile."[9] And I removed myself for awhile.
And then I came back and sat down again. Well, when I stood up
Noah and the other elders sat there, and then Chief Beiman said:
"Everything that you bring along, I want to hear, but I don't want to
listen to church talk." And when he had said that, I, Johannes King,
joined them again and Chief Beiman proceeded to say: "I won't have
it. I don't want to hear any church talk in my ears. Because white
people came to me and I said to them: 'I have my magic and when I
hear church talk in my ears, then I shall immediately die. My ancestors
and my gods will kill me. I don't want any church in my village. But
I won't hold anyone from going to church. Let each village headman
who so wants allow a church in his village. I don't forbid them to do
that. But you mustn't utter church talk in the house you live in.
I will give you no permission for church talk in my house either."
But when Chief Beiman spoke thus all the others took exception, also
the village heads, because Chief Beiman did not want to hear God's
word and message. Many of them went outside and spoke to each
other. And then they came to call the chief and said: "May the chief

8. This is a literal translation, which will be used throughout the story. The
peace is actually concluded when they drink each other's blood. In the event
of a breach of promise the people who drink will die.

9. King now knows that the second part of their mission will be discussed.
By going out he creates an opportunity to introduce the subject in his absence.
This may not be a sign of modesty but rather the opposite: he makes it possible
for the chief to oppose him as a prophet without being hampered by his presence. The chief later proceeds to say that he already opposed white people
(perhaps white missionaries) in this respect.

pikinso na sé. Èn granman Beiman hopo go na den, en den kapiten
nanga granman Beiman pikin srefi go taki nanga hen, den taki:
a moese jere na boskopoe foe Gado. Efi a no wani go na kerki
srefi, tokoe a moe jere na tori foe Gado-man. We, di granman
Beiman kon sidon baka, a taki gi ala den kapiten: oen alamala
go na wan tra hoso go sidon jere na tori disi den tjari. Èn wan
bigi hipi soema hopo, wi alamala go na wan tra hoso go sidon.
Ma di wi ben taki foeroe tori kaba, foe dati hede mi nanga Noah
taki gi den soema: meki na tori tan tide. Te tamara wi sa taki
nanga oenoe. Èn den alamala taki: ja, a boen na wi, èn den hopo
gowe solanga.

Tori foe na boskopoe foe Gado na Djoeka,
na granman Beiman pranasi, na Dritabiki

23. /augustus/

Débroko mamanten froekoe den alamala kon sidon foe jere na
boskopoe foe Gado. Èn mi Johannes King ferteri den soema
na heri tori, fa Masra Gado srefi ben tjari kerki kon na wi,
èn a no libisoema seni wi kon na oen, na Masra Gado srefi seni
wi kon na oenoe. We, di mi kaba foe taki na boskopoe foe Gado,
disi a ben seni mi, dan mi hori kerki. Mi lési na Evangelium foe
Njoen Testament, dan mi fermane den nanga foeroe wortoe
foe Masra Jesus Kristus, (gi den) fa a ben dede foe wi hede, èn
fa a ben pai na hebi boetoe foe wi alamala sondoe, nanga hen
santa diri broedoe, èn fa den ben kiri hen na kroisi foe wi hede.
Èn ke, loekoe, den pôti heiden soema, fa den ferwondroe foe
jere so wan tori, èn noiti den ben sabi efi wan Masra Gado
pikin de, disi den kari hen nen Jesus Kristus. (Èn na) na na
nen Masra Gado Jehova wawan den ben sabi. Ke loekoe, fa na
tori dangra den pôti heiden soema ferstan krin-krin. We dati
meki den haksi mi foeroe sani, fa den moese doe foe den kan
go na Gadokondre. We, dati meki mi poti foeroe fermane na
den jesi: na blesi foe Masra nanga den froekoe. Èn dan mi sori den
na kroisi prenki foe Masra Jesus. Na srefi dridewroko mamanten
froekoe, granman Beiman seni na bigi manpikin foe hen kon na Noah,
èn a taki: mi papa taki meki mi kon begi joe gi hen. A taki: joe no
moese mandi nanga hen, foe di hen krasi so esrede, èn a no foe taki
hen no wani jere na boskopoe foe Gado, disi joe tjari, ma hen jere
taki hen sisa pikin Petrus Lonmoesoe go na kerki, a trowe wan
gado foe hen, disi a ben habi, na dati meki a dede. We di hen jere

be permitted to hear them for a little while outside?" And Chief
Beiman stood up and went to them. And the village heads and even
Chief Beiman's child came to speak to him and said that he must
hear the message of God. Well, when Chief Beiman came to take
his seat again, he said to all the village heads: All of you go to the
other house and go and sit there and listen to the message they have
brought along. And a great many stood up and we all went to sit
down in another building. But because we had already spoken so
much, Noah and I said to the people: "Let things be for the day.
Tomorrow we shall speak with you." And they all said: "Yes, we
agree with that," and went home for the time being.

*The story of the message of God to the Djuka
in the village of Chief Beiman at Dritabiki*

23 August

The next morning they all came and sat down to hear the message
of God. And I, Johannes King, related to the people the whole history
of how the Lord God himself had brought the church to us. No
people have sent us to you, but the Lord God himself had sent us.
And when I was finished with the message of God for which purpose
I was sent, then I conducted a service. I read from the New Testament
and testified to them in many words about the Lord Jesus Christ,
how He had died for us and how He had paid the heavy penalty for
all our sins with His holy and priceless blood, and how they had
killed Him on the cross for our sake. And oh! see the poor heathens,
how surprised they were to hear such a story. Never before had they
known that there was a child of the Lord God who was called Jesus
Christ. They were only familiar with the name Lord God Jehova.
Oh! see how the story confused the minds of the poor heathens. For
this reason they asked me many things, what they had to do to enter
into God's kingdom. Therefore I gave them many admonitions: the
blessing of the Lord and the curse. And then I showed them a picture
of the Lord Jesus.

That very same Wednesday morning, very early, Chief Beiman
sent his big son to Noah and he said: "My father says that I must ask
you something in his name. He says you must not be angry with him
because he was so violent yesterday. It does not mean that he does
not want to hear the message of God which you have brought, but
he has heard that his sister's child, Petrus Lonmoesoe, has gone to
church. He had cast aside an idol and that has caused his death. Well

so, dati meki hen kon frede toe. Sonten, efi hen meki Johannes King
taki Gado tori na ini hen hoso, sonten na gado foe hen sa kiri hen toe.
Èn na foe dati hede hen frede. Ma te ala soema gowe kaba, Noah wawan
moe kon na hen safri kon taki gi hen na boskopoe, hen sa jere. (Èn di)
Noah taki: a boen, mi sa go na hen. Ke loekoe fa den pôti heiden habi
wan toemoesi doengroe prakseri; (na) den denki, te joe doe wan sani na
kibri fasi, dati Masra Gado hai no kan si hen, boen ofoe ogri. Na so granman
Beiman ben de wan granman, ma tokoe di a ben de heiden soema a ben habi
na srefi prakseri toe. Èn a taki: efi Johannes King taki Gado Masra tori
gi hen, na ala tra soema fesi, hen sa dede, (èn) na kroektoe Gado foe hen
sa kiri hen. Na foe dati hede granman Beiman no ben wani jere na boskopoe
foe Gado na ala soema fesi. We, Gado wortoe no kan lé, na wortoe di
boekoe taki: na soema, disi soekoe foe hori hen libi, hen sa lasi hen libi,
ma na soema di wani lasi hen libi foe Masra Gado nen ede, hen sa hori
hen libi. Èn di granman Beiman ben denki hen srefi sa helpi hen srefi,
foe hori hen libi, dati meki a lasi. Bikasi a ben de wan granman disi poti
ala hen fertrow toemoesi tranga na tapoe den kroektoe gado nanga den
obia sani foe hen. Ma pôti, den dati no ben helpi hen na noti. Èn mi
Johannes King de getoige foe Masra Jesus Kristus, di hen ben meki foe
mi getoigi foe den kroektoe Gado sani, di mi hai si na ini granman
Beiman hoso ini. Den foeroe toemoesi: popki nanga ala sortoe obia sani,
den foeroe toemoesi foe wan enkri soema moese habi so sani. Èn heiden
soema de foeroe sortoe. Ma den heiden soema di de libi na Djoeka,
den de dipi na ini didibri wroko, moro leki son foe den tra heiden boesi
kondre, troe-troe.

Tori foe na sweri na granman
Beiman pranasi na Dritabiki
Den 24. augustus 1865

Na wan fodewroko mamanten granman Beiman kari ala soema
kon makandra foe kon meki fri nanga wi. Èn a poeroe dri soema, èn
Noah poeroe dri soema toe. (Èn) Atamaren nanga Majoro, nanga
Kansi, (èn) den dati dringi sweri foe granman Josua sé, foe Matoewari.
Èn Mefle-Kwakoe, nanga Tinga, nanga Majoro-Gwandra, (èn) /den/ dri
soema dati dringi sweri foe granman Beiman sé, foe Djoeka. Èn ala nanga
ala a meki 6 soema, mansoema, di dringi na sweri, (èn) na aiti joeroe
mamanten. Èn dati ben prisiri na ala soema, foe di den dringi sweri meki
fri nanga Matoewari-nengre. Bikasi ala Maripaston-nengre na pikin foe
den Djoeka-nengre, nanga pikin foe pikin, na famiri foe den Djoeka-
nengre wawan. Èn dati meki den hati ben prisiri leti-leti, foe di wi dringi

now, when he had heard this he too was afraid. Perhaps if he allows
Johannes King to utter God's word in his house, perhaps his God
will then also kill him. For this reason he is afraid. But when the
others are gone, then Noah must come to him on the sly and alone
to transmit the message to him and then he will listen. Noah said:
"Good, I shall come to him." Alas, see what dark thoughts are in
the poor heathens. They think that the eye of the Lord God can't
see when you do something in secret, be it good or evil." Thus
Chief Beiman was a chief, but because he was also a heathen he
harbored like thoughts. He said that if Johannes King utters God's
words to him in the presence of all the others, he will die. His idol
will kill him. For this reason Chief Beiman did not want to hear the
word of God in the presence of others. Well, God's words can't lie,
the word of the Bible. He who tries to protect his life, he will lose
his life, but he who will lose his life for the sake of the Lord God's
name, he will retain his life. And because Chief Beiman thought
that he could help himself and retain his life, this caused him to lose
it. He was a chief who put all his faith in his idols and his magic. But
alas, they helped him in no way, and I, Johannes King, may testify
about idolatrous things which my eyes have seen in the house of
Chief Beiman. They were very many: idols and diverse magical things.
It was too much for one person to have. There are many types of
heathens, but the heathens who live amongst the Djuka are steeped
in the Devil's work, more so than some of the other heathen bush
tribes forsooth!

> *The story of the oath which was taken at*
> *Chief Beiman's village at Dritabiki*

24 August 1865

On a Thursday morning Chief Beiman called together all his
people to conclude peace with us. And he selected three persons, and
likewise Noah chose three persons. Atamaren and Mayoro and Kansi
partook of the oath on behalf of Chief Joshua of the Matuari. And
Mefle-Kwakwu and Tinga and Mayoro-Gwandra—these three—
drank an oath on behalf of Chief Beiman of the Djuka. All in all there
were six men who partook of the oath, at 8 o'clock in the morning.
And it pleased everybody that they had taken the oath and concluded
peace with the Matuari. For all the negroes of Maripaston are children
of the Djuka, and their children's children. They are all related to the
Djuka. For this reason they rejoiced in their hearts that we had taken

sweri/meki/fri makandra noja. (Ma) na owroeten den soema foe
Matoewari no ben de boen nanga den. (Èn) foe wi kan libi boen nanga
wi srefi sondro foe frede wi na wi, (èn) wi alamala kon wan makandra
noja.

*(Èn) wan tra tori foe den Djoeka-nengre
nanga den Matoewari-nengre:*

Mi sa ferteri oenoe pikinso foe dati toe. (Ma) na owroeten den
gransoema foe Matoewari no ben wani hori leti gemeenskap nanga
den papa foe wi, (èn) alwasi den tata foe wi na Djoeka ben soekoe
toemoesi foeroe tron foe hori friendskap nanga den Matoewari gransoema,
tokoe den no ben wani. (Èn) alwasi den gransoema foe Djoeka ben kon
libi so foeroe na bilo foe Saron-posoe, (ma) toekoe te den Djoeka-nengre
ben go na hoposé foe Saron-posoe foe go wroko; te den meki kampoe,
den go na wroko libi ala sani na den kampoe, kaba te den Matoewari-
nengre de pasa kon na foto, (èn) den si den kampoe nanga sani na ini,
dan den Matoewari-nengre de poti faja na den Djoeka-nengre kampoe,
bron ala sani foe den Djoeka-nengre na na kampoe, alamal.

*Tori foe granman Kodjo ofoe Bojo
Na so na granman nen ben de na ten di den Matoewari-nengre
ben de bron den kampoe pori ala sani foe Djoeka-nengre*

(Èn) dan den gowe foe den, èn dati ben de den bigi prisiri. (Èn) te
den Djoeka-nengre komoto na wroko kon na kampoe, den si ala den
kampoe bron, nanga den amaka, den njanjan, èn den pagara, sribi krosi,
èn ala sani di den habi bron krin-krin. (Èn) na so den Matoewari-nengre
ben de doe nanga den tata foe wi foe Djoeka. We, jere fa Masra Gado
ben sori mi granpapa, di ben de granman daten, èn Masra Gado ben
sori hen wan bigi skreki sani en marki. Èn granman Kodjo, na hen ben
de Matoewari granman daten di den soema foe hen ben de doe na ogri.
Ma granman Kodjo no ben wani warskow den soema foe hen taki:
oenoe no moe doe na ogri. Èn na foe dati hede den folkoe foe granman
Kodjo hori doro foe doe na ogri nanga den Djoeka-nengre.

We, jere fa Masra Gado ben strafoe granman Kodjo wan hebi strafoe.
(Èn) wan lési granman Kodjo go na foto. Lanti gi hen foeroe ransoen
nanga someni tra sani moro. A ben lai wan grofoe boto ofoe bigi boto
(èn) nanga foeroe sani, (èn) nanga nofo foe den soema disi ben tjari
hen. Ma den alamala ben waka na na wan boto. Èn di den ben tjari so
foeroe sani, na boto foe den ben lai nanga sani. (Èn) we, di den komoto

the oath and had concluded peace together. Formerly, the Matuari
were not on good terms with them, so that we could live well with
one another without fear. Now we became united again.

Another story about the Djuka and the Matuari

I shall also tell you something about it. Formerly the elders of
the Matuari did not want to consort with our fathers. Although our
fathers often tried to be friendly with the Matuari elders, yet they
did not want to. The elders of the Djuka often came to live south
of the outpost Saron. The Djuka went to work upstream from Saron.
After they had constructed a camp they proceeded to their work
and left everything behind in their camps. Then the Matuari negroes
came along on their way to town and saw the camps with all the
possessions. Then the Matuari negroes set alight the camps of the
Djuka negroes and burnt down everything in the camp of the Djuka
negroes.

Story of Chief Kodyo, also known as Boyo
*This was the name of the chief at the time the Matuari negroes
burnt the camps and destroyed all the possessions of the
Djuka negroes*

Then they went away. That was their greatest sport. When the
Djuka returned from work to their camp, they found everything
burnt down, their hammocks, their food, the pagaras containing all
their possessions, their sleeping clothes and everything they owned,
totally destroyed. This was how the Matuari treated our Djuka forefathers. Well, listen how the Lord God at that time admonished my
grandfather. And the Lord God revealed a terrible sign to him. It
was about Chief Kodyo, who was chief at the time when the Matuari
did this evil. But Chief Kodyo did not want to warn his people and
say: "You must desist from doing evil." As a result the people of
Chief Kodyo continued to behave badly to the Djuka.

Well, listen how the Lord God meted out a heavy punishment to
Chief Kodyo. Once Chief Kodyo went to town. The government
supplied him with a liberal ration and many other things. His big boat
was loaded with many things and with a considerable number of
people who came with him. All of them traveled in the same boat.
And because they brought back so many things the boat was over-
loaded. Well, when they came back from town on their way back to

na foto de gowe baka na Matoewari, den go te den pasa Saron-posoe
gowe te (farawe) moro farawe na hoposé. Èn watra ben bigi na liba.
Di den go foe go pasa na wan tranga lon watra, nomo na boto kanti,
a soengoe nanga ala den lai, èn so na boto gowe krin-krin na ondro
watra nanga ala den sani di de na ini, na boto gowe krinkrin.

Èn mi granpapa nanga den soema foe hen swen go komopo na
sjoro, èn den no ben sabi no wan rai, fa den ben moesoe doe. We,
helpi no de, den ben moesoe foe waka na foetoe na ini boesi, te go
doro dape, den Djoeka-nengre de na wan kampoe de wroko. Èn granman
Kodjo nanga den soema foe hen, den no ben habi noti foe pasa den
libi. (Èn) den no habi faja, no njanjan, no krosi, no owroe, no nefi srefi,
boiti pari wanwan, /di/ den ben hori na den anoe. We, di granman Bojo
ben sabi wan wroko kampoe foe den Djoeka-nengre de na wan presi
na fesi, no toemoesi farawe, (èn) den sa waka na foetoe doro dape na
srefi dé. We, na so granman Kodjo nanga den soema foe hen waka na
foetoe go doro dape den Djoeka-nengre kampoe de. Èn di den Djoeka-
nengre jere den Matoewari nanga granman Bojo de waka na ini boesi
de kon na den, (èn) den no ben si den nanga hai ete, den ben denki na
loweman de kon na den. Den ben seti den srefi klari de loekoe hoesortoe
fejanti kon na den tapoe. Èn now den si wan dagoe foe granman Bojo
waka na fesi kon doro na den, èn dati meki den kon sabi (èn) wanten
dati a no loweman, bikasi den Djoeka-nengre ben sabi na dagoe foe
granman Bojo. Èn na baka granman srefi kon doro na den, a taki den odi.

Èn den Djoeka-nengre haksi granman, den taki: granman, san doe joe
so? (Èn) granman taki: mi soengoe, ala sani foe mi gowe nanga mi boto,
alamala gowe. We now den Djoeka-nengre bigin foe haksi granman Bojo
noja foe ala den kampoe di den Matoewari-nengre ben bron. Èn den
taki: granman, a no joe ben bron wi kampoe na so wan presi? A piki: ja,
na mi. Èn den taki: granman, a no joe ben bron wi kampoe na so wan
presi? A taki: ja, na mi. Granman, a no joe ben bron wi kampoe na so
wan presi? A piki: ja, na mi. Èn a no joe ben bron wi kampoe na so
wan presi, nanga ala sani foe wi na ini? A taki: ja, na mi. (Èn) granman
no ben sabi san foe doe moro. Èn den Djoeka taki: we, granman, na
joe nen granman, a ogri. We, tide ogri miti joe. Tide ogri nanga ogri
miti oenoe srefi, èn Masra Gado pai joe, granman Kodjo. A taki:
ja, na troe mi pikin, ogri miti mi tide, troe-troe. We noja den

the Matuari, they passed the outpost Saron and went farther upstream. The river had risen, and when they came to a strong current, the boat capsized and sank with all the possessions. The boat disappeared completely under the water with everything it contained.

My grandfather and his people swam to the bank. They did not know what to do. There was no help in sight. They were forced to trek through the forest on foot. At last they came upon a working camp of the Djuka. They were completely down and out, had nothing —no fire, no provisions, no clothes, no matches, not even a knife— nothing except the paddles which they had in their hands. Well, when Chief Boyo found out that there was a camp of the Djuka not too far away and that they could still reach it by foot that day, well then, Chief Kodyo together with his people went on foot to the place where the Djuka negroes were. Now when the Djuka negroes heard that the Matuari with their chief, Boyo, were approaching them through the forest, they had not yet spied them. They thought that runaways were coming to them.[10] They prepared themselves to see what kind of enemy was descending on them. And then they saw the dog of Chief Boyo walking in front. Thus they immediately knew that these were no runaways, because the Djuka negroes were familiar with Chief Boyo's dog. Then the chief himself came into view and greeted them.

The Djuka negroes asked the chief: "Chief, what has happened to you?" The Chief answered: "My boat has capsized and sunk, and with it all my possessions." Well now, the Djuka negroes started questioning Chief Boyo about all the camps which the Matuari had razed to the ground. And they said: "Chief, did you not burn down our camp at this place and that place?" And he replied: "Yes, it was me." And they said: "Chief, did you not burn down our camp at this place and that?" And he replied: "Yes, it was me." "Chief, did you not burn down our camp at this place and that?" And he replied: "Yes, it was me." "And have you not burnt down our camp at this place and that together with all our possessions?" And he said: "Yes, it was me." And the chief knew no way out. The Djuka negroes said: "Well, chief, you are called chief. You've done wrong. Well, today you've met your Moses. Today, you've really hit the bottom. And the Lord God has repaid you." And he answered: "Yes, my child, it is true. Evil

10. This event took place before emancipation. In the peace treaties the bush-negroes had promised not to accept future runaways, so henceforth runaway slaves were considered enemies who had to be caught and sent back to their masters.

Djoeka-nengre bigin foe pina en spotoe granman Bojo nanga nofo
takroe wortoe, foe na ogri di den soema foe hen ben doe nanga den
Djoeka-nengre. We, granman Kodjo ben teki ala den ferwéti disi den
Djoeka-nengre ben ferwéti hen, alwasi granman Bojo, a no hen srefi
ben doe den ogri. A no ben bron no wan enkri kampoe, na den folkoe
foe hen ben doe ala den ogri. Ma tokoe na granman Kodjo ben (kisi)
/teki/ ala na ferwéti na hen tapoe nanga pasensi. Èn a no ben piki den
Djoeka-nengre no wan takroe wortoe baka, ma a gi den leti, a ben
piki den krin taki: na hen doe den ogri troe-troe. Èn dati meki den
Djoeka-nengre hati ben kowroe nanga hen. Den ben doe hen, granman
Kodjo, nanga ala den soema foe hen wan toemoesi bigi-bigi boen (wa-)
wanten. Èn den gi den boto nanga njanjan èn sowtoe, krosi foe weri,
nanga amaka foe sribi, èn sribi krosi, patoe foe bori njanjan, preti,
spoen, krabasi foe dringi watra, èn ala pikin-pikin sani, disi de fanowdoe
foe den kan pasa den libi na pasi go doro na den kondre. We, den sribi
na den Djoeka-nengre.

Débroko mamanten granman Kodjo nanga ala den soema foe hen
hopo teki na reis baka foe gowe te na den kondre, na Matoewari. We,
granman Kodjo libi na dagoe foe hen gi den Djoeka-nengre foe solanga.
Èn di granman Kodjo go doro na hen kondre, a kari ala soema, èn den
kapiten nanga ala den tra gransoema, èn ala den jongoewan kon
makandra, a taki gi den alamala san miti hen, èn fa pikinmoro den
alamala soengoe dede na ini watra. Alwasi den no ben dede na ini watra—
den alamala swen go komopo na sjoro, den no dedena ini watra—ma
tokoe, efi den Djoeka-nengre no ben de pikinso krosibé, foe den waka
na ini boesi go doro na den, na dede den alamala ben moesoe dede nanga
hangri na ini boesi. We, dan granman Kodjo bréti—ala den soema foe
kondre poti wan fast wet gi den dia alamala—a taki: efi wan Matoewari-
nengre (di) sa prefoeroe foe bron wan Djoeka-nengre kampoe moro,
hen sa strafoe na soema wan hebi strafoe. Èn dan granman Kodjo meki
den soema foe hen soekoe foeroe njanjan, a meki den soema foe hen
lai boto nanga someni tra sani moro, èn a seni den Djoeka-nengre foe
presenti. (Èn) ma di granman Bojo ben libi wan dagoe foe hen na den
Djoeka-nengre, (èn dan) granman seni teki na dagoe baka. We, di
granman Kodjo seni presenti gi den Djoeka-nengre, a seni taki den
grantangi foe na bigi boen disi den Djoeka-nengre ben doe hen. We
dati meki den Matoewari-nengre kaba foe bron den Djoeka-nengre
kampoe te leki tide, den kaba krin-krin.

has met up with me today, it is true." Well now, the Djuka negroes
started to embarrass Chief Kodyo and revile him with many dirty
words, because of the harm his people had wrought upon the Djuka
negroes. Well, Chief Kodyo accepted all of the reproaches which the
Djuka negroes flung at him, even though Chief Boyo had not com-
mitted the evil himself. He had not burnt down a single camp. His
people had done all the harm. Notwithstanding this, Chief Kodyo
patiently accepted all the reproaches and he uttered no evil word
to the Djuka. But he conceded that they were right. He answered
them clearly that he had really done harm. And this caused the hearts
of the Djuka to mellow. They did lots of good to Chief Kodyo and
his people. They supplied them with boats, gave them food, salt,
clothes to put on and hammocks for sleeping, sleeping clothes, pots
for cooking their food, dishes, spoons, calabashes from which to
drink water, and all those small things necessary to sustain themselves on their way home.

Early the next morning, Chief Kodyo and his people rose to return
to their land, to the Matuari. Well, Chief Kodyo left his dog in the
custody of the Djuka, and when he arrived in his own land, he
summoned all his people, the village heads and all other elders and
young ones. And he related to them what had happened and how
they were nearly swallowed up by the waters. And even though they
did not drown in the waters—they had all swum to the river bank
and did not die in the waters—yet if the Djuka were not within walking distance, they would all have died of hunger in the forest. Well
then, Chief Kodyo rejoiced and all the people in the land proposed
a law which would apply to everybody, namely, if a Matuari again
dared to burn down a camp of a Djuka negro, then a heavy punishment would be imposed on such a person. Then Chief Kodyo ordered
his people to collect lots of food. He asked his people to load a boat
with still many other things and he sent these to the Djuka as a
present. But since Chief Boyo had left a dog with the Djuka, he sent
for it. Well, when Chief Kodyo sent these presents to the Djuka, he
also sent his heartiest thanks for the many good things the Djuka had
done to him. Well, that was the reason why the Matuari stopped
burning down the camps of the Djuka even to this very day. They
stopped it completely.

CHAPTER 5

J. G. A. Koenders

As a teacher in Surinam working for the government, Koenders was forced to toe the line of colonial educational policy. The educational system of the Netherlands was faithfully copied in Surinam and was believed to be the best way to transmit European knowledge and skills. Dutch schoolbooks, fitting the needs of Dutch children in their European environment, were shipped to the colony and used in the Surinam schools. Creole culture and language were generally regarded as obstacles to a better future. It was thought that the use of the mother tongue would negatively influence the children's command of Dutch. Therefore the children were not allowed to speak Sranan Tongo, their own Creole language, at school. Even at home, parents were expected to discourage their children from expressing themselves in this language. Teachers and parents alike sincerely believed that this was for the benefit of the children.

Consequently, as we noted in the Introduction, Creoles developed an ambivalent attitude toward Creole language and culture. They were taught that anything that was their own must of necessity be inferior. They were inclined to adhere to the official viewpoint, though it seldom became a deep-rooted conviction. One can easily understand that parents and teachers often had to violate these self-imposed rules and in practice could not avoid using Sranan Tongo.

However, it still took great courage to go against the policy publicly. This was what Koenders did. He actually tells us in one of his articles that it became clear to him how, through the school system, the children were being trained to become stupid parrots: "Ever since my early thirties I have known what sort of knowledge parrot knowledge is, to wit, many words, only words, instead of comprehension" (*Foetoe-boi,* July 1946).

Around 1943 some women of the organization Pohama (short for Potie hanoe makandra, literally "Join hands together") enlisted his cooperation. This organization tried to raise the poor from their inhuman conditions and stimulate them to aspire to greater heights. It was officially founded in 1944 and initiated many activities, such as inducing Creoles to save money through the suborganization Praktama (short for Prakserie tamara, "Think of tomorrow"), developing

nurseries for lower-class working mothers, and organizing an annual
Creole cultural evening on Emancipation Day. Koenders actively
participated in the organization. He published three booklets for it,
the first in 1943 under the title *Foe memre wi afo* (In memory of
our forefathers), which is mainly concerned with the Creole language
and its orthography; at a later date *Aksie mie, mie sa piekie joe foe
wie skien* (Ask me, I will answer you about our body), in which he
tries to explain elementary biological facts to people with an imperfect knowledge of Dutch; and finally *Sieksie tintien moi en bekentie
siengie* (Sixty beautiful and well-known songs).

Foetoe-boi (Servant) was ostensibly a periodical put out by
Pohama. It was regarded as Koenders's brainchild, although other
authors were involved. But Koenders unmistakably controlled the
journal as the editor responsible for it. It was written in Dutch and
Sranan Tongo. Many articles were clearly inspired by Koenders's
ideals. He wanted Surinam Creoles to be self-assured and spiritually
independent. The word *Creole* embraces the whole colored population of African descent, however remote, and Koenders preferred
another term. He called himself a negro and addressed the people
to whom he wrote as negroes, deliberately ignoring the touchiness
of many of them about the term.[1] On many occasions he explained:
"I am addressing myself to those who are great-grandchildren of
the negroes imported from Africa as slaves, and who don't wish to
deny this" (*Foetoe-boi*, May 1946). In fact, almost everyone tried to
deny it in one way or another. The nearly white-skinned Creole had
more opportunities to deny his background than the pure black, who
could not hide his skin but could, and often did, conceal other marks
of his slave past.

Koenders addressed himself mostly to blacks and to the inhabitants
of the backyards of Paramaribo.[2] He taught them to be proud of their
skin, their history, their language, and their culture. Yet a close
scrutiny of ten years of *Foetoe-boi* discloses a contradiction. Ironically,
Koenders often resorted to artificial constructions more reminiscent
of ponderous written Dutch than of the natural flow of Creole speech.
He had a tendency to make an unnatural distinction between homonyms,

1. Twentieth-century Surinam has seen more revivals of negro identity.
Koenders evidently was not the first to use this term.
2. The slaves of Paramaribo were lodged in small houses built in the backyards of their master's home. This pattern continued until quite recently.
Houses that front on the street, even rather modest ones, have a backyard
where small shacks are built and rented to the poor.

for instance. His ardent wish to prove the value of his mother tongue caused him to fall prey to the very thing he so severely criticized in others. Yet the fundamental tenets of his belief—his insight into the deepest roots of Creole frustration, his protest against the injustice of the colonial educational system—remained unshaken. It was up to the younger generation to free themselves completely from cultural oppression. This new generation was greatly stimulated and encouraged by Koenders and his *Foetoe-boi*.

In reading through all the numbers of *Foetoe-boi* one gets a vivid picture of Koenders as a highly intelligent man with strong personal convictions, never impressed by authority, title, or position. For ten years he was engaged in a private war against intimidation and ignorance. For ten years his voice was heard reiterating the same themes: Never be ashamed of your own background, trust your own common sense more than those beautiful authoritative phrases, and most of all respect yourself! By imitating others, by hiding your own ways, you only turn yourself into an object of ridicule and become a party to your own enslavement. His favorite proverb, cited many times in *Foetoe-boi*, was: *Yu kan kibri granmama, ma yu no kan tapu kosokoso* ("You may hide your grandmother, but you cannot prevent her from coughing").

Foetoe-boi, May 1946

Wi kondre

Dati no wani taki na kondre di wi abi èn pe wi abi fu taki. Nanga wi
kondre wi de meyne: na kondre di bow na tapu sweti, watra-ay nanga
brudu fu wi afo, den nengre di den ben tyari komopo na Afrika leki
kakalaka na fowru mofo, fu meki stampu busi kon tron moy Sranan.
Wi ala di de pikin-pikin fu den nengre disi èn di *wani* sabi dati, meki
fu dipi lespeki fu wi afo ede, wi lobi wi kondre leki nomru wan, so
leki ala tra nasi, te na den moro lagi wan, e du. Ibri pipel abi na ini
en libitori takru, ogri, fisti momenti, na wan moro leki na trawan.
Dati wi afo ben de srafu no de wan sani fu syen: den no ben du dati
nanga den fri *wani.*

Syen a de te wi frigiti wi afo, te wi trapu den sweti, watra-ay,
brudu nanga futu. Wan nasi di trowe en libitori, frigiti en afo, so
wan nasi te fu kaba a sa tron figi futu. Meki wi poti anu makandra
fu wi no tron figi futu.

Wi tongo

Dati a no san den kari *neger-engels* ofu *nengre-tongo.* Neger-
engels dati na a broko broko Engels, san wan nengre e taki: *mi no no*
na presi fu *I don't know.* Nengre tongo na a tongo fu ala nengre èn
dati wi tongo no de tu, bika dia na Sranan kaba, den abra sula nengre
abi den eygi tongo. Wi tongo na Sranan *nengre-tongo,* dati na a tongo
fu na moro bigi ipi Sranan nengre. Nèt so leki na ini ala tra tongo yu
abi wortu, di den ben teki fu trawan, so na wi tongo tu, ma broko
broko fu wan tra tongo a no de; a abi en eygi fasi, a e meki wortu
na en eygi fasi.

Wan pipel di libi ofu lasi en tongo ofu afrontu en fu wan tra
tongo ede, awansi sort'wan, na pipel dati don moro den afo fu wi;
bika den ben koti na odo kaba taki: *yu kan kibri granmama, ma yu*
no kan tapu koso koso. Efi fu yu brede ofu prisiri yu mu leri wan

Foetoe-boi, May 1946

Our land

That is not to say, the land that we own and where we have the say.
By "our land" we mean the land which is founded on the blood,
sweat, and tears of our forefathers, the negroes who were brought
from Africa, trapped like cockroaches in the beak of a chicken, to
transform the impenetrable jungle into beautiful Surinam. All of us
who are children's children of these negroes, and who want to admit
that, let us with profound respect for our forefathers love our land
first and foremost. Just as all other nations, even to the lowest ones,
do. Each nation has in its own history unpleasant, ugly, and dirty
periods, the one more than the other. That our forefathers were
slaves is nothing to be ashamed of; they were not such of their own
free will.

It is shameful when we forget our forefathers, when we trample
on their blood, sweat, and tears. A people which rejects its history,
forgets its forefathers, such a people will eventually become doormats. Let us join hands so that we don't become doormats!

Our language

That is not what they call negro-English or Negro tongue. Negro-
English is that broken English which a negro speaks: "mi no no"
instead of "I don't know." The "Negro tongue" is the language of all
negroes. And that is not what our language is, for in Surinam alone
the negroes in the interior have their own language.[3] Our language
is the Surinam negro language, that is, the language of most of the
Surinam negroes. Just as you find in other languages words that are
borrowed from others, so also in our language, but it isn't a broken
variant of another language. It has its own manner, makes words in
its own way.

A people that has neglected its language or lost it, or heaps insults
on it for the sake of another language, whichever it may be, is more
stupid than our forefathers, because they were wont to use the expression: "You can hide your grandmother, but you can't prevent

3. Koenders refers to the fact that even in Surinam negroes speak different
languages: coastal Creole and several bushnegro tongues. The appellation
negro tongue cannot be applied to coastal Creole exclusively.

fremde tongo, leri en bun, ma a no fu dati ede yu mu ferakti yu eygi
tongo èn trowe en . . .

> Taki san di yu wani,
> suma sani a no yu sani,
> suma pe a no yu pe,
> sor' mi pe di f' yu de!

Foetoe-boi, June 1946

Wan srafuten tori

Soleki fa wi ben yere nofo tron, den grantata fu wi, fu tron friman,
ben de lonwe libi den pranasi go na busi. So den srafu fu Coronie ben
de du tu. Den ben de teki boto, seyri go te na mofo Nickerie liba.
Drape den ben de wakti, te den feni wan bun kans fu koti na bradi
Corantijn liba go na abra sey, pe den kon fri, bikasi Berbice no ben
de seni den go baka na Sranan. Dati de wan fu den reyde, di meki
Coronie nanga Nickerie busi no ben sabi san di den de kari Marrons
(dyuka's). Ma no ala ten a ben de waka den bun. Nofo tron den ben
de kisi den na Nickerie seni go baka na Coronie. Dati ede den ben kon
na makandra na wan konparisi, fu luku san fu du, te den feni wan fasi.
Na sekanti, bijna ala ten skuna fu den pranasi eyginari ben de didon.
Wan bun dey ofu moro betre wan bun neti, te gron kowru dan ala
suma fu den difrenti pranasi, di ben meki na barki nanga makandra,
de kon na sekanti teki wan skuna lonwe gowe. Fu dati no kan pasa
moro, den eyginari poti wakti na ini den skuna: srudati nanga lay gon.
Nengre taki: *hontiman de pramisi busimeti, busimeti de pramisi
hontiman.*

Na da ten, di wi de taki, wan masra na Coronie ben abi wan futuboy
nen Philip, di ben abi so wan switi fasi, dati en masra nanga trawan,
èn den tra srafu, ya te den srudati srefi, ben lobi èn fertrow en. Wan
dey Philip meki wan barki nanga someni trawan taki, srudati ofu
no srudati, den sa si wan fasi, fu teki wan fu den skuna, lonwe gowe.
Fu di ala suma ben lobi Philip, sodati den bakra no ben sa abi sospisi
na en tapu, Philip teki na en tapu, fu seti na tori nanga wan tu trawan

her from coughing." When, for the sake of maintaining yourself or purely for pleasure, you must learn a foreign language, see to it that you do it well. But this is no reason for despising or rejecting your own language.

> Whatever you may say:
> Things of others are not yours,
> Abodes of others are not yours.
> Show me where your own are.

Foetoe-boi, June 1946

A tale of slavery

As we have so often heard, our forefathers fled from the plantations and went into the jungle in order to be free. Thus was it with the slaves of Coronie. They took a boat and sailed to the mouth of the Nickerie River. There they waited for a good opportunity to cross the wide Corantijn River to the other bank, where they became free, because Berbice did not send them back to Surinam. That was one of the reasons why the jungles of Coronie and Nickerie never saw any maroons. But it did not always run smoothly. Often they were caught in Nickerie and sent back to Coronie. Therefore they arranged a meeting to see whether they could find an answer to this. Almost invariably schooners belonging to the plantation owners were moored near the shore. One day after sunset, when all was quiet, all those from the various plantations who had hatched the plot came to the shore and fled in a schooner. In order to prevent it from happening again, the owners put guards on board the schooners—soldiers with loaded guns. The negroes say: "The hunted is wary of the hunter."[4]

At the time about which we are talking, a master in Coronie had a trusted valet named Philip, who had such pleasant manners that his master and others, as well as the other slaves, even the soldiers, loved and trusted him. One day Philip plotted with many others to find a way, soldiers or no soldiers, to capture one of the schooners and make a getaway in it. Because all the people loved Philip, and the whites harbored no suspicion against him, Philip, with the help of some others, took it upon himself to arrange the matter. They operated

---

4. The Creole proverb quoted here says literally: "The hunter promises the game, the game promises the hunter." "Promises" must be interpreted as "promises to watch out for."

makandra. So den wroko safri-safri, ondro-ondro, te na yuru doro.
Mofo fu mofo na boskopu waka: So wan neti, so wan yuru na so
wan presi. Na dey dati, Philip du ala en wroko leki fa a ben gwenti,
sondro fu misi wan. Di en masra de go na bedi, a waka go nanga en
te na da kamra mofo doro, dan a taki kuneti, a dray baka. Philip
now no ben de futuboy moro, ma edeman fu en srudati. Esi a feti
go na sekanti, pe a feni ala sani na order. Èn a teki neygi steyfi man
na ini wan srupu fu lo go na wan skuna, di ben de fu en masra. Fosi
den doro, na wakti si den, a teki en gon, dan a bari: he drape, suma
na un, san un wani? Bun suma, na mi Philip, wi kon, fu kon du wan
pikin krawerki.

Di den srudati yere na Philip, den poti den gon na sey, libi den,
meki den kon na ini na skuna. Den tra neygi, leki fa na barki ben
meki, panya den srefi, ala di Philip ori na Kapten nanga tori, te a
si ibri wan man na en posu. Dan a gi kumando, seni go. Fosi yu
denki, Philip naki na Kapten trowe na gron. Den matrosi, di ben
de srafu tu, ben de tu na ini na barki, den nanga den tra neygi poti
anu makandra, tay na Kapten fasi nanga na mast, tay den srudati
anu nanga futu, libi den didon na tapu na dèk. Na baka dati, den
opo seyri, den trowe fu Demarara, pe den doro eri bun. Di den doro
dape, den go na lanti, go ferteri na tori. Lanti libi den fri èn so na
Kapten nanga den srudati ben abi fu dray baka sondro den lonwe
man, go na Coronie, fu tyari na nyunsu gi na masra fu Philip. So wi
de si taki, Venezuela abi en *Urbina,* ma Sranan abi en *Philip* tu.

Now wan suma sa taki, Philip de wan takru suma, fu di a meki
misbruik fu na fertrow fu en masra nanga trawan. Dati na so, ma
Philip na libisuma, nèt so leki ibri trawan. Te wan libi suma de feti
fu en fri ofu fu en libi, dan no wan suma de prakseri den moy tori
disi. Fransman taki: à la guerre comme à la guerre, nengre taki: feti
no abi kondisi. Mi denki ala tu tan a srefi, Fransman na libisuma,
nengre na libisuma.

Foetoe-boi, July 1946

Wi tongo

Na Srananneti M'ma B'be meki wan ferwijti na den tata, mama

surreptitiously until the moment of action. The message was relayed by word of mouth: On this night, at that hour, at this place. On this day Philip performed his duties as usual, omitting nothing. When his master went to bed he accompanied him as far as the door. Then he bade him good night and turned round. No longer was Philip a valet but a commander of soldiers. Quickly he hastened to the shore, where he found everything under control. He took nine sturdy men in a shallop and rowed out to one of his master's schooners. Before they arrived, the guard spotted them, raised his gun, and shouted: "Hey there, who are you, what do you want?" Philip replied, "Good people, it's me, Philip. We have come to do a little job."

When the soldiers heard that it was Philip, they put down their guns and left them in peace, so they could board the schooner. The nine scattered, as had been agreed, while Philip kept the captain talking until he saw that everyone was in position. Then he gave the order: "Off and away!" Before you could say "Jack Robinson," Philip knocked the captain to the deck. The sailors, who were also slaves, were in the plot as well. Together with the nine, they joined hands, bound the captain to the mast, bound the soldiers hand and foot, and left them lying on the deck. Then they hoisted the sail and departed for Demarara, where they arrived safely. On arrival they went to the government to tell their tale. They were allowed their freedom, and the captain and his soldiers returned to Coronie without the runaways to impart the news to Philip's master. Thus we see that Venezuela has its Urbina, but Surinam also has its Philip.

Somebody might perhaps say that Philip was a mean person, because he abused the confidence that his master and others had in him. That is true, but Philip is only human like everyone else. When a living soul fights for his freedom or life, then nobody gives a thought to these highfalutin principles. The Frenchman says, "A la guerre comme à la guerre." The negroes say, "All is fair in war." I think both have the same meaning. Frenchmen are human, negroes are human.

Foetoe-boi, July 1946

Our language

On Sranan neti[5] M'Ma-B'be berated the fathers, mothers, and

5. *Sranan neti* ("Surinamese evening") was a performance organized

nanga meester fu den Sranan pikin. A taki, en no de puru tiki,
meester Kundrusu de na ini tu. Na den meki den pikin sabi Andrisi
fu Denmarki, ala di den no sabi M'ma B'be fu No-mer-mi-kondre.
Krin taki, na bun libi M'ma B'be, ma fu meester Koenders sey yu
abi wan bigi aboysi. Di mi ben de wan yongu meester fu 20 yari, mi
ben abi na law, ma dati pasa mi langa ten. Na skoro mi ben e tanapu
na den pikin tapu fu taki Hollands, fu di den musu leri na tongo,
*ma noyti mi ben kisi na mi ede fu strafu wan pikin fu di a ben taki
en mama tongo.* Sensi 40 yari kaba, meester Koenders ben frustan
san agu taki: *tyakun tyakun, fu yu na fu yu.*

Dati ede nofo tron mi no ben syen, te mi firi taki wan pikin no
ben frustan san a leysi, fu aksi en taki, fa yu sa taki dati na Sranan
tongo? M'ma B'be, yu sabi san ben e pasa dan? Den pikin ben e
luku fruwondru, dati mi aksi so wan sani, bika na oso den ben leri
taki, yu no mu taki Nengre ofu Neger-Engels, soleki fa wi ben e kari
Sranan tongo na a ten dati. Ma mi no ben store mi srefi no wan yuru
na san den pikin ofu den mama nanga den tata ben denki fu dati,
bikasi sensi mi tron wan yonkuman fu 30 yari, mi ben sabi sortu
leri na popokay leri de, d.w.t. furu wortu, soso wortu, na presi fu
na frustan san den wortu wani taki. Yu yere mi tori M'ma B'be?
Wan tra leysi yu sa abi fu puru tiki.

Now di mi abi na okasi, mi sa teki en fu tagi den suma di e kon
na Srananneti wan sani. A sori leki furu fu un no e frustan san de
na ede sani fu den Srananneti. Meki den suma dati yere bun.
Srananneti wani taki *Sranantongo neti,* d.w.t. wan okasi fu sori taki
wi tongo no hey, a no grani, a no gudu, ma toku a kan du san den
tra tongo e du. Te den suma na Srananneti bari lafu, klop na ini
anu, dan mi de seyker taki, den sabi fu san ede den e du dati. *Den
frustan san den yere.* Efi den Srananneti ben e ori na Hollands,
dan mi de seyker taki, furu fu den suma di ben sa klop, ben sa de
leki skapu: na wan bari bè, na trawan no sabi fu san ede, a piki bè.

teachers of Surinamese children. She said that she would brook no
exception, not even for master Koenders. They have seen to it that
the children know about Andrew of Denmark while they don't even
know who M'ma-B'be of No-mer-mi-kondre is.[6] It's good to call a
spade a spade, M'ma-B'be. As for master Koenders, you miss the
boat by miles. When I was still a young teacher about twenty years
old, I too was not devoid of such madness. But that was long ago. At
school I stood in front of the children to teach them how to speak
Dutch, because they had to learn how to speak that language. But
never did it cross my mind to punish a child because he spoke his
mother tongue. For forty years master Koenders has understood what
the pig says: "Slop, slop, that which is yours is yours."

For this reason I very often did not feel ashamed to ask a child
who did not understand what he was reading to say it in Surinamese.
M'ma-B'be, do you know what happened then? The children were
amazed that I asked them such a thing, because at home they were
taught you must not speak the negro language, as we then called
Surinamese. But not for a moment did I pay any attention to what
the children or their parents thought of this. Ever since my early
thirties I have known what sort of knowledge parrot knowledge is,
to wit: many words, only words, instead of comprehension. Do you
understand what I am driving at, M'ma-B'be? Next time you should
make an exception.

Now that I have the opportunity I shall use it to tell something
to those who frequent Srananneti. It appears that many of you
don't know what the real purpose of these Srananneti is. Listen carefully: Srananneti is Surinam language night, that is to say, it is an
opportunity to show that our language is not that elevated, not that
old, not that rich, but is still capable of doing what other languages
are capable of. When people burst into laughter and applause at a
Srananneti, then I know for sure that they know the reason for doing
so. They comprehend what they hear. When the Srananneti were
held in Dutch, then I knew for sure that many of the people who
applauded were nothing but sheep: the one says "Baa!" The other
does not know why, but he answers "Baa!"

---

annually on the evening of July 1 to commemorate the emancipation of the
slaves.

6. *No-mer-mi-kondre* (literally "Don't-touch-me country") is a mythical
land, situated somewhere near the capital, where it was possible for runaways
to become invisible. Many stories circulate about the place.

Foetoe-boi, February 1947

Fruku?

Yu abi suma, Nengre nanga trawan, di e taki wan fruku de na
Nengre tapu. Na tru dan? Ya, so a de, fruku de na furu furu Nengre
tapu, no na ala. Na fruku di de na den tapu, dati de disi: na don, law
bribi di den abi taki fruku de na den tapu. Na bribi disi den teki fu
srafuten, ala di na baka srafuten, trawan steyfi na bribi disi na den
ini èn san wan suma e bribi, bun ofu ogri, fu en srefi, na dati a sa
de tu. Mi no e bribi na wan fruku fu Nengre, èn mi abi bigi èn dipi
sari fu den Nengre di abi na bribi disi. Fu san ede? Fu di na don law
bribi e dompu den go na ondro, a e broko den kindi, a e lan den
anu, a e tapu den ay, a e swaki den baka, a e dofu den, a e dungru
den frustan, a e masi den geest, a e kwinsi den siel.

Wan dey wan bakra leriman ben kari en gemeente kon makandra
fu taki wan saak nanga den. Te un yere leriman, dan un kan frustan
wanten taki na tori disi a no disiten tori, bikasi disi ten leriman no
de moro. Ma efi suma de, di wani denki taki den tori leki den disi
na fu owruten nomo, dan a spijt mi gi den, bika dan den sa kori
den srefi, te leki na dey fu tide trawan de luku Nengre leki pikin,
di den kan tagi sani, di den no sa dorfu tagi trawan. Te leki na dey
fu tide furu furu Nengre de, di lasi lespeki fu den srefi, dati nanga
prisiri den e teki afrontu fu trawan, di e luku den "als niet vol."
Suma sa wani twijfel na den tori disi, mi e ferseyker taki dusin fu
dusin mi abi den. Trawan fu den suma dede kaba, trawan de na libi
ete, so, efi a de fanowdu, mi kan kari nen, ofu mi kan sori san den
skrifi, braka na tapu weti. Meki wi go doro.

Di na leriman kaba taki san a wani, den suma, den ben sa de wan
50 so, sidon sondro fu piki wan wortu. Dan wan fu den teki man-ati,
a opo fu taki, ma di na leriman si taki a e lo na boto go na wan sey
di a no feni bun, a bari na Nengre: A nofo now, ori yu mofo!

Foetoe-boi, February 1947

Curse?

There are people, negroes and others, who say that there is a
curse on negroes. Is it true? Yes, it is so. There is a curse on very
many negroes, but not on all of them. The curse resting on them is
the stupid, insane belief they have that there is a curse on them.
They have taken over this belief from the period of slavery, while
others, later confirmed it. And that which one believes of oneself,
be it good or evil, will also be true. I don't believe in a curse on the
negro. And I have a deep compassion for negroes who harbor this
belief. Why? Because this stupid, insane belief pulls them down,
forces them to their knees, paralyzes their arms, blurs their vision,
blocks their ears, clouds their thinking, crushes their spirit, and
wrings out their soul.

One day a white leriman[7] called together his congregation to
discuss something with them. When one hears the word leriman,
one will immediately know that this story is not of recent date,
because at present there are none of them. But if there are people
who prefer to think that the present story took place only in former
times, then I feel sorry for them, because they're fooling themselves.
Right up till today people regard negroes as children to whom one
can say things that one would not dare say to other persons. Right
until today there are many negroes who don't respect themselves,
with the result that they accept with pleasure insults from people
who don't take them *au sérieux.* If there are people who mistrust
these stories, then I can assure them that I have dozens in my possession. Some of the people in question are dead; others are still alive.
If necessary I can quote chapter and verse from their writings. Let
us proceed further.

When the leriman had said what he wanted to say, the members
of the congregation remained seated as mum as mice. Then one of
them plucked up courage, got up, and spoke. But when the
leriman saw he was steering an unsafe course he yelled at the negro:
"That's enough. Shut up!"

7. The Moravian missionaries were formerly called *leriman* ("teacher").
Later, when Creoles were also ordained, a difference was created between
the title *dominee* or *domri,* for people who studied theology in Europe, and
the title *leriman,* used for evangelists trained in Surinam. Koenders might
have made this remark about the former title *leriman* with some ironic after-
thoughts.

San a Nengre du? A teki en ati opo gowe, ala di a taki: Yu kari
mi fu taki, efi mi no kan taki, dan san mi e tan du? Dan a gowe fu
en. Man srefi! Te leki na dey fu tide mi abi lespeki fu a Nengre disi,
bika a no ben abi na don law bribi taki fruku de na en tapu, di e
meki lasi lespeki fu en srefi. Den trawan, san den du? Den seti fu
krutu na trawan fa a abi hey memre, na presi fu den du san den ben
abi fu du, opo gowe libi na leriman. Ma pôti, di den ben abi na bribi
taki fruku de na den tapu, den tan sidon.

Wan dey wan pastoru ben e taki en gemeente odi. "Na ten di
Bisschop kari mi, tagi mi taki en e seni mi go na . . . , di mi prakseri
taki mi mu go na . . . na den agu mindri, mi go na ini mi kamra, mi
krey." San den suma du? Den du leki suma di e bribi taki fruku de
na den tapu. Den sidon arki na pastoru èn di den komopo na kerki,
dan den piri en skin gi en. Na en baka. San den ben sa du, efi den
abi lespeki fu den srefi? Den no ben sa kosi na baka, ma den ben
sa opo wan na baka trawan gowe libi na pastoru nanga en kerki èn
den no ben sa trapu futu na ini na kerki te Bisschop ben seni wan
tra pastoru gi den.

Efi so Nengre ben du, efi so den ben leri den pikin fu den, taki
un mu gi ibri wan suma san a mu abi, ma un no mu meki wan suma,
awansi na Bakra, awansi na pastoru ofu leriman teki un meki dagu,
dan tide na bribi no ben sa de moro taki fruku de na Nengre tapu,
meki no wan bun den no abi, noti den no kan, den gebore fu tan
na trawan ondro. Den Nengre di e taki so, na den tapu na fruku de,
fu di den abi na bribi taki fruku de na den tapu. Mi ben taki kaba
san na law don bribi disi e meki fu wi. Wan fu den ogri di na bribi
disi e du, a e dungru wi frustan. Efi wan Nengre no wani du wan sani,
di kan tyari en na fesi, kaba a go du na srefi sani gi wan trawan
meki na trawan kon na fesi, dan na Nengre dati frustan dungru
fu tru.

Nengre kondreman, mi teki Gado begi unu, trowe na bribi
disi na ini faya, teki na asisi trowe na ini liba, dati nomo kan steyfi
yu futu, lusu yu anu, tranga yu baka, opo yu ay nanga yu yesi, krin
yu frustan, nanga wan wortu tron wan man fu karakter, di e lespeki
en srefi. Sondro lespeki fu yu srefi, noyti trawan sa lespeki yu.

What did the negro do? He took his hat and went away saying:
"You've called me to speak. If I can't speak, why should I stay?"
Then he left. What a man! Until today I have had respect for this
negro, for he did not have that stupid, insane belief that there was
a curse on him which caused him to lose his self-respect. And what
did the others do? They started at once to talk behind his back,
saying how arrogant he was, instead of doing what they should have
done: get up, leave, and let the leriman be. Poor suckers, because
they were imbued with the belief that there was a curse on them,
they remained seated.

One day a priest delivered his opening sermon: "When the bishop
called me and told me that he would send me to . . . When I realized
that I was to go to . . . among those pigs, I went to my room and
wept." What did the people do? They behaved like persons who
believed that there was a curse on them. They kept on listening to
the priest, and only when they had left the church did they tear him
apart, behind his back. What should they have done, if they had any
grain of self-respect? They should not have reviled him behind his
back, but should have, one after the other, gotten up and left the
priest and his church. And they should not have set foot in the
church again until the bishop had sent them another priest.

If negroes would behave thus, if they would educate their children
in this way, saying that you must grant everyone that which is his
but must not allow anyone to treat you like a dog, not even if he is
a white man, or a priest, or a leriman, then today this belief in a
curse on the negro, that there is nothing good in negroes, that they
can't do anything, that they are born to be lorded over would not
exist. The curse rests on those negroes who speak in this way, because
they firmly believe that there is a curse on them. I have already told
you what this stupid, insane belief has done to us. One of the evil
things this belief does is to cloud our thinking. If a Negro does not
want to do that which will help him to make headway, but does the
very same for another so that he makes headway, then the thinking
of this negro is really clouded.

Negro countrymen, I plead with you, for God's sake, cast this belief into the fire, take the ashes and throw them into the river. Only
that can cause your legs to stand firm, free your arms, straighten your
backs, open your eyes and ears, unclog your minds. In one word,
transform yourself into a man of character who respects himself.
If you don't respect yourself, others will never do it.

Foetoe-boi, March 1949

Mama Afrika e krey fu en pikin

Pe den alamala go?
Amba, Kwami èn Kodyo.
Farawe fu oso, farawe na abra se
den opo ay e suku pe den oso de.

Trangaman fufuru den,
trangaman fufuru den,
seti den leki elen
ondro dungru sipi, koti se
go farawe na abrasey,
go srafu neti nanga dey.

Bigi busi, makti bon
Yaw mu fara kon na gron.
Kwami diki gotro, bantaman,
fu trangaman tron guduman,
fu busi kan kon tron Sranan.

Adyuba e drasi ken.
Wans' en skin e krasi en
ten no de fu krasi: Futuboi fu trangaman
tanapu nanga langa wipi na en han.

Tobo lay nanga kofi
fu Akuba èn Afi.
Wasi den mu wasi: afu bere, swaki skin,
so den mu wasi ala tobo fre fre krin.

Kofi, katun nanga ken
den mu prani,
ma no f' den.
Sipi nanga sukru lay
gowe fu trangaman,

Foetoe-boi, March 1949

Mother Africa weeps for her children

Wither are they, all of them?
Amba, Kwami, and Kodyo—[8]
far from home, far across the sea,
they lift their eyes, search for their huts.

Powerful ones have snatched them away,
Mighty ones have stolen them all,
stacked them like herrings
in the darkness of the ships, making way
across the sea, far away,
so that they would slave night and day.

Huge forests, mighty trees,
Yaw is now forced to fell.
Kwami digs ditch and trench,
that the powerful ones may be rich,
that the forest become Surinam.

Ajuba thrashes the cane,[9]
though she itches so.
There's no time to scratch, for a servant of the powerful ones
stands with a long whip there!

Tubs filled with coffee
by Akuba and Afi.
They must wash: weak and famished.
They must wash, scrub clean all the tubs.

Coffee, cotton, and sugarcane
they must plant,
not for themselves.
Ships for the powerful ones
loaded with sugar leave.

8. Koenders here uses the so-called "day names," which are still used in Surinam. The child gets a name according to its sex and the day of the week on which it was born. The names match those of such Gold Coast languages as Twi and Ewe. For instance, a girl born on Saturday is called Amba, a boy born on the same day is called Kwami. See *Encyclopaedie,* s.v. Naamgeving.

9. The word for *thrash* is creolized to *trasi.* There is a slight possibility that Koenders uses an old word *drasi* for the English *dross.* We failed to find this word in the dictionaries.

fu masra Jan, fu di en de na trangawan.

(Ma pasyensi, san fu du,
wan dey, masra Jan, yu tu,
yu tu sa tron srafu.
Moro trangawan lek' yu
sa tek' lefensi
fu Kwasiba èn Afi.)

Diaso . . . Sranannengre libitori de. Leki fa Hollander e kari dati: in een notendop. A no de fanowdu fu tagi un taki wi libitori na wan fu sweti, brudu nanga watra-ay, dati un sabi nèt so bun leki wi, ya, a kan de moro betre srefi. 300 yari langa den afo fu wi ben tan na ondro na ebi katibo disi, sondro fu sabi wan dey payman. Now mi denki un sa kan ferstan taki so wan katibo, so wan ebi leki di a ben poti na wi tapu, no de fu puru na ini 86 yari. Meki wi luku ma na den Hollander, feyfi yari nomo den ben de na ondro wan katibo, di no kon na di fu wi bakafutu èn arki den, fa den e kragi fu san na katibo disi ben meki fu den pikin fu den.

Ma den no sidon e kragi nomo, ma na ala fasi den e broko den ede fu kweki den pikin fu den, fu puru den fasi di na feyfi yari katibo ben tyari gi den. We un leki Sranansuma di now mu tiri na kondre, wi denki taki a de un prekti, no fu kisi atibron fu den fowtu fu un masanengre, ma fu broko ede èn fu abi pasyensi nanga den, no fu dini den leki fa pori pikin wani fu den mama èn papa dini den, ma leki fa a fiti wan frustan papa di abi na prekti fu kweki en pikin.

Fu san ede wi e skrifi ala den sani disi? Fu di na ini na tori fu den yonkuman fu Srotweki sani taki, di ati wi leki Nengre. Meki wi no

Alas for Master John, for power does he have.
[But have patience, there's nothing one can do,
One day Master John, even you, even you
will be a slave.
Stronger ones
will take revenge
for Kwasiba and Afi.][10]

Here is the history of Surinam negroes, according to Dutchmen, in
a nutshell. It is not necessary to tell you that our history is one of
blood, sweat, and tears. You know that as well as I do, and maybe
even better. For three hundred years our forefathers suffered under
this heavy slavery without seeing a day's wages. I think you will
understand that such slavery, such a burden which has weighed us
down, cannot be wiped out in eighty-six years. Let us but look at
the Dutch. For only five years they lived under a form of slavery
which does not even bear any comparison to ours. And listen how
they complained about this slavery and what it had done to their
children.[11]

Not only did they complain, but in various ways they took the
trouble to educate their children in order to wipe out the mentality
that five years of slavery had inculcated in them. Well now, you
Surinamese who must now govern the land, it is your duty, so we
think, not to take exception to the shortcomings of your countrymen, but to take up responsibility for them and to have patience
with them: not to serve them as spoilt children would want their
mother and father to do, but as befits a sensible father who has
the responsibility of educating his child.

Why do we write all this? Because things have been said about the
young men of Slootwijk which caused us as negroes pain.[12] Let us not

10. This poem by Koenders was translated into German and published
in the German anthology *Schwarzer Orpheus* by Jahn-Heinz John (1954).
Koenders added some final lines after 1949, which he published in *Foetoe-boi*,
March 1955. They are added here between brackets.

11. Koenders refers to the German occupation of Holland during the
Second World War.

12. Slootwijk was an agricultural project intended to counter the growing
urbanization, especially of Creoles. The first Surinam government, the newly
appointed CAB (Committee for General Affairs), wanted to bring Creoles
back to agriculture. The project failed, and the Creoles were blamed.
In this article Koenders tries to analyze the failure in a more comprehensive
way.

frigiti taki, na baka na ebi katibo libi, di ben koti, so leki fa den e
taki, na 1863, no wan sortu muyti ben meki, fu kweki den afo fu
wi fu tron leti borgru fu na kondre. Na baka na kontraki ten den
lusu den na wey, libi den abra na den lot, ma dati no de ala ogri
ete. Na moro bigi ogri, na moro bigi kruktu di den ben du na wi
èn di e wroko te tide, dati de, dati fosi wi kisi wi srefi pikinso baka,
den gi wi sani na anu, fu di wi no ben abi ferstan kweti kweti, fu
kari na nen, wan koloniale Staten. Na presi fu lanti ben sorgu,
awansi a ben de nanga tranga srefi, fu kweki wi, den gi wi skoro
di kiri wi te tide. Meki ala suma ferstan wi bun, wi no de kondemi
leri, ma wi e kondemi den skoro, na fasi fu na leri.

   Fu bigin, den feti fu wi lasi wi mamatongo, fu wi frigiti wi
eygi tongo, fu meki wi tron Hollander, wan sani di noyti no kan.
Den afo fu wi, pôti, den no ben sabi betre, ben denki taki dati na
a moro bigi bun di den ben kan du wi, ala di a ben de wi dede, te
leki na dey fu tide, bika te now yu abi furu fu wi di no man fu ferstan
taki wan pipel di no abi wan tongo, noyti kan de san di fiti na nen
fu wan pipel. Efi wi teki wan skorobuku na anu, dan wi no e si
noti na ini leki Holland-libitori, Holland sabana, Holland foto,
Holland winti miri, Holland osolibi e.s.m.f. Nofotron yu kan yere
suma e taki fa den skoro fu wi de so bun skoro, èn fu san ede den
de so bun? Bikasi, te den pikin fu wi gowe na tra kondre den e feni
bun wroko tangi fu na bun skoro di den kisi. Mi fu mi denki taki
wan skoro, di e leri pikin fu go wroko gi wan tra kondre, libi na
eygi kondre, meki a go na baka, mi no feni dati wan bun skoro. Mi
no denki taki wan kondre de na grontapu, funamku wan kondre
di no abi furu suma, di e ori skoro fu tra kondre prisiri. Sranan e
du dati, fu di wi no kisi kweki. Suma ben mu gi wi na kweki? A
ben de na prekti fu lanti, bikasi den suma di ben lasi wrokoman,
di ben e wroko fu soso, noyti ben sa du dati, ibri wan suma kan
ferstan dati. Furu yari na fesi, di den suma disi ben si taki sani de
kon, tru tru, den Nengre ben e go kisi fri, den dwengi lanti na den
foordeel. Den suku fu lanti seni teki tra suma, di ben kan wroko
moro bunkopu, kon na a kondre. Dia na bigi fowtu, na bigi kruktu

forget that after the heavy period of slavery, which as people main-
tain came to an end in 1863, no attempt was made to educate our
forefathers to become full-fledged citizens of this land. After their
contract period they were sent packing and abandoned to their fate.
But that was not even the worst that befell us. The worst, the most
abominable they did to us, which even to this day shows its effects,
is that before we found our feet they entrusted us with things of
which we had not the foggiest notion, namely, a mock parliament.
Instead of the government taking care that we receive an education,
they provided us with schools which to this very day kill us. Let each
and every one know this: we don't condemn the education, but we
condemn the schools, the teaching methods.

To begin with, they tried to make us lose our mother tongue,
forget our very own language, turn us into Dutchmen, something
which is impossible. Our forefathers, however, didn't know better
and thought that that was the best they could do for us. In effect it
rang the deathknell for us right up till this very day, because at present
there are many who don't understand that a nation without a language
can never be anything which is worthy of the name nation. When we
pick up a schoolbook, we find nothing but Dutch history, Dutch
meadows, Dutch cities, Dutch windmills, Dutch domestic life, and
so on. Often persons are heard to say that our schools are good. And
why are they so good? Because our children, when they go to other
countries, are able to secure good jobs thanks to the good schooling
they have had. I think however that a school which teaches the
children to go and work for other countries, to leave their own country
so that it falls into decay, is not a good school. In my opinion, there
is no country in the world, especially not one with such a sparse
population, which keeps a school going for the benefit of another
country. That is what Surinam is doing, because we have not had
any education. Who should have given us this education? That was
the government's duty, for everyone will understand that those persons who had lost laborers who were toiling for nothing could never
have done it.[13] Many years ago when these people realized that things
were really happening, that the negroes would have their freedom,
they forced the government to tip the scales in their favor. They
tried to get other people into the country who would provide cheap
labor.[14] Here lies the big fault, the great injustice which the govern-

13. Meaning the former slave owners just after emancipation.
14. Koenders here refers to the Asian immigrants who were imported under
contract as cheap laborers.

de di lanti du na den suma, di opo Sranan nanga den brudu, den
sweti, den watra-ay. Tide ala suma e taki Nengre no wani meki gron,
trawan e skrifi taki den no wani fu du dati, fu di a e memre den taki
den grantata fu den ben de srafu. Now wi denki taki den lespeki
masra fu na C.A.B., nanga nen masra Waller sabi nèt so bun leki mi
taki furu furu fu den afo fu wi, na baka di na katibo koti, ben go
meki gron na Sramacca, na Commewijne, na Cottica, sondro fu den
ben abi yepi nanga moni ofu bun lay fu sabi san den mu du èn fa
den mu libi.

Lanti libi den leki pikin di no abi papa ofu mama. Èn toku wi
ala, mi denki un tu, mi lespeki masra fu na C.A.B. nanga nen
masra Waller sabi fa den ben wroko den srefi kon na fesi. Efi den
suma disi di no ben kisi no wan sortu yepi, ben kan lepi den srefi
so, kaba tide den pikin pikin fu den gowe libi den gron, dan mi
denki a musu abi wan oorzaak èn leki fa wi ben taki na ini no.
10 fu Foetoeboi, wan bun datra no e feti nanga ede-ati, ma a e suku
fosi san e tyari na ede-ati. We, awansi den lespeki masra fu wi no de
Nengre ofu no e firi den srefi Nengre, toku wi denki den de
Sranansuma, den kumbatetey beri dya, den sabi Nengre libitori, den
sabi na kruktu di pasa wi, wi denki pe leti de èn pe den kisi na kari
fu tiri na kondre, den abi wan bigi prekti na wi Nengre, den abi na
prekti, no fu frufri gi den, ma leki bun datra, di sabi na oorsaak fu
wi siki, fu broko ede feti nanga na siki nanga pasyensi, nanga lobi,
nanga wan wortu fu meki bun san Hollander pori na wi.

Èn efi a mu de so taki den mu du wan extra sani gi Nengre di
den no sa du gi tra ipi di de na ini na kondre, dan wi denki taki
dati de nanga leti, bikasi san di wi ben taki na ini na nomru fosi
disi, wi e taki dya baka: Sranan, ya eri Amerika abi wan payman
na Nengre, di a no abi na no wan tra ipi fu na kondre.

Foetoe-boi, November 1949

Oen sa wani sabi, mi denki, san na wan yobonengre? Wan
yobonengre na den sortu Nengre di bun ofu ogri no sabi wan tra
sani fu piki leki yes yobo, yes.

Kwaku, Gado no fruku Nengre?
—Yes yobo, yes.

ment did to those people who opened up Surinam with their blood, sweat, and tears. Nowadays everyone says that negroes don't want to work on the land. Others allege that they don't want to do that because they don't want to be reminded that their forefathers were slaves. We, however, are of the opinion that the respected gentlemen of the C.A.B., and especially Mr. Waller, know as well as I do that very many of our forefathers worked on the land in Saramacca, in Commewijne, and in Cottica after the period of slavery without any help and money or good advice as to what to do and how to live.

The government abandoned them to their fate like children who have no father or mother. And yet we all know, even you I think, respected gentlemen, and especially Mr. Waller, how they have worked themselves up. If these people who received no help whatsoever could fend so well for themselves, and if today their grandchildren leave the agricultural lands, then in my opinion there's a reason for it. And as we have already stated in *Foetoe-boi* number ten, a good doctor does not fight against a headache, but tries to establish what causes the headache. Well, although our respected gentlemen do not feel themselves negroes, we think that they are at least Surinamese. Their umbilical cords are buried here. They know the history of the negro. They know the injustice which has befallen us. We think that where there is justice and where they have received the call to govern the country they have a great duty toward us negroes—a duty not to lose patience with them, but like a good doctor who knows the causes of our illness to be concerned and to combat the illness with patience, with love, in a word, to set right what the Dutch have messed up.

And if it should mean that they would have to do something extra for negroes, which they would not do for others who live in the country, then we think it is only meet and right, for what we have said in the first issue we say once more: Surinam and the whole of America owe a debt to the negro which they don't owe any other group.

Foetoe-boi, November 1949

You may want to know, I think, what an Uncle Tom is. An Uncle Tom is a person who, good or bad, knows no other way of behaving than saying: "Yes, boss, yes."

> "Kwaku, has God not damned the negroes?"
> "Yes, boss, yes."

Nengre no meki fu tan alaten na trawan ondro?
    —Yes yobo, yes.
Te Nengre e lon fu go na fesi, tra Nengre no mu go lon frekti den
futu, ari den fadon?
    —Yes yobo, yes.
Den no mu tay Nengre anu nanga futu nanga ketin, srepi go na hemel?
    —Yes yobo, yes.
Awansi den ketin e koti den, dat' n' a trobi?
    —Yes yobo, yes.
Awansi na srepi e piri den skin, dat' n' a trobi?
    —Yes yobo, yes.
Nengre no mu seri en famiri, en masanengre, en karakter?
    —Yes yobo, yes.
Fu wan pikin nyanyan, wan pikin sopi ofu wan pikin piri tifi nanga
den?
    —Yes yobo, yes.

Ma tangi fu Gado, a no soso yobonengre de na grontapu . . .
    Foetoe-boi no abi na wroko fu srepi Nengre nanga ketin go na
hemel. Wi e du muyti fu seki den komopo na ini na dipi sribi di den
de, meki nanga krin opo ay den kan si na hel di wi ala de na ini èn
fu gi anu makandra feti komopo na ini. Wi e feti fu meki Nengre no
lasi lespeki fu den srefi ofu fu makandra, fu wi no tron figi futu fu
saka saka. Dati na wi wroko. Ofu na bun ofu ogri wi e du, dati wi
no kan taki, dati no wan suma di de now kan taki. Den suma di sa
de na wi baka, tentin tentin yari, na den wawan sa man krutu wan
leti krutu. Bakra taki: De wereldgeschiedenis is het wereldgericht.
Wi no e fruku no wan suma, wi no e kari wan suma satan. Suma du
bun, na fu en, suma du ogri, na fu en.

Foetoe-boi, July 1952

Sranan

Kondre fu sweti, watra-ay, brudu.
Doti pe wi fadon na gron,
    pe wi kumba tetey beri.
Wi sabi taki yu mandi nanga yu pikin.
Wi sabi taki yu abi leti,
    bigi leti fu mandi.
Wi sabi taki wi du ogri,
    bigi ogri.

"When negroes make progress, then the other negroes must grab hold of
their feet and drag them down."
    "Yes, boss, yes."
"Must one not tie the negroes hand and foot and drag them off to heaven?"
    "Yes, boss, yes."
"Even if the chains cut into their flesh, it doesn't matter."
    "Yes, boss, yes."
"Must the negroes not sell their family, their associates, their character?"
    "Yes, boss, yes."
"For some food, for a glass of wine or a wee smile from them?"
    "Yes, boss, yes."

But, thanks be to God, there are not only Uncle Toms in this world.
    Foetoe-boi does not have as its task to drag the negroes off to
heaven in chains. We try to jostle them from their deep sleep to see
with clear eyes the hell in which all of us find ourselves, so that we
can join hands and wrest ourselves from it. We fight so that the
negroes shall not lose their self-respect or their respect for each other,
so that we shall not become the doormat of the dregs. That is our
task. Whether we do good or whether we do evil, we cannot tell.
Nobody who lives at present can say that. The people who come some
decades after us, they will be able to judge. The white man says:
"History will tell." We curse nobody, we call nobody Satan. He who
does good, it is his business; he who does evil, it is his business.

Foetoe-boi, July 1952

Surinam[15]

Land of sweat, tears, blood.
Earth on which we descended,
where our umbilical lies buried.
We know that you hold it against your children.
We know that you are right,
very right, to be so vexed.
We know that we have perpetrated harm,
great harm.

15. In our opinion Koenders is not an original poet, although he produced
some remarkable translations of Dutch poems in Sranan. He was a very
modest man, with a low opinion of his own poetic abilities. His article
"Sranan," however, which he reprinted in *Foetoe-boi,* June 1955, has highly
poetic qualities. H. F. de Ziel, the poet Trefossa, mentioned this to us and
arranged the article in the way it has been published here.

Nanga wi du wi spiti na ini yu fesi,
mama fu sweti, watra-ay, brudu.
Wi sutu ala wi tu anu
dipi na ini doti, morsu, fisti,
fringi na wi srefi tapu,
    gi yu bigi syen na ay fu eri grontapu.
Wi sabi yu kon weri nanga wi.
Yu lusu wi,
yu libi wi,
meki wi tron moro saka saka fu saka saka,
leki san wi de kaba.
Yu libi wi,
meki wi meki wi srefi frowa.

Yu libi wi gi grontapu
meki den spotu wi,
lafu wi,
dagu wi,
meki den spiti den moro fisti spiti na wi tapu,
aladi wi abi fu tapu wi mofo.

Bun mama Sranan,
doti fu sweti, watra-ay, brudu,
yere wi:
kaw wi no abi fu srakti gi yu,
brudu wi no de gi yu,
bika dati yu dringi nofo,
ma wan pikin kowru watra,
Gado alenwatra,
na ini wan nyun krabasi.

No fu wi srefi,
ma fu den pikin fu wi,
fu den suma
di de kon na wi baka.
Fu den wi de begi yu:
kowru yu ati,
no strafu den tu.
Den no du noti.

Efi den du,
dan na san den si wi du;
den spiti na ini yu fesi,
fu di den si wi du dati.
Den no abi lespeki fu den srefi,

With our deeds we have spat in your face,
Mother of sweat, tears, blood.
Both our hands we've pushed
deep down into the earth's dirt and slush,
flung upon us,
    debasing you in the eyes of the whole world.
We know that you are weary of us.
You have left us alone,
forsaken us,
so that we've become even viler
than we already were.
You have forsaken us
so that we have turned ourselves to chaff.

You have abandoned us in the world
so that it can have fun with us,
laugh at us,
treat us like a dog,
spew the vilest spittle on us,
while we had to keep our tongues.

Good Mother Surinam,
earth of sweat, tears, blood,
hear us:
We have no cows to slaughter,
blood we do not give,
for you have drunk your fill of it.
But a little bit of water cold,
rain water of God,
in a new calabash.

Not for ourselves,
but for our children,
for them
who come after us.
In their name we plead with you:
harden not your heart,
chastise them not,
they have done naught.

If they are at fault,
then it is what they have seen us do.
They spat in your face, because they saw us do so.
They respected not themselves,

fu di wi no de teri yu.
Ala fowtu de na wi,
den bigi wan,
di kisi leri
nanga di no kisi.

Wi de nati yu fu den ede.
Bun mama,
doti fu sweti, watra-ay, brudu,
luku den pikin nanga den yongu suma.
Kibri den,
opo den ay,
krin den frustan,
meki den no waka
na wi futustapu baka,
gi den gusontu kabesa
fu den si,
taki na pasi di wi ben waka
de tyari go na ferdumenis,
meki den no waka en.
Bun mama,
gi den karakter,
meki den lespeki den srefi.

because you did not count with us.
All guilt devolves on us,
the elders,
those who had schooling,
and those who had none.

We sprinkle[16] you in their name.
Good Mother,
earth of sweat, tears, blood,
Behold the children and the youth.
Protect them,
Open their eyes,
Illuminate their brains.
Let them not follow
in our wake.
Grant them sound minds
so that they see
the path that we have trod
leads but to purgatory.
Let them not walk it.
Good Mother,
give them character,
let them respect themselves.

16. Water is sprinkled on the earth in a ritual ceremony to honor and
appease the earth mother.

CHAPTER 6

Eddy Bruma

Eddy Bruma was born in 1925. He finished his studies in Surinamese law after World War II. He was for a short time president of a nationalistic youth club in Paramaribo, which must have been a rather frustrating experience. In Creole society there existed an especially strong urge to assimilate to the Dutch way of life, as is so typical of a colonial society. As we have seen, this often gave nationalistic feelings a certain ambiguity. Bruma believed that Surinam would never be able to shape its own future, to solve its own problems, and to make a valuable contribution to mankind, if the Dutch way of life continued to be the ultimate norm. The physical emancipation of 1863 had to be followed, he believed, by a psychological one. These ideas brought him into close contact with the work of Koenders, who also tried to convince the Creoles that they had to respect themselves.

There was, however, a clear difference in their general aims. Bruma not only wanted to educate the underprivileged Creoles, but also regarded a change in the basic outlook of the whole society as a prerequisite for social change. Political independence could be based only on cultural and psychological independence.

Bruma's basic ideas were unacceptable in Surinam. After his departure to Holland to finish his studies at the university level, he teamed up with a group of Surinamese students, recruited from all walks of society, who proved more susceptible to his ideas. They had been confronted in Holland with the failure of their assimilation ideals. They were not regarded as Dutch students with a slight tropical touch but remained foreigners who rather surprisingly also spoke Dutch. This inspired them to search for their own identity.

Bruma already had a strong conviction that Surinam should have its own identity. Now he was given the chance to shape the new ideas of his countrymen. In Amsterdam he founded the cultural nationalistic movement Wie Eegie Sanie (Our own things) in which for the first time intellectuals and laborers pooled resources on an equal basis. The laborers were in the privileged position of having a better mastery of Creole and a more intimate knowledge of lower-class Creole culture. Thus they could help the students to find a non-European identity.

After the completion of his studies in Holland, Bruma returned to
Surinam. With the help of the other members of Wie Eegie Sanie he
now succeeded in disseminating these new ideas. It was a period of great
activity, witnessed and described in 1962 by an outsider as follows:

> The leader of the Nationalists and possibly the most discussed
> person in Suriname is Eduard Bruma, a Negro lawyer in his
> middle thirties. He is dark brown, of medium height and build,
> with an unusually striking face: his brow puckers easily above
> the nosebridge and he has high eyebrows that slope steeply
> outwards over deep-set intense eyes. When he drives around in
> Paramaribo in his monster green Chevrolet boys and men
> wave, and there is a hint of conspiracy in their greeting. For
> though the Nationalist agitation is carried on openly, the
> Nationalists have as yet no official positions and the move-
> ment has a touch of the underground.[1]

The government, although politically almost independent, was indeed quick to recognize the political implications of these new
cultural ideas. If this movement succeeded, the old colonial elite was
bound to lose its prominent position in society. In the multiracial
setting of Surinam, the movement, interpreted as a struggle for
Creole supremacy, brought forth reactions from other racial groups.
It must be said that Bruma himself always stressed his national, and
therefore multiracial, approach. He did not succeed in proving this
unequivocally.

It seems only natural that Bruma was gradually drawn into the
vortex of politics, although he never became a true dyed-in-the-wool
politician. He always remained an outsider, refusing to be drawn into
political schemes and accepting successive losses with good humor.
Politics to him did not seem a serious business in itself, only an instrument for social change.

In the cultural battle Bruma started to use Creole as a means of
literary expression. He has been extremely careless with his manuscripts. A few poems have been published in *Foetoe-boi*,[2] and one
short story has been published in *Tongoni*,[3] but that is about all of

---

1. Vidia Naipaul, *The Middle Passage* (London, 1962), p. 178.
2. Some of his early poems are reproduced in chapter 8.
3. *Tongoni* 1 was published as a separate issue of *Vox Guyanae* 3, 1 (1968),
cf. pp. 10-17. A Frisian translation of this story has been published in *De
Tsjerne*, Suriname-numer, September 1952, pp. 276-86. A Dutch translation
appeared in a Dutch anthology, *Meesters der Negervertelkunst*.

his literary production which has found its way into print. His most
valuable contribution to Creole literature may perhaps be in the field
of drama. Bruma had already produced a play in Holland around 1952,
but on that occasion he was forced to express himself in Dutch.[4] Back in
Surinam he took over Koenders's job of annually producing a play in
Creole on July first, Emancipation Day. He has for some years written
and produced plays in Creole with his own group. He continued the
tradition of popular, mainly improvised drama on well-known themes
of slavery, produced by local groups, but he introduced a more
sophisticated structure. In this way he has greatly influenced local
plays. His own plays have never been published, and they may on the
whole have been written in too great a hurry to be published in full.
By mere chance we managed to lay hands on one of his best plays,
Basja Pataka, produced about 1958 in Paramaribo.

In this play Bruma treats the problem of collaboration during the
period of slavery. The peace treaties concluded with different groups
of maroons contained a paragraph in which the maroons solemnly
promised not to shelter runaway slaves any longer but to send them
back to their former masters for punishment. Today Creoles tend to
interpret their own past in Surinam as a constant battle for freedom,
fought openly by the maroons and surreptitiously by the slaves. The
above-mentioned paragraph in the peace treaties is difficult to accept
and could even be interpreted as treasonous. Bruma paints two different types of collaborators among the slaves against this general background of the peace treaties. There is the rather simple character of
the old doctor, who has had his own revolutionary past, and is ready
to volunteer witty advice, but does not want to get involved in any
way in revolutionary activities. He is in a way the intellectual, dis-
cussing freedom on a highly abstract level but mortally afraid of the
possible consequences if his words are taken literally. More complex
is the hero of the play, Basja Pataka. As the unscrupulous driver, he
is in a sense the prototype of the collaborator, the right hand of his
white master. He extracts the utmost from his fellow slaves for the
benefit of their master. But he is at the same time the fanatic worker,
devoted to his task, not to his master. In fact, neither master nor
slave exists in his eyes, only the task, which constitutes his only ethos
in life. This makes him a lone wolf, feared and respected by all. When
in a critical moment, he fails, he loses even his power of speech and
lives in a pig sty like a pariah.

4. This play was called in Dutch *De geboorte van Boni* (The birth of Boni).
A Creole adaptation was later produced in Surinam around 1957.

Two years later, when the slaves had lost all hope, and when the maroons refused to help them and they were on the point of giving up, Pataka is shaken from his lethargy. He regains his power of speech and takes the lost cause of the slaves upon himself with the same fervor with which he formerly embraced the cause of his master. He becomes the head of a slave uprising, which is doomed to failure. He has a purpose no longer dependent upon its success.

Different historical data have been used in constructing this play. The slave uprising in Coronie in 1836 served as a model. The leader of this slave uprising, a certain slave Colin, lost his power of speech and only regained it to start a hopeless struggle for freedom (Renselaar 1963, Voorhoeve Renselaar 1962). He has been identified with the hero of a story from the time of slavery, Basja Pataka.[5] To explain the crisis on the plantation during which Pataka loses his speech, Bruma used data from a court case against a certain Cameron, who killed a slave for dancing the forbidden Congo Tombe on the plantation.[6] We reproduce here part of the first act of Bruma's play.[7]

5. This story was published in *Tongoni* 2, *Vox Guyanae* 3, 6 (1959); 18-20.
6. Cf. the manuscript journal of A. F. Lammens in the Surinam Museum 868 VI (vol. XI, part B, no. 13). Cf. Voorhoeve 1960.
7. An analysis of this play is to be found in Voorhoeve 1966.

Basya Pataka

Act 1

*[Na fesi den oso Amba nanga a boy fu Sera sidon. Kwasi nanga Kofi
sidon toe na wan tra presi. Dan Kwaku doro. A go honti. A e singi
nanga den tra suma a singi disi.]*

> A ningi ningi ba busara,
> ningi ningi ba busara,
> hey a ho, ningi ningi ba busara
> ningi ningi ba
> ningi ningi ba
> ningi ningi ba busara-o,
> ho a ho, ningi ningi ba busara.
> Di moni no de, Akuba lowe,
> ma ningi ningi ba busara,
> ho a hey, ningi ningi ba busara-o.

Kwaku. Tsye! We i si, a tori di u yere e singi de, a ningi ningi ba
busara. A no now uma e gowe libi man. Sensi a fosi ten i ben a wan
basya, den e kari basya Pataka. A pranasi kon broko now, a biro
kawna. Now skowtupost kon drape de, a Kunofru. We, dape ben de
a moro hogri presi, pe den ben e tyari srafu gowe go makti. Efi i de
wan hogri srafu, dan den tya i gowe go makti a Kunofru. Ma den
ben e poti ton a den mofo hari ken pondo. We, a basya fu drape ben
de basya Pataka. We basya Pataka . . . ho! Pataka a wan sani, a de a
libi, efi i meki wan grap nanga en, a e beti tumusi takru. A dede,
toku a e beti. Bika efi i abi a drey pataka, dan i anu misi go na en
tifi sey, a sutu i kaba. Yu e nyan hen srefi, toku a e beti yu. Dùs pataka
a wan hogri sani. A man ben de wan hogri nengre, ne a teki a nen fu

Basya Pataka[8]

Act 1

*Amba and the son of Sera sit in front of the houses. Kwasi and Kofi
sit somewhat apart. Then Kwaku arrives. He sings the following song
with the others.*[9]

> A ningi ningi ba busara
> ningi ningi ba busara.
> Hey a ho, ningi ningi ba busara.
> Ningi ningi ba
> Ningi ningi ba
> Ningi ningi ba busara-o.
> Ho a ho, ningi ningi ba busara.
> When there was no money, Akuba walked away.
> But ningi ningi ba busara,
> Ho a hey, ningi ningi ba busara-o.

Kwaku. Well, you see, the song that you've heard here is "ningi
ningi ba busara." It's not only nowadays that women run off from
their husbands. Long ago there was an overseer called Basja Pataka.
The now dilapidated plantation is somewhere in the lower Commewijne.
Now, there was a police outpost at Kunofru.[10] Well, there you had
the most fear-inspiring place, where slaves were sent to be broken in.
If you were an evil slave, then they sent you to Kunofru to be tamed.
They put a bridle in your mouth so that you could pull the pontoon
filled with cane. The overseer at that place was called Basja Pataka.
Well, Basja Pataka! Ho! Pataka! That is something! When he is alive
and you joke with him, then he bites you in a terrible manner. When
he is dead, he still bites you. For if you have a dried pataka and your
hand should accidentally come near the teeth, then he's at you at
once. Even if you eat him up, still he bites you. Therefore a pataka
is a terrible thing, and that man was a terrible negro. Therefore he

---

8. *Basya* is a creolization of "overseer." It is used exclusively for the black
overseer who is himself a slave. The name *pataka,* a sort of fish, indicates the
fierce character of the man.

9. The recurring line *ningi ningi ba busara* is, according to informants, an
old African proverb meaning "people [negroes?] are ungrateful."

10. The Frederikshoop plantation was called by the slaves Kunofru or
Knofru. See chapter 8, note 8.

Pataka. Dan a ben kon de basya. Dan ala suma e kari en taki basya
Pataka. We, te a kon na oso, ala dey a mu nyan dri sortu tonton. Den
tonton den tan na ini baki ini. Wan sey weti kasaba tonton, wan sey
bâna tonton, wan sey kokori tonton. Kap-kapu yarabaka ede nanga
katfisi, stimofo, bonyo-bonyo sowtu meti de na ini wan krabasi.
So ala dey s'sa Akuba be e bori tonton. Efi a dey di a kon, s'sa
Akuba bori bâna, a e kisi s'sa Akuba, a e fon en. No fon en prey-
prey fonfon, a e fon en bun fonfon.

    Kofi. [*E bari lafu.*] Wakti! A sibi u e sibi bâna, now mi sabi suma
a e taki. Na wi eygi basya. Ma a bun a no e pasa fu yere yu, noso
yu ben sa kaba fu gi den dreygi tori disi.

    Basya. [*Komoto na ini a dungru.*] Ala pondo lay kaba?

    Kwasi. No wan no tan abra. Lay te fu sungu.

    Basya. Dati bun!

    Kwasi. Sensi mi de, mi no si pondo lay so hesi ete. Fruku
mamanten u o hari den na fesisey. Un libi waktiman a baka fu sorgu
fu a frudu no koti a tetey.

    Kwaku. Basya, a gersi den srafu wani aksi wan sani.

    Basya. Noti den no abi fu aksi mi. Efi na pansboko den wani,
dati den kan kisi.

    Kwaku. Ma basya, den wroko tranga!

    Basya. Na fu dati den de. Mi denki dati i ben sabi dati kaba.
[*Basya e koyri pikinso.*] Un tya seyri go na bakadan fu tapu den
boto?

    Kwasi. Ala dati seti.

    Basya. Mi e si wan basra alen hipi en srefi a dati sey. Efi a sa lusu,
den boto sa sungu.

    Kwasi. Ala dati seti tu. . . . Sensi mi de a firi, mi no man kaba fu
luku a loktu. Mi no man futrow en. Mi no man tagi wan suma san
mi e firi. Mi skin e piki mi, dati dineti no e go de wan bun neti gi unu.

    Basya. Fa so! San yu wani taki. Piki mi, meki mi sabi sortu
hogri un poti na un ede fu du. Ma mi dya e wakti unu. Mi e warskow
unu.

    Kwasi. A no dati basya. Na di mi ben de a tapu na dan na libasey,
wan safri draywinti ben way, mi skin ben gro.

    Basya. Wan draywinti?

assumed the name Pataka, and when he became overseer, all the
people called him Basja Pataka. Well, when he comes home every day
he had to eat three types of dumplings. The dumplings were in a
calabash. On the one side dumplings made from white cassava. On
the other dumplings from plantain. And then dumplings from bitter
cassava. And then in the one calabash there are chopped up heads of
the yellow backfish, catfish, meat, and bony salted meat. Thus
sister Akuba prepared dumplings every day. When he came home one
day and sister Akuba had cooked bananas, he grabbed hold of her
and gave her a thrashing. Not for a joke, he gave her a hell of a
beating.

    Kofi [*bursts out laughing*]. Wait! We were sifting the plantains,
but now we know who you're referring to. It is our very own overseer. It's a good thing he doesn't hear you. Else it would have been
over with your pestering.

    Basja [*emerges from the dark*]. Are all the pontoons loaded?

    Kwasi. They're all loaded to the top. Every one.

    Basja. That's good.

    Kwasi. I've never seen pontoons loaded in such a hurry. Tomorrow
morning early we'll pull them to the front of the plantation. We have
left the guards behind to see that the tide does not break the ropes.

    Kwaku. Basja, it seems the slaves want to ask you something.

    Basja. They have nothing to ask. If they want to feel the Spanish
buck, they can.[11]

    Kwaku. But Basja, they've slaved hard.

    Basja. That's their purpose. I thought you already knew that.
[*Basja walks to and fro.*] Have you taken canvasses to the back to
cover up the boats.

    Kwasi. Everything has been seen to.

    Basja. I see foul weather approaching over there. If it breaks, the
boats will sink.

    Kwasi. That has also been taken care of. The whole day in the
fields I've been anxiously watching the sky. I don't trust it. I can't
say what I think. I have a feeling that this night will bring us no good.

    Basja. What do you mean? Answer me. Tell me what you're up to.
I'm prepared for you. I warn you.

    Kwasi. It isn't that, overseer. When I stood on the dam near the
river, a soft wind eddied from all directions. It gave me goose pimples.

    Basja. Eddied, you say?

11. A cruel punishment. Cf. chapter 3, note 5.

Kwasi. Na so basya. A ben frede mi. A ben dray leki wan fini
froyti na ini mi yesi, mi ben firi en, mi ben yere en.

Basya. Wan winti leki wan fini froyti? Boy, yu sabi bun san yu
e taki? Yu wani mi krawasi yu te yu fadon dede, dineti? Hesi taki
a no tru. Hesi noso mi sa broko yu bakabonyo! [*A e opo na wipi fu
naki. Kwasi bukundu.*]

Kwasi. No naki basya! No naki! A no tru! Mi no yere noti!

Basya. Oooo! Yu leyman yu! [*Na basya e koyri go doro, Kwasi
e luku en, a e seki en ede.*]

Kwasi. Efi yu no wani bribi, na yu mu sabi. Den gado mu kibri wi
na san mi e fruwakti no go pasa dineti. Draywinti na wan tumusi
takru sani. Furu nengre sa krey, furu bakra sa krey. Draywinti no
sabi papa, no mama. A no sabi srafu, a no sabi basya.

Kofi. Yu o ferteri mi draywinti tori. Mi boy, wan yari ten, di mi
ben de na mamakondre ete, wan draywinti ben way neti. Efi a no
ben de so, taki wi ben abi wan trangawan na wi mindri di ben sabi
fa fu kowru na atibron fu den gado disi, no wan fu wi no ben tan.

Kwasi. Brada, nanga san a man ben kowru na atibron fu den gado?
Na fosi tron mi yere so wan tori.

Kofi. We, draywinti . . . u e kowru en nanga wan steyfi kongo
tombe. Te un dansi en so, un dansi en wan pisi, dan na draywinti
e kaba way.

Sera. Un no kan kaba nanga den tori disi? Fu san ede ala sortu
takru winti mu go way dyaso na wi kondre? Kande na srafu libi disi
no tranga nofo gi wi? Dan ete un wani draywinti nanga marawinti
mu kon broko wi masanga? [*Sera e dray taki nanga Kwaku.*]
Na heri mamanten kaba mi pruberi fu feni wan piki na tapu den
sani, di yu aksi mi esrede. Mi mu tagi yu leti mi no man feni.

Kwaku. Yu no abi fu suku moro, mama. Awansi fa yu sa suku,
yu no sa man feni.

Amba. San na dati? San a ben aksi yu?

Sera. A aksi mi efi mi sabi, san na a sani di du wi nengre, meki
un no kan komopo na ini katibo. Ne mi e suku, mi no man feni san
a wani taki.

Kwaku. Mi aksi yu wan sani moro.

Sera. Na so, olanga mi denki wi Koroninengre e go tan, meki den
e du nanga wi san den wani.

Kwaku. A no tru! A no dati mi aksi yu. Mi aksi yu olanga wi o
teki en.

Sera. Yu abi leti. Olanga wi sa swari dati! Yu sabi a boy fu mi. A
abi twarfu yari. Tra dey neti, na leti dya mi nanga en sidon, di ala

Kwasi. Yes, indeed. It frightened me. It eddied like a soft whistle in my ears. I felt it, heard it.

Basja. A wind like a soft whistle? Boy, do you know what you're saying? You want me to beat the hell out of you tonight? Quick, take it back. At once, or I break your spine. [*He raises his whip to beat. Kwasi ducks.*]

Kwasi. Don't beat, Basja, don't beat. It's not true. I never heard a thing!

Basja. Ah! Liar that you are. [*Basja walks on. Kwasi stares after him, shakes his head.*]

Kwasi. If you don't want to believe it, it's your business. May the gods prevent what I expect from happening tonight. Whirlwinds are something terrible. Many negroes will weep. Many whites will weep. Whirlwinds make no distinction. They know no father, mother, slave, or overseer.

Kofi. You're telling me! Boy, once when I was still in the motherland, a whirlwind blew at night. If there wasn't a powerful one among us who knew how to help the anger of those gods die down, then none of us would have been left.

Kwasi. Brother, with what did he soothe the anger of the god? It's new to me.

Kofi. Well, a whirlwind . . . we soothed it with a spirited Kongo-Tombe. When we had danced it for awhile the whirlwind stopped blowing.

Sera. Can't you stop? Why must all kinds of dangerous winds blow here on our plantation? Isn't this life of slavery enough? Do you also want whirlwinds and typhoons to destroy our huts? [*Sera turns to Kwaku.*] All morning I've been trying to find answers to the things you asked me yesterday. I must honestly tell you I can't find them.

Kwaku. You don't have to look any longer, mother. No matter how you try, you won't find the answer.

Amba. What did he ask?

Sera. He asked me whether I knew what happened to us negroes that we can't overcome our slavery. Since that time I've been looking for the answer. I can't find it.

Kwaku. I asked you something else.

Sera. That's right: how long, in my opinion, the negroes from Coronie will allow them to treat us as they please.

Kwaku. Not true. I didn't ask you that. I asked you how long we will accept it.

Sera. You're right. How long will we suffer it! You know my boy? He's twelve years old. Last night he and I sat precisely here, when all

suma go sribi kaba. A neti ben kowru, na sewinti ben way so switi.
Fosi tron sensi mi kon dyaso mi ben firi so wan rostu na ini mi ati.
A ben gersi na Afrikan kondre mi ben de baka.

Kwaku. Afrikan kondre, Mama kondre! Ay, mi Gado!

Sera. Dan a boy pasa en anu na mi baka, leki a ben wani mi firi,
taki mi nanga en na wan. [*Amba e geme.*] Dan a aksi mi:

Boy. M'ma, fu san ede den bakra moro tranga moro wi?

Sera. Mi no ben sabi san mi musu piki en. Mi tagi en taki den no
tranga moro wi, ma a no bribi mi. A piki taki:

Boy. Ma . . . someni nengre, so pikinso bakra, dan ete den na
basi.

Sera. Mi tagi en na di unu ben prati, na fu di wi ben feti nanga
un srefi na Afrikan kondre, ne wi no ben kan wini den bakra, di den
kon fufuru wi tya gowe. Na now wi kon ferstan wi srefi moro betre.
Ma en ati no ben sidon. A aksi mi:

Boy. Efi dati de so, dan fu san ede basya e makandra nanga den
bakra fu makti wi?

Sera. Na wan sani nomo mi ben kan tagi en, dati basya na wan
takru libisuma. A kan tanapu e arki mi efi a wani, mi no kan yepi,
ma na so mi ati gi mi fu piki na boy.

Kwaku. Yu ben mu tagi en taki disi sani a kon miti, na bakapisi
fu katibo. A no kaba mi kaba fu ferteri un Kunofru tori. San mi eygi
ay si dya a tapu na pranasi furu tumusi fu mi mofo ferteri. Yu ben
mu tagi en taki tra nengre fu wi kondre sori kaba, taki den no moro
mendre leki den bakra. Den wini den, den kiri den, den makti den
sote, te den ben abi fu kon begi fu tapu na feti. Dati meki den nengre
dati, fa mi yere a tori, kisi fri. Den kan go te den wani, den kan kon
te den wani. A so mi yere. Mi ay no si den, ma mi e bribi.

Kofi. Fa a sa man tagi a boy so wan sani. Wi alamala dyaso yere na
tori. Na letiwan fu en wi no man sabi. Ma efi na mi, mi sa syen fu
meki den pikin fu wi sabi na tori. Na wan syen tori.

Kwaku. Fa so? San yu wani taki?

Kofi. San mi wani taki? Mi wani taki disi. Na wi alamala kon dya.
Den ben kon fri fosi wi. Dan den fergiti, taki wi tan na ini a sari.

Kwaku. Fa so?

Kofi. Den fergiti ya! Mi yere taki den sweri fu seni wi gi den bakra,
efi wi sa lowe na den kampu.

people had gone to sleep. The night was cool. The sea breeze blew
so nicely. For the first time since my arrival here, I felt peace in my
heart. It seemed as if I were back in Africa.

Kwaku. Africa! Motherland! Oh God!

Sera. Then the boy stroked my back as if he wanted to make me
feel that we were one. [*Amba sighs.*] Then he asked me:

Boy. Mother, why are whites stronger than us?

Sera. I did not know how to answer him. I said that they were not
stronger than us. But he did not believe me.

Boy. But . . . so many negroes, so few whites. And they're still
the boss.

Sera. I said to him that this is so because we are divided, because
we fight each other in Africa, that for this reason we couldn't win
against the whites when they stole us. Now we understand each
other better. But he was not satisfied. He asked me:

Boy. If that is so, why does Basja take the white man's side to
tame us?

Sera. I could only tell him this, that Basja is a bad person. Even
if he stands right here listening to me I can't help it. For so my
heart told me to answer.

Kwaku. You should have told him that such things happen
in the times of slavery. I'm not yet finished with my story about
Kunofru. That which my own eyes saw here on the plantation is more
than my mouth can tell. You should have told him that other negroes
from our plantation have shown that they are not inferior to the
whites. They've conquered them, killed them, made it so difficult for
them that they had to beg them to stop fighting. Therefore those
negroes, so I have heard, gained their freedom. They can go wherever
they want. So I have heard it. I have not seen them personally. But
I believe it.

Kofi. How can she tell the boy such a thing? We all of us here have
heard it. But the truth of the matter we'll never know. In my opinion
I would feel ashamed to tell this story to our children. It's a shameful
story.

Kwaku. What! What are you trying to say?

Kofi. What am I trying to say? Simply this. We have all come here.
They were free before us. And then they forgot that we were still in
trouble.

Kwaku. How so?

Kofi. Yes, they've forgotten it. I've heard that they have sworn an
oath to send us back to the whites if we run away to their villages.

Ala suma. Oooo!

Kwasi. Na so mi yere. A no wan syen tori?

Amba. We, dan efi wi wani lowe, dan na frey wi sa abi fu frey.
Ma yu abi leti, ef a de so, dan na wan syen tori.

*[Wan ipi suma e lon pasa na tapu na background, man nanga
uma nanga pikin. Den pikin e krey. Den umasma e kragi. Alamala
e tyari bondru nanga tra sani na den anu. Den e luku na den baka
ala di den e lon gowe, èn wi kan si taki na wan frede sani den e lowe
gi. Den srafu skreki di den si den. Den dyompo go e luku san de fu
du nanga den.]*

Uma 1. [Te na bakasey.] Mi Gado! Mi Gado! San e pasa nanga wi.
Ala wi oso, ala wi sani go. Mi si fa mi masra nanga mi pikin fadon
komopo na ini en oso go na gron. Ala tu dede. San pasa! San pasa!

*Uma 2. [E waka go na alamala e suku wan sani, dan a e kon na
fesi pe den srafu de. A e go na den wan fru wan.]* Masra, yu no si
mi pikin? Masra, yu no si mi boy Kofi? Tagi mi no? Yu no si Kofi?
Dri yari nomo a abi. Yu no si mi boy? Pe a de? *[Nowan suma no e
piki, dan a e gowe. Ma fosi a gowe, a e seki wan fu den ete, ma a
no e aksi noti moro. Dan den tu wetiman komopo na barkon kon
tanapu e luku tu san e pasa.]*

Masra. [E taki nanga basya.] Basya, aksi den nengre san pasa
nanga den. Pe den e go? San yu e wakti?

Basya. Mi e go kaba. *[A e go tu stap, dan a e tanapu. A e bari.
Ma no wan suma no e piki en kari. Dan a e broko go na bakasey. A
e teki wan na en skowru hari en kon na fesisey. A man e go nanga
en sondro a wani.]* Masra nengre! San du unu? Pe u e lowe gowe?
Piki mi. San de fu du?

Nengre. Masra, a betre un seti lon na wi baka. Den Gado ati bron.
Takru winti e dray kon na birosey. Ala wi pranasi kon tron wan doti
ipi. Lusu mi, meki mi gowe. Suma wani kan tan.

Basya. Wakti! Suma na yu? Pe yu komopo?

Nengre. Mi na Novari nengre.

Basya. Na winti broko Novari, leki fa mi ferstan?

Nengre. A broko en, a broko en. Noti noti no tan abra. A opo wi
kampu tya go hey na loktu. Noyti moro wi no si den. A opo na
granmasra oso tya go hey na loktu. No wan planga fu en no kon na
gron moro. Kronoto bon e seyri a loktu gowe se. A ben tranga fu si.

Basya. Èn den srafu?

Nengre. Den dede. Den dede leki agu. Na wi so, den tu ay suma

[*All people present cry out "Oh!"*]

Kwasi. That I have heard. Isn't it a shame!

Amba. Well, if we want to run away, we will have to fly. But you're right, if it's true, it's a shame.

A group of people in the background consisting of men, women, and children run past. The children are crying, the women are complaining. All of them have small bundles of clothes and other things on their heads. They look back while running. One can see that they have run away from something terrible. The slaves are frightened when they see them. They jump up to see what's wrong.

First Woman [*in background*]. God, my God, what's happening to us. All our houses, everything is lost. I saw my husband and my child flung out of the house, both of them dead. What's really happening to us!

Second Woman [*walks to them and searches for something. Then comes to the fore where the slaves are sitting, moves from one to the other*]. Mister, haven't you seen my child? Mister, haven't you seen my boy, Kofi? Say something. Have you seen Kofi? He's only three years old. Have you seen my boy? Where is he? [*Nobody answers. Then she leaves. Before she goes she shakes one of them, but doesn't ask a thing anymore. Then two whites come from the balcony and watch the scene.*]

Master [*addresses Basja*]. Basja, ask the negroes what has happened? Where are they off to? What are they waiting for?

Basja. I'm off already. [*He walks two paces, then stands still. He calls. No one answers. Then he walks quickly to the back. He grabs one of them by the shoulder and brings him forward. The man accompanies him unwillingly.*]

Basja. Man, what's eating you people? Where are you running to? Answer me. What's up?

Negro. Mister, it would be better if you followed us. The gods are mad. An evil wind turns and approaches. Our whole plantation is in ruins. Leave me, let me go. He who wants to stay, let him.

Basja. Wait! Who are you? Where are you from?

Negro. I'm a negro from Novar.

Basja. Do I understand you well, that a storm has destroyed Novar?

Negro. Destroyed! Yes, destroyed! Nothing is left. It has flung our huts into the air. We haven't seen them back again. It has flung our owner's house into the air and into the sea. It was terrible.

Basja. And the slaves?

Negro. Dead! Dead like pigs! Only us left. A few grains of us remained.

disi tan abra. Gado srefi meki wi ben de na firi ete, di a winti bigin
way. Noso wi tu ben dede leki dagu. Ne wi seti lon.

Basya. Pe na granmasra fu na pranasi de?

Nengre. Noti fu en wi no si di wi kon na fesisey. Trawan taki a
ben de na ini oso.

Basya. Dan suma gi un pasi fu lon libi na pranasi?

Nengre. Na winti ben takru tumusi. Fa wi ben sa man du wan tra
fasi? Na pasi wi e lon kon, ne wi miti ala den tra nengre. Bonse
nengre, Oxford nengre. Den alamala grabu san den ben kan teki. Ne
yu si wi kon pasa dya. Ma wi futu weri. Wi lon kaba pasa wan yuru.

Basya. Na winti kaba way?

Nengre. No ete. A e way wan pisi, dan a e dray go na sekanti.
Efi yu si fa na watra e spoyti kon na loktu te a dorosey. A ben
frede fu si. Baka wan pisi ten a e dray kon baka. Wi di ben e lon
na tapu na pasi, wi ben e firi fa na gron ben e seki na wi ondro. A
gersi na pasi ben sa way komopo na ondro wi futu. Efi wi no ben
trowe wi srefi nanga bere na gron, a ben sa teki wi, opo wi go trowe
na ini den swampu. Masra ef yu ben si san a meki nanga Kwami, di
ben e lon na mi sey. Mi bari gi Kwami. Dukrun! Ma a ben weri so
te. A no man dyompo go na bantama. A tanapu langa langa na tapu
na pasi. Watra ay e lon na en fesi. A winti dray en leki wan maraston.
En futu na loktu. A iti en wan pisi dan a fanga en baka, e dray en
tya gowe na se. . . . Dati ben tranga fu si.

Kofi. Basya, wi mu tapu en. Wi mu tapu en fu a no kon. Wi mu
naki wan kongo tombe gi en. A sa kiri wi. Basya, taki no!

Basya. En srefi kon, en srefi sa gowe. Na tapu na pranasi disi pe
mi de basya, no wan winti no e kon broko mi wroko. Na Afrikan
kondre marawinti e arki kongo tombe, dyaso a e arki mi!

Kofi. A sa kiri wi, basya.

Basya. Solanga mi de basya, noti no sa pasa.

Kofi. Ma ef yu dede basya? Ef na winti kiri yu, basya?

Basya. Mi sa tranga moro en. [*A e dray fu taki nanga na granmasra.*]
Masra, mi basya sa tranga moro en. Mi sa luku yu pranasi gi yu. Yu no
abi fu frede. A no mi fara den busi disi meki na pranasi? A no mi meki
yu pondo bigi moro ala den trawan? A no mi meki yu sukrumiri de
na moro bigiwan fu heri Koroni?

Kofi. [*A e fadon na en futu, begi en.*] Libi wi, meki wi dansi na
kongo tombe.

Basya. [*E skopu en komoto na en tapu. Na man e fadon na gron e
krey.*] Komopo! Frede meki den e kroypi leki dagu. Mi no wani kongo

God has seen to it that we were in the field when the storm started,
else we would also have been killed. So we are away.

Basja. Where's the owner of the plantation?

Negro. We did not see a speck of him when we came to the front
of the plantation. They say he was in the house.

Basja. Who then gave you permission to leave the plantation?

Negro. The storm was so terrible. What else could we do? We ran
down the road. Then we came across all the other negroes. Negroes
from Bonse, negroes from Oxford, all of them grabbing what they
could. Then we passed this place. And we are tired. We have run for
more than an hour.

Basja. Has the storm stopped?

Negro. Not yet. It blows for a little, then turns to the sea. You see
how the water splashes in the air. It was terrible. After some time,
it turns back. We who ran along the road felt the earth under us
shaking. It seemed as if the trembling road was being blown from
under our feet. If we hadn't flung ourselves to the earth, it would
have grabbed us and chucked us into the swamp. Mister, if you'd
seen what it did with Kwami who was walking next to me! I called
to Kwami "Dive!" but he was so tired he couldn't jump into the
trench, he remained standing on the road. Tears rolled down his face.
The wind turned him like a millstone, feet upward. It cast him some
distance, caught him again, and then turned him sideways. It was
terrible.

Kofi. Basja, we must keep the storm away. Keep it away that it
doesn't come here. We must do a Congo-Tombe for it. It will kill us.
Basja, say it please.

Basja. It came on its own, it will go away on its own. On this
plantation no wind will come to destroy my work. In Africa the
whirlwind listens to the Congo-Tombe. Here it listens to me.

Kofi. It will kill us, Basja.

Basja. As long as I'm Basja nothing will happen.

Kofi. But if you're no longer here, Basja, if the wind kills you . . .

Basja. I'll be stronger than it. [*He turns to speak to the owner.*]
Master, I, Basja, will be stronger. I'll look after your plantation.
Don't be afraid. Have I not felled the bushes to create this plantation?
Have I not made your boats bigger than all the others? Have I not
turned your sugar mills into the largest in all Coronie?

Kofi [*falls at his feet and begs him*]. Let us, let us dance the
Congo-Tombe!

Basja [*kicks him away. He falls on the ground crying*]. Shut up!
Quiet! [*In their fear they crawl like dogs.*] I don't want the Congo-

tombe dansi na tapu na pranasi. Mara winti kan kon! A sa miti mi!

Kofi. [*E opo, go na en tapu.*] Yu no wani! Ma wi wani! Wi sa dansi na kongo tombe. [*Basya dray en wipi, naki en. A fadon na gron baka. Na granmasra e kon na mindri.*]

Masra. Basya, fu san ede yu no wani den dansi?

Basya. Masra, kongo tombe na watramama. Efi a dansi wan leysi na tapu yu pranasi, dede, malengri nanga takru du sa de wan aladey sani tapu yu pranasi. Kande na kongo tombe sa de wan tapu gi na marawinti, ma lespeki nanga koroku no sa de moro na wi mindri. Feti nanga dede sa de wan moro hogri marawinti di sa broko yu pranasi, te noti no tan. Kande na marawinti di sa kon na en presi sa tergi yu pranasi nomo nomo. Masra, yu kan go sidon baka nanga yu fisiti.

Tombe to be danced on the plantation! Let the whirlwind come.
He'll find me ready.

Kofi [*gets up and walks to him*]. You don't, but we want to. We
will dance the Congo-Tombe. [*Basja lifts up the whip and strikes him.
He falls down again. The owner intervenes.*]

Owner. Basja, why don't you want them to dance?

Basja. Master, Congo-Tombe is a water spirit. Danced once on the
plantation, then death, sickness, and bad behavior will be an everyday
thing on your plantation. Maybe the Congo-Tombe will stop the
whirlwind. But there will be no respect and happiness among us.
Strife and death will be a more terrible whirlwind, which will destroy
your plantation until nothing is left. Maybe the whirlwind which
comes in its place will only disturb your plantation. Master, you can
go and sit down again.

CHAPTER 7

Wie Eegie Sanie

Wie Eegie Sanie (Our own things) is the name of a nationalistic cultural movement founded around 1950 by Surinamese students living in Amsterdam. In the multiracial society of Surinam, it is difficult to determine precisely what "our own things" are. They might be something quite different for the descendants of Javanese immigrants than for maroon descendants in the bush. The name might best be interpreted as the expression of an ideal: we want to have "our own things," our own Surinamese culture, our own identity as an independent nation. The movement was clearly a reaction against the imposition of the Dutch language and culture. As such it had much in common with the reaction in 1932 of the Martinique students in Paris, who wrote a flamboyant manifesto, *Légitime Défense,* which might be regarded as the birth of the new cultural ideal centered on the concept of "négritude."[1] But compared with *Légitime Défense,* Wie Eegie Sanie represented a much more balanced reaction. Its spokesmen always stressed their essential openness to influences from other cultures. They even accepted Dutch culture as part of their cultural heritage, but they wanted to shape their own national culture, in which all Surinamese people could participate.

In order to understand this kind of reaction against the language and culture of a colonial power, one has to remember that the typical colonial society lacks an indigenous elite. The most prominent people in the colonial society are those born in Europe, who have a different set of cultural values. But at the same time they function as the colonial elite and therefore exert a normative influence in society. They are followed and imitated by other groups. Acculturation therefore seems an inevitable phenomenon in colonial society.

The generation of Wie Eegie Sanie was raised under these conditions,

---

1. This manifesto was published in Paris and contained statements such as the following by Etienne Léro: "The Antillian, stuffed to the neck with white moralism, with white culture, with white education, with white prejudices, displays the puffed-up image of himself. To be a good copy of the pale man has for him social as well as poetic self-justification. He can never be decent enough, starched enough in his own eyes." (Translated from the French)

and to say that they were greatly encouraged to assimilate to the
Dutch way of life is an understatement, as we have already seen.
Students with the best results at school (which also means the most
acculturated pupils) were given the chance to go to Europe to complete their studies in Holland. There they discovered that their ac-
culturative efforts were not nearly so greatly appreciated as at home.
Especially among fellow students the soulless imitation of Western
habits was scorned, and non-European behavior was applauded as
something new and original. What might have been a reason for pride
back home became a badge of shame and disgrace.

Mr. Bruma, explaining the cause of Wie Eegie Sanie in a public
speech, goes even further. He considers language and culture as an
agreement or civil contract between people. We *agree* to call a cat
"cat" and a dog "dog." If now these same people are forced to ignore
their agreements, they feel themselves guilty of treachery. This
makes them unhappy and calls forth resistance. Wie Eegie Sanie tries
to free every individual from biases against his own language and
cultural values, not in the belief that it is better than any other but
that it is equally valuable. This movement teaches self-respect as the
essential basis for mutual understanding between different groups.

Vidia Naipaul, comparing the situation in Surinam with that in
other West Indian countries, writes:

> The Dutch have offered assimiliation but not made it obligatory.
> This tolerance and understanding of alien cultures is greater than
> the British, and the very reverse of the French arrogance which
> makes the French West Indian Islands insupportable for all but
> the francophile. And one cannot help feeling it unfair that the
> Dutch should have their own cultural offerings spurned by their
> former colony. Suriname has come out of Dutch rule as the only
> truly cosmopolitan territory in the West Indian region. The
> cosmopolitanism of Trinidad is now fundamentally no more
> than a matter of race; in Suriname diverse cultures, modified but
> still distinct, exist side by side. The Indians speak Hindi still;
> the Javanese live, a little bemused, in their own world, longing
> in this flat unlovely land for the mountains of Java; the Dutch
> exist in their self-sufficient Dutchness, the Creoles in their urban
> Surinam-Dutchness; in the forest along the rivers, the bush-
> Negroes have re-created Africa (Naipaul 1962:170).

Naipaul may have underestimated the fierce cultural reaction in
some French West Indian islands, as shown for example by the group
that published *Légitime Défense,* and by the work of Aimé Césaire

and his contribution to the négritude movement (see Kesteloot 1965). It remains a fact, however, that Wie Eegie Sanie is an exceptional movement, unparalleled in the Caribbean, and for which there is as yet no fully acceptable explanation (but see Voorhoeve and Renselaar 1962).

The language problem has been one of the most important issues in Wie Eegie Sanie. Surinam Creole was regarded as the only true national language because it lacked roots elsewhere. Moreover, it already served the very useful purpose of a contact language between ethnic groups, more so than Dutch or any other indigenous language. So they decided that Creole should become the national language. They started to use Creole on all occasions and indeed succeeded in turning it into a respected language.

One of the most convincing arguments of Wie Eegie Sanie has been the achievements of Creole poetry. Members of Wie Eegie Sanie had started to write poetry in Creole in Amsterdam, and in 1952 the Frisian cultural periodical *De Tsjerne* devoted a complete issue to the new Creole literature.[2] At that time only a few acceptable poems existed in Creole. We reproduce in this chapter some of those first poems. Following chapters will show how rapidly Creole found acceptance as a means of literary expression.

2. *De Tsjerne,* Suriname-numer, September 1952.

EDDY BRUMA

Mi braka mama

Mi braka mama
na tap' hen bangi e dyonko,
ala pikin go sribi kaba.
Mi owru mama, kon, opo go sribi,
mi sab fa yu weri mama.

Now fosi mi de si
pe yu wiwir e weti,
èn den proy na ondro yu ay.
Kon, mek mi grat den safri-safri
fu mek yu no wiki, mama . . .

Èn noya di y'e lafu na ini yu sribi,
m'e si yu takru tifi, o lobi mama.
Kon, wiki, go na yu bedi,
yu dyonko nofo kaba.

Waran-neti dren

Kon sdon, dineti,
di neti fadon,
na mi mofo-doro, mi p'kin.
Winti e way,
a e wunwun wan singi
gi wi . . .

S'don tiri, no dray-dray,
dungru fadon.
Safri na singi e kroypi
e kon
na mi.

Wan kondre ben de . . .
A no dya,
a no yana,

EDDY BRUMA

My black mother

My black mother
dozes on her bench,
all the children have gone to bed.
Old mother, come rise, go to sleep,
I know how weary you are, mother.

Now only do I see
where your hair to white has turned,
and the creases beneath your eye.
Come, let us softly smooth them out
that you do not wake up, mother . . .

And now that you laugh in your slumber
I see your ugly teeth, Oh dearest mother.
Come, wake up, go to bed,
you've dozed enough for the while.

A warm night's dream[3]

Come sit then tonight,
now the night has ascended,
on my threshhold, my child.
The wind is blowing,
it hums a song
for us . . .

Sit silently, do not stir,
dusk has ascended.
Softly does the song creep on
and comes
to me.

There was once a land,
not here,
not there,

3. The poem tells a well-known story dating from the time of slavery, in
which a certain lady, Suzanna Duplessis, is said to have drowned the child of
a female slave during a boat trip on the river because she was irritated by its
incessant crying.

no na farawe presi.
Wan dey . . .

Wan mama ben de . . .
A no dya,
a no yana,
no na farawe presi.
Wan dey . . .

Suma no pari,
suma no hari,
mi boto mu go,
suma pikin
no tap na babari
sa go.

Sribi mi p'kin,
sribi mi brudu.
Neti fadon.
Mama sa hor wakti,
te sribi kon.

Nengre, un pari,
uma, un hari,
mi boto mu go.
Watra sa swari
na p'kin,
te mi boto
no lo.

Ma winti no wani.
A no dya,
a no wani.
Na farawe presi
a gwe.

Na watra ben kowru.
Na neti ben kowru
sote.
Gado n'e meki pikin tide
fu tamara
a dede.

Mama, no sari,
yu, pikin fu doti,
mama fu wan dey.

not in places far off,
on a day . . .

There was once a mother,
not here,
not there,
not in places far off,
on a day . . .

Who does not row,
who does not pull
—my boat
must row—
whose child does not stop to howl,
will die.

Sleep my child,
sleep my flesh,
the night has ascended.
Mother will watch
till sleep has arrived.

Negroes row!
Women pull!
My boat must go.
Water will devour
the child,
if my boat
does not row.

But the wind is unwilling.
It's not here,
it's unwilling.
To places far off
it has blown.

The water was cold.
The night was cold,
excessively so.
God creates no child today
so that tomorrow
he dies.

Mother, be not sad,
you child of the earth,
mother for a day.

San yu kisi tide,
tamara yu lasi
agen.

Kon sdon dineti
—neti fadon—
na mi mofo-doro, mi p'kin.
Winti e way,
a e tyari wan tori,
wan tori
fu er-tin-tin . . .

CHR. H. EERSEL

December

Gron nati, kowru, fini alen de kon.
Fara baka busi stondoyfi de soktu . . .
Wan fru wan mi de yere fadon
den dropu alen na tapu mi fensre.

Grontapu de sari sondro son:
langa watr'ay de lon na strati.
Mi de si den dungru spuku-bon
moksi so safri tron blaka loktu.

Dan neti de saka blaka didon,
leki wan bigi dedekrosi
tapu na kowru nati gron.
Dan tiri de regeri ala presi.

JO RENS

Opo-oso

Sortu prisiri sa gi doti
di de brenki na trawan ay?

What today you received,
tomorrow you'll lose
again.

Come sit then tonight,
now the night has ascended,
on my threshhold, my child.
The wind is blowing,
he brings a tale,
a tale of
once upon a time . . .

CHR. H. EERSEL

December

Moisture-seeped and cold is the earth.
     Gently does it drizzle.
Far off in the forest ringdoves coo . . .
One by one I hear the patter
of raindrops on my window.

The world is morose without sun:
long tears roll down the street.
I see the dark trees apparition-like
slowly merge and lose themselves
     into the darkening sky.

Then black night descends
like a large shroud of death
on the wet, cold earth.
Then silence reigns supreme.

JO RENS

Opo Oso[4]

How can a feast give off specks of dirt
which blind another's eyes?

---

4. It is customary among the workers in the building trade, to have a party
and to pass drinks around when they have reached the roof of a house.
This party is called *opo-oso*. In all probability the image of the building of a
house refers to the building of an independent Surinam.

Luku busi, luku birbiri,
kriki, swampu pe fisi lay.

Firpenki na tapu den bon sidon
de bari lafu fu den;
watra de singi na mindri den ston
de kari wi nanga hen sten.

Na liba de kowru na faya fu son
di weri den bromki sote.
Kankantri ben kari wan winti kon
fu prati katun alape.

Pitani, na ondro den bon
pe na fosi libi ben seti,
pitani pikin, fu san yu de krey?
Tide na Gado feeste-dey.

TREFOSSA

Bro

No pori mi prakseri noyaso,
no kari mi fu luku nowan pe.
Tide mi ati trusu mi fu go
te na wan tiri kriki, farawe.

No tak na lon mi wani lon gowe
fu di mi frede strey èn krey nomo.
Ma kondre b'bari lontu mi sote.
San mi mu du? Mi brudu wani bro.

Na krikisey dren kondre mi sa si
pe ala sani moro swit lek dya
èn skreki-tori no sa trobi mi.

Te m' dray kon baka sonten mi sa tron
wan p'kinso moro betre libisma,
di sabi lafu, sabi tya fonfon.

Behold the forest, behold the shrubs,
the creek, the swamp where it teems with fish.

Firpenki[5] sits laughing
in the trees;
Water gurgles between the stones
and calls us with its voice.

The river cools the fire of the sun
which saps the flowers so.
The cotton tree had beckoned a wind
to help disperse his cotton everywhere.

Pitani,[6] under the trees
where life at first came about,
pitani my child, why weep you so?
Today is a feasting day of God.

TREFOSSA

Repose

Do not come between my thoughts just now,
and call me not to look elsewhere.
My heart today is urging me
to a far-off quiet creek.

Say not that I'm intent on flight
because I fear the struggle and can only weep.
But the worldly din has overwhelmed me so.
What must I do? My blood is hankering after peace.

There at the creek
   I shall a realm of dreams espie
where everything is lovelier than here
and tales which frighten me will not confuse.

When I return again
perhaps I shall become a slightly better man
who knows to laugh and take a beating too.

---

5. *Firpenki* must be a kind of bird unknown to us.
6. *Pitani* is the Carib word for "child." It is used in this poem to indicate
the true Surinamese, born and raised on Surinamese soil.

CHAPTER 8

Trefossa

The Creole teacher Henny F. de Ziel, born in 1916, published the first
book of Creole poems in 1957 under the pseudonym Trefossa, a
name that is apparently a Creolization of the name Tryphosa in Romans
16:12. In 1951 his poem "Bro" (Repose) was published in *Foetoe-boi*.[1]
It was written around 1949, and more or less by chance fell into the
hands of a friend, who published it in a teachers' periodical. Written
in the traditional sonnet style, it made a tremendous impression and
was recognized as something completely new. Until then a few existing Creole poems were mostly translations from other languages and
written in the stilted literary language used in church services. This
church Creole was generally considered to have a higher social status
than the broad, vulgar, street patois. In "Bro" for the first time
this patois was used with obvious mastery to express the highest
poetic intentions, a daring cultural achievement.

The poet was raised in Paramaribo. When he received his teacher's
certificate, no post was available. He served in the army and worked
for some years as a male nurse in the government hospital. Finally
he found a post as teacher in an institution for lepers. This period of
confrontation with human misery colored his whole vision of life.

Teachers in Surinam often start their profession in small outposts.
District and town constitute two different worlds in Surinam. De Ziel
was born and bred in town and had spent many years in a Moravian
institution, so when he finally received the chance to embark on his
teaching career in the district he found himself in a completely different environment. His life up to that time had pretty well isolated
him from the life of the lower-class Creoles. Creole life in the district
made a big impression on him and instilled in him a great love for
his own race and language. To reach the district children, he used
small poems in Dutch and Creole, made up on the spur of the moment.

In 1953 De Ziel was sent to Holland to take a course in librarianship.
The great wealth of information on the smallest details of Creole life
and history that was stacked away in the vast Dutch libraries made an
indelible impression on him. He studied Surinam's history avidly, and
in 1956, on receiving his certificate, he returned home to take a post

1. It is reprinted in chapter 7.

as librarian of the Cultural Center. Here he had an opportunity to transmit his newfound knowledge to his countrymen. His office was often filled with lower-class Creoles who wanted more information on their own history. The results of these contacts were sometimes seen on stage in the popular drama. De Ziel was appointed director of the Cultural Center, but he became so disillusioned with petty local cultural politics that he resigned after a time and returned to his old profession. During a period of sick leave in Holland, he undertook the editing of Johannes King's works. The samples of King's writings in chapter 4 were edited by him.

Between 1953 and 1956 De Ziel wrote more poems. After the poem "Bro" in 1951, three other poems were published in *Foetoeboi* in 1955 and 1956. In 1957 a small collection of nineteen poems was published under the title *Trotji* (a technical term in the musical culture of Creoles). The poems were published in scientific disguise as part of the publications of the Bureau for Linguistic Research in Surinam (University of Amsterdam), with translations in Dutch and a study of one of his poems by J. Voorhoeve. The book was dedicated to J. G. A. Koenders.

De Ziel will always remain a poet with a remarkably small poetic output, but all of his poems are well-nigh perfect. Since *Trotji,* in which were also printed the poems that first appeared in *Foetoe-boi,* he has published only three more poems and one poetic story. He has shown other poems to intimate friends, but these will probably not find their way easily into print, as he regards them as essentially repetitions of earlier poems. His range is relatively small. Many poems show an existential fear of losing contact with reality in an expanding universe. His poetry seems to represent a struggle to rediscover some kernel (a single word or a seed), which is supposed to justify or save his life. A careful analysis may reveal how serious his poetic intentions really are.[2]

While readers may wonder what is beneath the surface of these poems, they certainly cannot fail to be impressed by the poet's mastery of his language and by his intricate poetic forms. He seems to experiment with all kinds of free forms and subtle rhythmic patterns. These few poems have beyond doubt shaped the new poetic traditions of the younger generation in Surinam.

The only story ever published by Trefossa seems to be more a poem in disguise. Its complex composition, the abrupt transitions and com-

---

2. J. Voorhoeve analyzed some poems by Trefossa in his contribution to the collection *Trotji* and in Voorhoeve 1959 and 1971(b).

plicated chronology may easily confuse the reader. The story itself
is fairly straightforward. A young man called Luti has fallen in love
with a girl from the same village and wants to offer her a better
future. He therefore leaves the district in order to earn money in
town. On his way to town he passes a haunted spot, where during
slavery a vampire, said to have been maltreated, now angrily seeks
revenge. When he passes the haunted spot a sudden flash of lightning
causes Luti to panic, and he drowns. The friends back home improvise
a song about this event in honor of Luti.

The first six poems are taken from the collection *Trotji*. The poem
"Granaki" and the story "Owrukuku ben kari" were published in
Tongoni 2 (*Vox Guyanae* 3, 1959:6). The poem "Yu ay" was published in *De Gids* 9 (1970), 309. The poem "Humor in èksèlsis" was
written in 1973 and is published here for the first time.

Wan tru puëma . . .

wan tru puëma na wan skreki-sani.
wan tru puëma na wan strey te f' dede.
wan tru puëma na wan tra kondre
pe yu kan go
te yu psa dede fosi.

wan tru puëma na den wortu d' e tan abra
te ala trawan n' in yu libi wasi gwe:
wan koko soso,
ma wan di kan sproyti
nyun libi.

lon na mi abra dan,
Arusubanya fu grontapu.
kande wandey, wandey
mofo fu mi sa broko opo
fu taki gi onowsruwan tu wortu
di, te den gro, sa trowe lepi stari,
di mi de suku now.

way!

d' e opo den srefi gi son,
den grun wiwiri,
te angri fu gro
priti buba fu siri.

na mi?
piki . . . piki!
apinti, na mi?
san de lufru so,
san wiki?

korsu, korsu
de seki mi,

A true poem . . .

A true poem is a thing of awe.
A true poem is a struggle unto death.
A true poem is another land
where one sojourns
when one is past death's door.

A true poem is made of words that linger on
when all the others in one's life are washed away:
one single kernel,
but one from which can sprout
life all anew.

Stream then all over me
Arusubanya[3] of the world.
Perhaps one day, one day,
my mouth will burst asunder
to utter but two words for simple souls
which, as they grow, will sprout ripe stars
which even now I am searching for.

Leave off!

They open up themselves to the sun,
the verdant plants,
when their hunger to grow forth
has torn apart the seedling's coat.

Am I that?
Answer . . . answer!
Apinti,[4] am I that?
What is it that rumbles so,
what that awakens here?

Delirium, delirium
convulses me,

3. Arusubanya ("It loosens the ribs") is the name of a rapids in the Surinam River. Here it stands for the turbulent difficulties of life.
4. *Apinti* is one of the principal drums used in religious dances. There are definite allusions in this poem to religious experiences, especially the transition to a state of possession.

fu di na bita powa fu mi borsu
wani lusu kon.
way!
san keti na peti
sa broko tuka krin leti.

xxx

te den srenger mi puru na den prakseri
—den pimbadoti-wan—
mi sa grabu den noko fu den oso,
mi sa kwinsi den toren na mi borsu,
mi sa it wan ay na yu,
star na firmamenti,
di ben sori pasi na den koniman.

star fu den koniman,
gi mi wan presi na yu baka,
seyri nanga mi na den leygi loktu.
na den wèrder winti
mi sa hori mi srefi
na den faya-prin fu yu.
mi no sa fadon,
bikasi mi wani go,
mi wani go
te pe te yu sa tan tiri
na bigin-bigin,
pe Bun didon
nanga soso skin.

a yuru dis . . .

a yuru dis e bradi so su-u-un . . .
bigin, kroboy,
hey nanga dipi,
kruktu-, letsey
e dans-dansi gwe
lek te—na sabana—
son
e bron.

because this bitter power on my chest
will be released.
Leave off!
that which is chained in the pit
will break forth, touch the crystal light.

                                xxx

When they have flung me from their thoughts,
—they who are the white-earthed ones—[5]
then I'll grab the ridges of the houses,
clasp the towers to me,
fasten all my eyes on you,
star of the firmament
which to the wise the way did show.

Star of the wise ones,
grant me a place on your back,
sail with me through empty skies
through the wild, wild winds.
I shall hold on
to your fiery beams,
shall not fall,
for I would like to go,
would like to go
right to where you will halt
at the start of time
where the Good lies down
in all its nakedness.

                        This hour . . .

This hour droningly expands itself . . .
Beginning, end,
heights and depths,
right and left
obliterates
like when—on the savannah—
burns
the sun.

5. White earth is smeared on the face and body in certain rituals. The reference, however, seems more to white Europeans and to feelings aroused in
the victim of white discrimination.

te yu w'wan tan,
yu w'wan so kodo,
a libi weti,
weti lek wan dow.

mi anu frekti mi kindi,
ede boygi
—marawinti, marawinti!—
doisr' e teki mi.

mi m'ma, mi m'ma!
san sa kon so dyonsro-dyonsro?
yepi yu boy . . .

wan enkri gado-momenti . . .

wan enkri gado-momenti, nomoro,
e poko na wi mindri.
ma hen meti span
lek te hondro yari
sinta na wan.

Sisi, mi m'ma,
agen mi mu kari yu nen.
kibri mi!
mi na wan peyri
di sutu kon dya.
elu fu mi!
ef mi no doro
fu boro
buba fu ten.

mi go—m' e kon

te dreyten winti sa troki
na Mawnidan:
—krioro fa?

And if you finally remain,
you lonely soul,
then life is white,
white as the dew.

My arms clasp my knees,
head bends.
—Whirlwind, whirlwind!—
Giddiness o'erpowers me.

Mother, Oh my mother,
what will anon, anon take place?
Please help your boy . . .

Only a single moment . . .

Only a single moment and no more
between us eddies.
But the flesh is taut
as if a hundred years
are girdled into one.

Sisi, my mother,
once more I must invoke your name.
Protect me!
I am an arrow
which comes flashing here.
Woe unto me
when I don't succeed
to penetrate
time's hide.

I've been gone—I'm back

When the wind of the dry season starts to incantate
on the Mahoni lane:[6]
—Creole say!

6. The first three stanzas refer to three different stages in the poet's life:
the Mahoni lane in Paramaribo, where he lived as a little boy; the sacred cotton
tree, which seems to symbolize his religious experiences during adolescence;
and the big tree on the village center of Onverwacht (local name, Bose), a
small village in the Para District where he served as a teacher. Boyo is a sweet
manioc cake.

m' sa piki:
—dya mi de,
—banyi fu ba-m'ma seti keba:
—ertintin . . . ertintin. . . .

te dreyten winti sa troki
na kankantri:
—krioro fa?
m' sa piki:
—dya mi de,
—Eifeltoren hey pasa,
—m' a n' a yorka, a n' a yorka. . . .

te dreyten winti sa troki
na Moy-bon fu Bose:
—krioro fa?
m' sa piki:
—dya mi de,
—s'sa Mina, ptata bun,
—ma boyo fu yu kir-kiri. . . .

mi go—m'e kon,
sowtwatra bradi.
tak wan mofo,
ala mi mati,
tak wan mofo.
m' go,
m' e kon. . . .

Granaki

liba de lon
na mi ati lanpresi,
dungru de kon,
ma dineti
lampu sa leti.

na mi broki
lanteri sa brenki
fu sori
pe pori,

I shall chant back:
—Here I am,
—bench of Grandma is in readiness,
—once upon a time, once upon a time,

When the wind of the dry season starts its incantation
in the cotton tree:
—Creole say!
I shall chant back:
—Here I am,
—the Eifel Tower is so much higher,
—but it lacks a spirit, lacks a spirit,

When the wind of the dry season starts to incantate
in Moy-bon in the village of Bose:
—Creole say!
I shall answer:
—Here I am,
—Sister Mina, potatoes are so nice,
—but your boyo has no peer . . .

I've been gone, I am back.
The sea is wide.
Utter something,
all my friends,
utter something.
I've been gone,
I am back . . .

Granaki[7]

The river flows
along the mooring place of my heart.
Darkness comes,
but tonight
the lamp will burn.

On my pier
the lanterns will shine
to warn you
where it's decayed,

---

7. *Granaki* is a fancy name for a woman. The word literally means "garnet."

mek futu d' e kon
feni drey gron.

yu sa kon tideneti,
Granaki?

bika ef yu no kon,
dan agen mi mu waka
tapu ston, tompu-tompu,
waka èn suku
kibri timba,
fu wan dey mi kan doro
yu drompu.

Yu ay

Edewiwiri lontu yu fesi
so prisiri,
lek te dreyten e kon.

Ala den pkin-pkin wortu
d'e prey bonsbak
e syebi so brenki
te den dyompo kon baka.

Ay na wan esrede
wan tide
wan tamara
wan oten?

Ay na wan kontren
fu katun
di lontu mi siri so safri
so sroyti . . .

. . . so opo
lek a bun
f'wan armakti lun
na baka seybi-stari . . .

Humor in èksèlsis

Didibri fir a fârt tak bigi grani
byo psa grontapu her-es, mofo-yari.

to ensure that feet to come
will tread on dry ground.

Shall you come tonight,
Granaki?

For if you do not come,
then I must walk again
on stones, tree stubs,
walk and seek
for a crossing unrevealed
that I at your threshold
may arrive.

Thine eyes

Thy hair frames thy face
so festively,
like when the dry season is about to dawn.

All the little words
playing to and fro in us
are polished brilliantly
when they come bouncing back.

Thine eyes are a yesterday
today
tomorrow
a time unknown.

Thine eyes are a space
of cotton fluff
encasing softly the seed
so tightly . . .

. . . so open
like the benignity
of the endless void
behind the Pleiades.

Humor in excelsis

The Devil got wind of some big happening
soon at the end of the year in the world.

A manpkin f' Gado, so Tata ben wani,
byo tron wan libisma.—Oh gran friyari!

"M' e por a prey, m' e blèkout alasani."
Na so didibri opo mofo bari.
"M' e kot den drât a tap a heri plani,
d' e tyar elèktrik powa gi den stari."

Ma . . . wruts! Syatsroyti panya branti-faya.
Didibri kori hen krabyasi, baya!
A bron hen langa barba-kakumbe.

Èn engel singi: humor in èksèlsis!
Den lafu kwa-kwa: libi de pro vobis!
Èn beybi-Jesus krey a fosi: yè-è-è.

Owrukuku ben kari

Sonte mun no ben sa skijn so sari a neti dati, ef wan pkin worku
no ben drif kon let n' hen fesi.

Busi ben kon tron wan spuku-spuku dungru hipi; i ben kan yere
fa dowwatra b' e dropu fadon na den wiwiri, nèlek na dyumbi b' e
waka na tap den finga-ede.

Liba b' e lon, fu di yu sab tak a' e lon . . . noso yu ben sa prakseri
nomo tak na wan bigi spikri, di sontron na son presi b' e proy-proy
sorfru-sorfru, te wan safri winti saka kon te na ondrosey.

Ma ini saf-safu tiri disi, nèlek na now fosi grontapu b'e bigin, wan
gitar ben bigin prey èn wantu yonkman b'e singi na singi di wan f' den
ben meki so dyonsro-dyonsrode.

A singi b' e ferteri fa pranpran liba ben kon krasi, f' a opo mofo
swari na lay, bifo boto doro Posu . . . A lay di ben mus yep tyar a
moni kon, fu bow wan oso gi wan lobi-lobi uma.

Sonte, ef munkenki no ben skijn so sari, a singi ben sa de wan tra
fasi.

Ofu kande sani waka so fu di owrukuku ben kari, bika te owrukuku
kari, dan alaten yu prakseri e dray go n' a dungru fu dede.

—Suma n' a wroko mek a kon! —na so a fowru disi e kari. Na so
mama ben leri fu granmama, èn na so a ben ferteri hen pikin baka.

The Son of God, so the Father willed it,
would become a child of man. Oh! What a ball!

"I'll be a spoilsport, cause a total black out."
Thus the Devil with his loud mouth.
"I'll cut the wires at the plant,
supplying electricity to the stars."

But . . . presto. A short circuit and the fire spreads.
The devil found the tables turned on him.
He scorched his beard, his whiskers, everything.

The angels started singing: humor in excelsis.
They guffawed: ha! ha! ha! Life be unto you.
And the baby Jesus gave its first squall: wah! wah! wah!

The owl hooted

Perhaps the moon would not have shone so sadly that night if a
small cloud had not drifted right in front of its face. The forest
turned into a nebulous dark mass. The dewdrops could be heard drip-
ping on the leaves, as if they were ghosts walking on tiptoe.

The river ran because you know that rivers run . . . otherwise you
might have taken it for a big mirror that sometimes in certain places
unfolded in a silvery way when a soft wind settled down.

In this soft silence, as if the world were only starting now, a guitar
began to play and a few youths sang a song which one of them had
just composed.

The song told how the river had suddenly erupted, how its mouth
had opened to engulf the load before the boat reached Posu[8] . . . the
load that was to help earn the money to build a house for a beloved
woman.

Perhaps if the moon had not shone so sadly, the song would have
had a different mood.

Or perhaps it unfolded so because the owl had hooted. For when
the owl hoots, then one's thoughts turn to the abyss of death.

He who has no work, let him come!—thus calls this bird. So the
mother heard it from her grandmother, and so she handed it down

8. Posu (a creolization of "post") is a police post near or on the site of the
old Frederikshoop plantation, which has the Creole name Kunofru or Knofru.
The police post and plantation are also mentioned in Drie 1959 as terrible
places where slaves were sent for punishment. This is the haunted place, the story
of which is told by Dorsi shortly hereafter.

Èn na baka kari fu owrukuku alaten wan sari sani b' e pasa.

A no ala mofoneti Luti b' e tyar hen gitar kon, dan den no b' e
singi someni, ma Dorsi b' e ferter tori. Te hen sten ben kon na fesi,
ala trawan b' e tapu. Den ben lobi fa den skin b' e gro, te Dorsi sten
b' e saka gwe te wan frede-tori b' e kon. Te na tori ben kon span
let-leti, den b' e fergiti fu hari bro. Ma a watra b' e tan nak-naki
nomo-nomo na sey den kruyara na lanpresi. Dya den yonkman ben
kan luku go na liba, ma den ben kan si tu den redi-redi kokolampu
faya fu den pkin masanga.

—Yu no sa si kumakriki tak wan sma tay hen boto na Knofru—
so Dorsi b' e ferteri,—èn suma abi gron dape? Kaba fu taki leti, a
doti fu dape mu bun sref-srefi. Ala sma frede na bigi faya fu
owruten, di katibo ben de. A bigi faya di son neti pranpran ben
kan frey psa abra den kenfiri, ma di b' e dede, bifo yu sabi leti ef
yu si hen. Den waktiman b' e frede èn den dagu b'e knoru-knoru
safri nomo.

—Deybroko mamanten ala sma b' e taki fu na azema di kon
baka èn ala ongoloku den b' e fringi na hen tapu.

—Namku den takru-du fu driktoro. Brudu di hen ben lasi, a b' e
puru na trawan skin, bika sma ben sabi taki na fu soygi driktoro ede
azema b' e kon. Ma blank-ofsiri ben teki ray fu na owru kron
nengre Asabi, di ben de wan mati fu hen.

—Buba fu azema, di a sa puru kibri, yu sa suku na ini owru mata.
Dan yu sa poti sowtu.

We na so den weti man fu pranasi ben kon grabu azema wan
neti, ma na tra mamanten a ben gwe krin-krin komoto na den
mindri. Sens a ten dati a b' e spuku kfalek na Knofru. Wan baka
trawan den sma b' e dede, nanga ala di, lek fa den b' e ferteri
safri-safri, driktoro ben pay gron, dipi na mindri busi, nanga brudu
fu wan nengre, di a ben kiri.—

A neti fu na tori disi, di den yonkman b' e pari go na oso, den
skin b' e gro, ma no wan f' den b' e tak wan wortu f' dati.

Na munkenki neti Luti no b' e kon so fur-fur moro n' hen mati.

again to her child. And after the hooting of the owl, something sad
always takes place.

It was not every evening that Luti brought his guitar and on these
occasions they did not sing so much, but Dorsi told stories. When he
began to speak, a hush fell on all around. They enjoyed getting gooseflesh, when Dorsi's voice, telling a scary story, fell to a whisper.
When the tale chilled their bones, they listened with bated breath.
But the water kept on splashing against the canoes at the mooring
place. Here the boys could see the river, but also the red lights of the
oil lamps in their little huts.

—Someone who moors his boat at Knofru[9] is not easily seen—so
Dorsi told, and who has gardens there? To tell you the truth, over
there something is amiss.

All the people there are in awe of the big light of the days gone by,
when slavery still existed. The big light which on some nights could
suddenly shoot up over the cane fields, but which spent itself before
one knew precisely what he had seen. Then fear crept over the
guards and the dogs growled softly.

—The following day everybody talked about the vampire, which
had put in an appearance once again, and they ascribed all their
misfortunes to it.

Especially the wicked deeds of the director. The blood which he
lost, he sucked back from the bodies of others. For people knew that
the vampire came to suck the director's blood. But the white overseer consulted the gnarled negro, old Asabi,[10] who was his friend.

The skin that the vampire discards and conceals, one must look
for that in a mortar, and then pour salt on it.

Well, in this way the whites on the plantation cornered the vampire
one night, but the following day it had disappeared completely from
their midst. From this time onward the ghosts played havoc at
Knofru. People died one after another while, as whispered rumors
spread, the director appeased the spirits of the ground, deep in the
bush, with the blood of a negro he had killed.

On the night of this story, as the boys paddled home their flesh
crawled, but no one dared breathe a word.

After this, Luti seldom came on moonlit nights.

9. See note 8. Here follows a historic tale that is typical of the tales of
slavery. See chapter 3 for another example.

10. The name Asabi ("He knows") indicates already that this was a man of
great knowledge.

Den ben sabi f' a b' e weri, fu di a b' e wroko tranga; dan te
bakadina a b' e kot wan pis presi opo na libasey.

—Fu prani—so a b' e tapu den aksi fu hen mati, ala di a ben sab
tak a no ben kan dray den ede nanga dati.

Te wroko ben weri hen, a b' e go dray-dray pkinso na birman
oso. A ben mag fu bori hen nyanyan na birman brantmiri. Birman
no ben de guduman. Wi ala, so Luti b' e prakseri nofo tron, di e
libi na pranasi, suma fu wi na guduman? A no strey nomo wi abi
fu strey wi libi langa nanga grasi, kapuweri èn pina?

A moro pkin nofi sproyti fu birman b' e sdon n'a doti gron. A
b' e kwinsi na papa aleysi, di nanga beyf-beyfi anu a b' e tyar g' a
mofo. Ala hen fesi den aleyssiri b' e fas-fasi.

Te a pkin ben pusu na breki kan fadon, a b' e naki hen anu fu
prisiri na ini na watra. Dan wan fu den moro bigiwan b' e hari hen
go pkinso moro fara, nanga ala di a b' e lolo a doti empi tron wan
tumsi bigi kundu n' a pkin mindri baka.

No no, Luti b' e prakseri, no so! Na ini mi eygi oso ala sani
mu de moro moy.

Na den yuru a b' e sab taki, na opo liba wan sma b' e wakti hen
tranga-tranga.

Te a b' e prakseri den san disi, dan ala ten a b' e firi fa hen
brudu b' e kon moro waran.

Lek fa Luti ben gwenti, fos sabaten a b' e krin hen kruyara,
bika te a b' e go na doro, te neti hen krosi no ben mu doti. Den
yonkman ben sabi now bun-bun, san ben de fu du nanga den
mati, namku sens a grandinari-brada ben ori wan langa taki nanga
hen. Boyt dati, di domri ben kon, den ben si tak den mati ben go
na kerkikantoro nanga hen karta.

Luti ben sa go na waka, a byo go na foto. Te neti, te a b' e
si den redi-redi faya fu den kokolampu, dan a ben sab tak den
faya fu foto ben de tra fasi: moro furu, moro krin! Namku den
faya fu den kino a ben lobi, nanga den furu-furu sma, nèlek fa
sontron hondro-hondro azege b' e sanya na den stratilanteri.
Luti prakseri na hen srefi tak a b' o bay wan bun lampu.

Agen munkenki b' e dongo kon. Agen den mati ben kon na
makandra na ondro den waway fu den morisibon na lanpresi, fu
ferteri èn singi. Luti no ben de nanga den. A ben saka gwe nanga
kroboy fara.

They knew how tired he was, because he had worked hard; and then in the afternoon he cleared a piece of ground on the river bank.

For planting! Thus he was able to put an end to the questioning of his friends, though he knew full well that they were not taken in by his answers. When he was tired of working, he went to rest in his neighbor's house. He was allowed to cook his food on his neighbor's stove. This neighbor was not rich. Of all of us who live on a plantation, Luti often asked himself, is there one who is rich? Have we not struggled all our lives with grass, brushwood, and hardship?

The smallest newborn child of the neighbor sat on the mud floor. He grabbed the rice porridge and with unsteady hands brought it to his mouth. His whole face was plastered with grains of rice.

When the child had overturned the can, he gleefully smacked the water with his hand. An elder drew the child away and knotted his dirty cloth on his back.

No, not for me, Luti thought, not this for me! In my house everything must be more beautiful.

He knew then that upstream someone was waiting longingly for him.

When he pondered this, he felt the blood surging warm through him.

As was his custom, Luti cleaned his canoe in the early evening, for when he went out at night he did not want his clothes to be soiled. The boys knew full well what ailed their friend. Especially since the elder of the church had chatted with him for a long time. Moreover, when the minister came they saw their friend going to the office of the church with his membership card.

Luti was about to go on a journey. He was off to town. At night, when he saw the red glow of the oil lamps, he knew that those in town were different, more numerous, brighter. He loved especially the lights of the cinema and the masses of people like myriads of glowworms swirling round the street lamp. Luti made up his mind to buy a good lamp.

Again the moon came up and again the friends assembled under the fans of the palm trees at the mooring place, to tell stories and to sing. Luti was not among them; he had drifted down on the last ebb.

Saf-safri hen pari b' e pusu a pkin boto nanga lay. Toku
sontron a b' e hari wanwan steyf pari, te a watra di b' e dyompo
bun hey, b' e fadon lek bigi dropu na hen baka. Dat b' e psa te
a tiri breyti di a b' e breyti den ten disi, b' e beweygi na ini hen
skin. Dan a ben gersi lek a b' e sribi gwe, èn a b' e tan lek a watra
b' e tyar hen prakseri pasa den someni uku fu liba go lasi te n' a
kroboy lin fu loktu nanga se.
    Wan star ben sutu. No wet-weti, ma krin, nanga ala di munkenki
b' e skijn. Nèlek fumpeyri, krosbey. Wan momenti leti ben krin a
kontren, mek a kon tron wan pkinso moro tru sani. Na momenti
disi Luti kis hen srefi, tak a b' e psa watrasey fu Knofru. Now fosi
a b' e si den fayaworon nanga den azege di b' e gi faya. A prakseri
Dorsi.
    Azema. . . .
    Na tru?
    Now ten no ben de fu swit prakseri.
    Na ini a kowru-kowru neti disi sweti fu dede b' e broko hen
skin: a b' e psa watrasey fu Knofru èn a ben si wan faya.
    Luti no b' e pari moro. Hen boto b' e dribi nomo nanga farawatra.
Frede ben bradi hensrefi na hen tapu, nèlek busianansi e span hen
takru blaka futu na tapu wan n'nyan di a feni. A no ben sabi tak
hen boto b' e soygi watra now tu. A lapu fu toko-toko no ben yepi.
    Di a firi hen futu e kon nati, a frigiti tak kande a ben kan puru
watra ete. A dyompo g' a watra.
    Ma na watrasey fu Knofru un ben de. . . .
    Owrukuku ben kari èn den mati di b' e singi, ben panya nèlek
ibriwan fu den ben wan kibri hensrefi na ini eygi masanga.
    Ma baka fu dati ala sani b' e sribi na ini kowru fu munkenki.
Soso wan langaneki palmbon nomo b' e beweygi nèlek a ben wan
lakboru wan pkin dungru worku puru na loktu.

Softly he pushed off his small boat with its load. Yet now and then he would give a firm stroke or two, causing the water to splash high in big drops behind him. That happened when the quiet happiness he felt surged through his body. Then it seemed as if he dreamt away, and as if the water propelled his thoughts past all the many corners of the river and spent itself at the point where sea and sky converged.

A shooting star—not white, but radiant—shot up like a missile nearby, while the moon still shone. For a moment the surroundings were illuminated so that the whole area became more real. At that moment Luti came to himself and noticed that he was paddling past Knofru. Now he saw the glowworms and fireflies, which radiated light. He thought of Dorsi . . .

Vampire!

Was it true?

Now there was no time for sweet pensiveness.

In this cold night a deathlike sweat appeared on his body: he was passing Knofru and had caught sight of a light.

Luti had stopped paddling. His boat drifted along with the ebb. Fear had come over him as over a prey caught in the clutches of a bush spider's ugly black claw. He did not know his boat was taking water. The cloth soaked in mud was of no avail.[11] When he felt his feet getting wet he forgot that he might still be able to scoop the water out. He jumped.

Alas, it was the water near Knofru.

The owl had hooted, and the friends who had sung had dispersed as if each wanted to find a hiding place in his own hut.

Then all things slept in the black moonlit night. Only a palm tree with slender neck moved, as if to wipe away a small dark cloud in the air.

11. Holes in a canoe are repaired with cloth soaked in mud.

CHAPTER 9

The New Generation

"New Generation" is really a misnomer, for although these writers began writing later than Trefossa, some of them are his contemporaries and, in some instances, are even older than he. Some confessed that they discovered the possibilities of Creole as a literary language after reading Trefossa's poems. Trefossa in a sense paved the way for them. Today there are so many authors publishing in Creole[1] that we are forced to be highly selective. After studying all the published material, we felt that three of them proved to be of really outstanding quality: Johanna Schouten-Elsenhout, Michaël Slory, and Edgar Cairo. They represent at the same time three different generations: a grandmother in her sixties, a man in his thirties, and a student in his twenties.

We do not wish to suggest that others have not written remarkable poems. They have indeed, and we regret that we are unable to include some of them in this anthology. But the complete output of these other poets does not permit a substantial selection of really outstanding quality. Instead of presenting in this final chapter a panorama of the new generation, we have preferred a selection of the best authors and a representative sample of their work.

Johanna Schouten-Elsenhout, born in 1910 in Paramaribo, is older than Trefossa but has been influenced by his work. We do not suggest that she imitated him. On the contrary, she started writing poems without knowing that she had fallen prey to the muse. They were written down in a notebook, amidst the aromatic fragrances of her cooking pots, as bits of prose without punctuation or versification. Someone else had to enlighten her that these were poems, and with some help her work was transformed into poetry.[2] She can be

1. In addition to all the poets cited in this anthology, we must mention the names Eugène W. Rellum, Jozef Slagveer, J. Defares, and Edmundo, all of whom have published one or more collections of Creole poetry, and also Corly Verlooghen, R. Dobru, Wilfred Grimmèr, Johan Pont, Marcel de Bruin, Kawina, A. Gilds, Heo, Wati Deets, Vene, B. Ooft, Shrinivasi, and possibly many others, who have published one or more poems in Creole. An anthology of Surinam poetry was published in 1970 by Shrinivasi under the title *Wortoe d'e tan abra* (Words that remain).

2. She published *Tide ete. Fo sren singi* in 1963 and *Awese* in 1965. For

regarded as the Grandma Moses of Creole literature, but her work is
certainly far from naïve. Her poems are often very difficult to interpret. This may be due partly to her frequent use of special terms
from lower-class culture, and partly to her exploitation of lower-
class idioms and proverbs.[3] More often than not, however, her poems
seem to touch some subconscious depth, which demands from the
reader a deep understanding of the psychological problems of Creoles,
branded with the mark of slavery and colonial times and frustrated
in their hopes for a brighter future. We must confess that these
poems have deeply moved us.

Michaël Slory, born in Coronie in 1935, is a poet involved in
politics. Although his political poems can be highly effective ammu-
nition in the political struggle, as a poet he seems carried away far
too often by uncontrolled emotions, which harm or even ruin the
poetic balance. He started by using Dutch exclusively, even denying
his Creole background in a certain way.[4] Around 1960 he found himself in an emotional crisis as a result of his first contact with African
culture. He was then "converted" to Creole, although he still writes
Dutch poems. He published his first collection of Creole poems,
Sarka (Struggle),[5] under the African pseudonym Asjantenu Sangodare.
Here he gives expression to his political preoccupation with the injustice of this world. In the same period he prepared a second collection under the title *Fraga mi wortoe* (Signal my words). These poems
deal with more personal themes. Many refer to his youth in the
district, but they also show his concern with the national problems
of a multiracial society. The collection was accepted for publication
in Surinam, but the death of his publisher, and also the fact that the
latter feared possible political consequences, delayed publication for
several years and led to the poems remaining unpublished until 1970,
when Slory privately financed the publication of six collections of
poems, of which *Fraga mi wortoe* was one. The other collections are
Bonifoto (The fortress of Boni), *Nengre-oema* (Negro woman),

---

some years in succession she wrote by special request a Christmas poem in
Creole, which was broadcast. These poems have not been published.
  3. She collected more then a thousand proverbs, published in 1974 by the
Bureau Volkslectuur in Surinam under the title *Sranan Pangi*.
  4. His first poem was published in Dutch in *Tongoni* 1 in 1960. Many more
have been published since, for example the collections *Brieven aan de
Guerilla* (Letters to the guerilla) in 1968, and *Brieven aan Ho Tsji Minh*
(Letters to Ho Chi Minh) in 1969.
  5. Asjantenu Sangodare, *Sarka. Bittere strijd* (Bitter struggle) (Amsterdam,
1961).

Lobisingi (Love song), *Vietnam,* and *Memre den dé* (Remember the days).

Edgar Cairo, born in Paramaribo in 1948, is a young student who published his first novel, *Temekoe,* in 1969. He has published some collections of poems since then.[6] Prose production in Creole has always been meager, so this first Creole novel came as a big surprise to insiders. Cairo deals almost exclusively with his relationship to his father, a stern and lonely man, who distrusted everyone. In the last chapter of the book, presented here, he tells the story of his father's social life: about the only friend he ever had, his colleagues at the factory, his wife and children, his relatives. He led a completely independent but utterly miserable life. The chapter starts with a vision of a perfectly happy independent existence and ends on a haunting evocation of a lonely man trying to reach out to the world.

The examples cited in this chapter will make clear that the limited range of subjects treated by Trefossa has considerably widened. The authors are deeply concerned with the tensions of a multiracial society and are also deeply moved by the struggle for independence of developing nations and by the fight against the injustices of this world. They try to understand their own problems and their own history in terms of universal sorrow and glory. In this way, Creole literature in Surinam has gone beyond its boundaries without losing touch with its own Creole background.

---

6. A mimeographed collection, *Oroskopoe* (Horoscope), was published in 1969, and another collection, *Kra* (Soul), actually written before the preceding one, in 1970. Cairo is working on a new novel, *Sjoeroerwe.*

JOHANNA SCHOUTEN-ELSENHOUT

Awese

Kabra!
Troki gi den afkodreyman
a mindri n'akapu dyari
pe fodu e lolo
nanga santi ini en ay
lek papawinti
a mindri n' aladey son.
Wiki den, mi kabra,
ini a dofokampu,
mindri a doti f' sranan.
Troki mek kromanti
sekete nang' a pingi fu mandron
a mindri den awese.
Prisi a gronmama.
Opo frey mi nengrekopu mindri a watrapan.
A ten e kot' a greb' olo.

Mi dren

Yere mi sten,
lek wan grio e bari
a baka den bigi krepiston.
Mi ati e nak te dede fu frede.
M'e suk wan kibri olo
pe lobi de.
M' e frey lek wan sonfowru
mindri tranga winti
abra den moro hey bergi.
Sula e yere mi sten.
Mi skin e degedege.

JOHANNA SCHOUTEN-ELSENHOUT

Awese[7]

Forefathers!
Invoke for the pagan priests
amidst the commons
where the voodoo snake rolls
with sand in his eyes
like a snake god
amidst the sun of every day.
Wake them, my forefathers,
in the medicine house,
in the middle of the Surinam earth.
Invoke and let Kromanti
dance the sekete on the beat of the big drum
amidst the spirits of the awese.
Honor the earth mother.
Fly up nengrekopu from the middle of the pool.
Time runs its course at the grave.

My dream

Hear my voice,
like a grio calling
behind a boulder large.
My heart beats deadlike with fear.
I'm looking for a hole to hide
where love is to be found.
I fly like a sun bird
amidst strong blasts
far above the highest peaks.
Rapids hear my voice.
My body trembles.

7. *Awese* is difficult to translate. It is used in the non-Christian religion.
There seems to be no clear relation with the poem. The poem invokes the
pagan forefathers (*kabra*) and asks them to awaken the different gods such as
fodu or *papawinti* (names for the same snake god), *kromanti* (a group of
African gods), and *gronmama* (the earth deity). The bird *nengrekopu* may
also refer to a god but seems in this poem to be used more as a symbol for
the true negro spirit.

Loktu wawan e si mi
a mindri banawtu.
Mi kondre, mi pedreku bon,
mi nesi!
Sonten dede sa tuka mi
ini mi dren.

Arwepi

A gers
a no de f' bribi.
Den yuru doro man.
Kraswatra e broko
den bradi plana.
M' ede bigin dray
a mindri den worku.
A bot' ede opo mofo
kant' e tek watra ala sey.
Mi yeye
e sungu ondro wan bromki se f' howpu
pe m' e beg wan aladey brede
nanga aleluya fu agama.
Mindri doystri fu a mun
mi ati e tron pis'ati,
tek nyun weni
nanga winti fu stondansi
pe mi libi e syatu
mindri
den angri bere
d'e say ondro a son.

Yayofowru

Kompasi marki

The sky alone observes me
amidst this anxiety.
My land, my pedreku,[8]
my nest!
Perhaps I shall be touched by death,
within my dream.

Arwepi[9]

It's almost impossible
to believe.
The time has come, man.
Breakers cut up
the huge waves.
My head is given to a dizziness
amidst the clouds.
The open mouth of the prow
tips and lets in water on all sides.
My soul
sinks amidst a floral sea of hope
where I beg for my daily bread
and get only inanities in return.
Amidst an ominous moon
syphilitic my heart becomes,
then takes another turn
midst the excitement of Stondansi,
where my life ebbs away
amidst
the hungry bellies
strewn under the sun.

Yayofowru[10]

The compass has measured out

8. *Pedreku* (also pronounced *pegreku*) is a small tree where this bird is
supposed to have its nest.

9. *Arwepi* is the name of a white bead used in religious and medical
ceremonies. The name does not seem to be related to the poem, which instead
deals with the false hopes awakened by politicians. Stondansi is the name of
a great project that has given new hope to the poor.

10. We have left the title untranslated, but in the poem itself the word
yayofowru (literally "wandering bird") has been translated as "floozy."
Other untranslated words are *anamu,* a kind of chicken, and Awaradan, a
back alley in Paramaribo.

yu futpasi.
Yayofowru libi kron.
Ini yu dede
prodo trowkrosi,
drape grontapu libi
sor moro moy.
Te m' e si yu fesi
ini a gowtu munkenki,
dungru mun e boro gwe.
Pe m' e feti f' or a skin,
drape y' e grati lek anamu.
Te m' e si yu, yayofowru,
e frey psa a tapu awaradan,
mi sa begi fu deybroko
mek nyunfrudu
lon abra yu dan.

Sweti

Mi nyun oloysi
nanga prakiki
di brad' en frey a tapu,
di m' win lek
nomru wan a pren,
bigin nak yuru
e waka a baka.
A gers m' e firi f' go ler swen
nanga koni a mindri faya,
wins' a f' wan dey prisiri,
f' dukrun wan kefe
mindri a se f' asema brudu
f' marki soso wan enkri drop sweti f' mi libi
d' e lon lek kowru watra a mindrisey.
Frede bigin dangra mi.

your steps.
A floozy's life is not straight.
In your death
and bridal gown so proud,
there life on earth
reveals its loveliest side.
When I see your face
in the gilded shine of the moon,
dark moon fades away.
Where I try with all my might
    to hang on to the body,
there you slip away like anamu.
When I see you, floozy,
flit past on Awaradam,
I shall pray for the new morn
to let a new flood
pour itself o'er your dam.

Sweat

My brand new clock
spread under wings
of bird of prey.
This I have won
as prize on Queen's Birthday.
The hour begins to chime,
recedes . . .[11]
It seems as if I'd learn to swim
with magicality amidst the fire,
let it but be for one day long
to be submersed a fleeting time
amidst a sea of vampire blood
to set a mark on but a drop of my own sweat
and let it flow like water cold into the blood.
Fear then begins, usurps me whole.

11. This is one of the most difficult poems in the anthology. Our interpretation (and translation) hinges on the line *e waka a baka* (literally "walks back"), which may be translated in relation to a clock as "walks backward" or "is slow." We have assumed that the clock walks backward and takes the poet to past times, where she is confronted with the horrible age of slavery and eventually regains consciousness at the site of the old Jewish cemetery, Betkayn (Beth Chaim), amidst the bones of dead slaves.

Pre f' mi fadon nanga doro insey,
mi dyompo nanga tap' ay
a mindri Sranan liba.
Di m' op' ede a loktu baka,
mi si tak a owru Betkayn
mi fen mi srefi,
mindri a smeri
f' den srafu dedebonyo.

Duman

Mi no wani / wan ati
di n' abi kra,
mi wani / wan yeye d' e libi.

Mi n' e wer / susu
di n' e fit mi,
m' e wer / mi eygi krompu.

Mi n' e sdon / luku
a fesi fu sma,
m' e luku ini / mi eygi spikri.

Winti

A swit se winti
d' e way a Branspen
te doro ini
Sranan liba,
e mek mi yeye dyonko.
A naki f' den plana
a sey matros broki
e boboy mi gebre.
A lon watra
a mindri liba
d' e dray tron wan kolku

Instead of entering into yesteryears,
I jump with my eyes closed
straight into the river Surinam.
And when I raised my head again,
I saw that I was back once more
amidst the Jewish cemetery,
among the dank airs
of the rotten bones
    of slaves of yesteryears.

Man of action

I will no heart
without a soul,
I want a living spirit.

I wear no shoes
which do not fit,
I wear my very own clogs.

I do not look
at another's face,
but in my very own mirror.

Wind

A lovely sea breeze
which blows from Bramspoint[12]
into
the river Surinam,
lulls my spirit.
The splash of the waves
on the side of the mooring place
tames my tiger spirit.
The fast-flowing stream
amidst the river
which turns into a weir

12. Branspen is a place on the west bank of the Surinam River, close to the sea. Matros broki, also called in Dutch *Marinetrap,* here translated simply by "mooring place," is a small quay in the center of Paramaribo, near the old fort. This poem also seems to have definite political connotations. The poet does not want to be lulled to sleep by beautiful promises.

a mi ati lampe,
e broko mi dyodyo
saka gi doti.
Mi winsi
wan nyun dey opo fesi
fu wiki mi kra,
mek a dyompo a loktu,
di a swit se winti
e feti f' sribi.

Watr'ay

Luku!
Mi fini garden
e puru smoko.
Osey a faya seti?
Wan safri lafu
kibri a baka
pe mi brudu
e tron watra
f' kuku m' insey.
It' ay a mindri
a tranga lon watra:
mi langa watr'ay
e seni nyunsu go
gi den masanengre
f' mi n' abrasey,
tak mi bro
e feti f' tapu.
Wan pkin krabu
no de f' si, o-ten.
Tan bun, mi safri lafu.
Adyosi,
mi langa watr'ay.

Sekete uma

Oho,

at the mooring place of my heart,
breaks down my protecting spirit,
right down to the ground.
I would
a new day dawns
to wake this soul of mine,
so that it jumps into the sky,
now that this nice sea breeze
is almost laid to rest.

Tears

Look!
Smoke comes
from my thin mosquito net.
Whence comes the fire?
A soft smile
is hidden
there where my blood
to water turns
to heat up my innermost.
Fix your eyes to the middle
of the fast-flowing stream:
my long, long tears
send out a message
to those of mine
far across on the other side,
that my breath
is almost stilled.
Not even a scribble is returned,
never.
Stay well then, my soft smile.
Fare thee well,
my long, long tears.

Sekete woman[13]

Oh ho!

13. *Sekete* is a bushnegro dance. Here the word *awese* is also used with
a sort of generalized undefinable meaning (cf. note 7). The *kwakwabangi*
is a wooden bench played as a drum with wooden sticks. The poem deals
mainly with racial mixing.

mi sekete uma
a mindri a krin munkenki fesi
ini busi, ondro den taki
fu a mama kankantri,
pe mandron e boro doti sek mi gebre.
Not no de f' lus mi yeye
di spikri tanapu a fes den bromki
di yu awese futu e trowe gi gron.
Yu koti skin a tap kwakwa bangi
a mindri den difrenti
moy pangi strepi.
Brantmarki den tu blaw ay nanga
gowtu w'wiri fu a nyoni bromki a yu sey
d' e op' ede gro kon a loktu
fu wiki mi dyodyo a mindri
dipi sribi. Yu krusu w'wiri e bosro
mi frestan kon krin f' si den
toe brenki ay di was mi kra
mek a opo a dungru
f' dyompo fet a krin, suku
san lobi nanga brudu ben tay.

Kodyo

Mi no man moro,
Gronmama,
den sani di m' e si.
M' e fruferi
ala dey f' arki anans'tori
d' e prit mi ati a tu.

Mi no man moro
f' dray lontu soso saka
a mindri berefur libi

My sekete woman
amidst the clear shine of the moon
in the forest, under the branches
of the imposing cotton tree,
where the big drum shakes the earth
    and jostles my tiger spirit.
There is nothing to free my spirit
which stands nailed in front of the flowers
your awese feet trace on the ground.
Your sways cut the body
    on the beat of the kwakwabangi,
your body in the pretty stripes
of that wraparound of yours.
Observe those two blue eyes
and the little one's golden hair,
    that flower next to you
who raises his head on high
and wakens up my soul
from a deep sound sleep. Your kinky hair scrubs clean
my brains that I may see
    two eyes which sparkle so,
and washed my soul quite clean,
which cleaves the darkness here
and jumps and struggles toward the light
    to find out
what binds love and blood.

Kodyo[14]

I can no longer bear it,
Mother of the earth,
the things that I see.
I've had my fill of it
to hear tales every day
which cleave my heart in two.

I can no longer bear it
to be with empty pockets
midst this satiating life

14. Kodyo is a name given to a male child born on Monday. *Apinti* is a
certain kind of drum used in religious dances.

d'e bet mi tongo f' taki:
Pardon mi,
o masra Gado,
pinaman n' abi big' ay.

Mi no man moro,
Maysa,
a mindri den sraften katfisi
d'e swen mindri mi brudu ibri dey.

Mi no man moro,
Apinti dron,
den bakafutu banya
di y' e skopu f' or n' ati.
Mi n' e arki prey moro.

Mi wan' opodron
lek friman borgu.

Kondre,
dat' ede
m' e dorfu tide.

Amemba

Braka neti,
granaki ay,
takru triki
a mindri
kowru gron.
Yongu yari
d' e kor mi
a mindri prisiri.
Sabana bromki
di opo fesi
e waki mi so nya,
mek bigi dren
sor mi
wan futmarki,
pe a musdey stari

that I can hardly withhold from saying:
Forgive,
Oh Lord my God,
Paupers are not greedy.

I can no longer bear it,
Mother of the earth,
midst the catfish of the slave times
which daily swim in my blood.

I can no longer bear it,
drum of the Apinti,
the forbidden dance done in disguise[15]
which one dances to keep up faith.
I won't take part any more.

I want the drumming in the open
like a citizen who is free.

People!
For this
do I dare today.

Amemba[16]

Black night,
granite eyes,
ugly wiles
on the cold
ground.
Youthful years
seducing me
at the feast.
Savannah flower
lifting up the face
as red as blood eyeing me,
let the big dream
indicate
a footprint
where the morning star

15. Pagan religious dances were not permitted, and participants could
be punished. This law is, however, not enforced any more.
   16. Amemba is the name given to a female child born on Saturday.

e trowe krin faya
mindri a pasi
fu teygo dungru mun.

Granmorgu

Ini a pikin alen-ten dropu,
ay mi lobi,
a tapu a dyamanti pasi fu a neti,
mi si taki yu de
nanga dyomp' ati f' den dungru yari
f' mi libi. I dyompo tanapu
lek wan owru dren di kon tru.
Wan krioro di ben e sribi
a mindri dungru pasi f' libi,
frey opo lek wan kopro-prin maskita
fu suku a libi di kibri en srefi
a mindri son nanga alen,
a ondro den tranga rutu f' den bon-taki:
fa den e way fu tron draywinti
fu kanti den bigi bon ala sey.
Anu na anu ati e doro gron f' ati.
Brudu e katibo yu skin.
Ke, mi krinfesi sranan uma
nanga yu trutru granlobi,
yu sor i srefi a tapu a gowtu pasi:
granmorgu
a mindri den fayalobi bon.

Kresneti stari

Meki mi koyri
a ondro yu prasoro,
musudey stari,
a tapu a grati sorfu pasi
fu a libi,
a mindri rowsu nanga maka,
fu tuka a son fesi
di sa kori mi ati te gron.

casts a shining gleam
along the way
of an everlasting sombre moon.

New dawn

In the drops of the rainy season,
Oh my love!
On the diamond-studded path of the night
I see that you shrink
from the dark years
of my life. You have arisen
like a long lost dream which came true.
A Creole who slept
midst the dark alleys of life,
startled like a malarial mosquito
to look for life hiding itself
amidst the sun and rain,
under the strong roots dangling from the branches of a tree:
how blow they not to be a wind that whirls
and cause huge trees to sway from side to side.
Slowly the heart reaches the bottom of the heart.
The body becomes a slave to blood.
Oh my open-faced woman of Surinam
with your real, deep love,
you've dared to show yourself on the gilded path:
new dawn
amidst the fayalobi trees.[17]

Christmas star

Let me stroll
under your parasol,
morning star,
on the polished silvery path
of life,
amidst the prickly roses,
so that I may touch the face of the sun
which deeply mellows the ground of my heart.

17. *Fayalobi* is a bush with red flowers.

Luku fa mi e boro pasa
a mindri sneki
soso fu si yu fesi, mi gowtumun.
Ke, sor mi yu bigi grani
nanga krin faya,
fu mi feni a pkin stanfastesiri
fu say ini mi safu ati,
mek a opo gro.

MICHAËL SLORY

Fu memre

Di na oloysi meki na yuru sroyti,
mi firi fa mi libi lon gowe.
Na owruyari kakafowru froyti
wan enkri leysi, ma mi krey sote.

Memre

Strati
pe son marki ibri ay santi,
memre den futu di gwe moro fara.
Gotro di diki fu tyari lonwatra,
langa yu srefi, te skuma fu yu
yere mi nen.
Doti di meki mi
sa teki mi baka.
Ma mi sten di ben bari
mindri den bon,
a sa gwe?
Strati, no sribi!
Gotro, no drey!

Te pikinboy komopo na wenkri

A gersi
na mun e lon na mi baka.
A gersi
den bon e lontu mi.
Mama!

See how I stalk
between the snakes
only to see your face, my golden moon.
Ah, bare to me your greater glory
and clear bright light,
that I find a small seed of the everlasting flower
to sow it in my soft heart
and let it grow.

MICHAËL SLORY

To remember

When the clock announced the closing of the hour,
I felt my life streaming past.
The cock of the year gone by did crow
a single time, but I wept so.

Remembrance

Streets
where the sun has left its mark on every grain of sand,
think of the footsteps which have farther gone.
Gutters which were dug out to lead away the streaming water,
lengthen yourself, till your foam
hears my name.
Earth that shaped me
will take me back again,
but my voice which called
among the trees,
will it be lost?
Streets, sleep not!
Gutters, don't dry!

When little boys return from shopping trips

It seems
as if the moon is chasing me.
It seems
as if the trees are all around me.
Mama!

San grati pasa ondro den taki
go doro na dray-uku de?
Ondro na broki fu na gotro
wan kokro de . . .
Mama!

Wan man e waka na mi sey,
sondro wan skin, sondro wan futu.
Mi bro kon hey.
A sori skuma sa kon doro
fu lon fadon.
Mama!

Bamborita

Bamborita, bamborita!
Te den kokrontobon fadon,
sondro siri,
mi no e nyan.

Na wan grikibi e singi
te na noko
sondro frede.
Na wan grikibi e singi,
te den kokrontobon fadon.

Mi sa opo go na loktu
leki worku fu katun,
di e kroypi na mi baka,
na mi bere,
go na hey.

Ma den kokrontobon e kanti

What's gliding past under the branches
toward the corner over there?
Under the bridge over the gutter
lies a pipe . . .[18]
Mama!

A man is walking next to me,
without body, without feet.
I gasp for breath.
It seems as if foam appears
and downward drools.[19]
Mama!

Bamborita[20]

Bamborita, bamborita!
When the palms of coconut are falling,
without nuts,
I do not eat.

Sits a grikibi a-singing,
undaunted
in the highest tree.
When the trees of palm are falling,
sits the grikibi a-singing.

I will then be transported
like the clouds of cotton creeping
up my back
and stomach.

But the palms of coconut are falling,

18. Evil spirits may live in the metal or concrete pipes that allow the
water of a stream or gutter to pass under the road. Small children are afraid
to pass by them after sunset.

19. Probably the poet refers to the *bakru*, evil spirits that may take the
form of a human being but with some strange differences of appearance,
e.g., they may be half wood. The foam coming from an anthill betrays the
presence of a dangerous spirit, called *Akantamasu*.

20. *Bamborita* is the name for a brightly colored weekend shirt. The shirt
referred to in this poem has coconut palms on it, which make the poet think
of Coronie, the place of his birth. When the shirt creeps up on the body
(probably when the person wearing it starts dancing), the coconut trees seem
to fall sideways. This makes the poet think of the bad economic situation of
Coronie, which depends mainly on coconut cultivation. Palm disease threatens
to starve the whole population. A *grikibi* is a small bird.

safrisafri. Griki gwe.
Mi no e nyan, o bamborita!
Sondro siri
mi no e nyan.

Fa India . . .

Fa India
e tigri mi buba
nanga buy
na mi futu,
gowtu keti na mi neki,
brenki aka na mi noso.
Suma furu
mi baskita
nanga mamanten gruntu,
May?
Wanwan broko fensre opo.
Futulanki na lekdoru.
Faya santi dresi en.
Bakadan:
wan isri tromu.
Mindri foto:
dyari, oso.

Gi Dyewal Persad

Yu ros.
Yu krosi ros
leki na dey opo fruku
abra den kowsbantibedi,
nati, soso dow.

slowly, slowly. Grikibi has flown away.
I don't eat, Oh bamborita,
without nuts
I do not eat.

How India . . . [21]

How India
prickles my skin,
with bangles
on my feet,
golden chains round my neck,
glittering knobs in my nose.
Who fills
my basket
with greens for the morning,
May?
Here and there a broken window open.
The edges of the feet are nothing but corns,
healed by the heat of the sand.
Behind there in the backyard:
an iron cask.
In the midst of the town:
plots, houses.

For Dyewal Persad [22]

You are pink.
Your clothes are pink
like the day's early dawn
over the stringbean beds,
wet, dipped only in dew.

21. This poem deals with the racial tensions between Creoles and Indians
in Surinam. The poet is irritated and charmed by the Indians, who form the
economic backbone of the society. Unlike the Creoles, the Indians live in
very poor conditions but save a lot of money. East Indian women are often
called May.
22. Dyewal Persad is an Indian name. The pink color that pervades the
poem refers to the Indian *pagwa* ceremony, in which Indians throw a red
colored fluid on each other's clothes. This rosy optimism is contrasted with
the blue marks of slavery, which characterize the Creoles. The *tadya* is an
Indian drum.

Wan krin mamantenson
e leti
yu eri skin.
Na santa pagwa
e naki en tadya
te neti doro.
Mi baka blaw
te now ete. Den marki
no wani gwe.
Ma un sa si wan fasi.

Fu memre Guernica fu Pablo Picasso

Mi weri mi grun bruku.
Loktu blaka.
Sonfaya bron wan marki
ini mi ay.
Mi redi sak'angisa
nyan mi sweti.
Den bromki lila
tapu lantidan.
Ondro wan bon
wan burukaw e buku
wan man trowe.
Mi eri skin e gro.
Brudu didon so lala
tapu grasi.
San a sa du now?
Skreki tapu mi bro.

Mofoneti

Bakadinaredi
brasa na son gowe.
Den star e dropu
wanwan faya
kon na gron.
Ala penpeni e kenki
tron sorfru.
Munkenki e ferfi
nanga en sorfrukwasi

A clear morning sun
lightens up
your whole body.
The holy pagwa
beats his tadya
when the night descends.
My back is blue
from then till now. The marks
can't go away;
but we'll find a way out.

In memory of Pablo Picasso's Guernica

I wear my trousers green.
The sky is black.
Scorching sun has burnt a mark
in my eyes.
My red handkerchief
devours my sweat.
The lilac flowers
on the main road.
Under a tree
a bull tosses
a man away.
My whole body is gooseflesh.
Blood lies so spent
on the grass.
What will it do now?
Fear cuts off my breath.

Dawn

The red of the afternoon
embraces the sun away.
The stars trickle down
here and there a flame
to the earth.
All color changes,
turns into silver.
Moonlight paints
with its silvery brush

den dan fu grontapu.
Loktu blaw so tranga.
So mi kan si fa Gado fesi langa.

Rosalina

Den mormo fu yu ay,
den krin,
krin moro alenwatra,
tiri moro busikriki,
pe soso winti e sribi
ondro den taki.
Rosalina,
na yu sten tyari gowtu so?
Te mun srefi e bro
fu skreki?

Anda mi,
ankra mi na yu boto
tay na lin
di yu iti now na watra,
pe wi gro kon tron wan libi,
wan lobi.

Pasi langa

Pasi langa.
Mi e toptopu
te mi doro.
Titey fu mi skin
kon weri.
Wan doyfi, Simbolo
fu fri prakseri,
sutu go na loktu
fu go miti na blaw.
Porti sayans!
A sa naki en frey

the paths of the world.
The sky is such an azure blue.
In this I am shown
   how far God's eye can roam.

Rosalina

The beads of your eyes
are crystal clear,
clearer than rain water,
quieter than a creek in a bush,
where only the wind comes to doze
under the branches.
Rosalina,
does your voice store so much gold,
that even the moon pulls in its breath
for fright?

Keep me within the span of your hand,[23]
anchor me firmly to your boat,
tie the line fast
which now you let in the water sink,
where we'll melt into one life,
one love.

The way is long

The way is long.
I walk on my toes
until I arrive.
The sinews of my body
tire out.
A dove, symbol
of unfettered thoughts,
shoots into the sky
to meet the blue . . .
Small chance!
He will bash his wings

23. The expression *anda* is used in a game of marbles. The first marble
that is thrown to within a distance of another marble that can be bridged by
the span of the player's hand wins.

na grontapu skin
te a broko.

Te Budha

Te Budha lusu ensrefi
meki Kresi miti en,
nyun firi sa broko doro.
Sranan prakseri sa lolo
ala makandra
kon wan.

Un sa memre na dey
di den preykiman fruteri:
ertintin . . . ertintin . . .
Budha wawan bên tanapu
e luku den wey
furu nanga soso aleysi,
soso kaw.
Abra den bedi Kresi
ben anga so langalanga
naki fasi ini en eygi brudu
na en kroysi,
so sari.
A ben weti ete.

Ma now
na toko kaba.
Rostu wini.
Makandra nomo un sa go
na hey.
Makandra nomo
un sa brasa den dangra
di tergi wi kra.

Fraga mi wortu

Fraga mi wortu
gi den di de na baka.
Opo den ay,
no libi den didon.

'gainst the crust of the earth,
till they break.

If Buddha . . .

If Buddha rises
for a meeting with Christ,
a new feeling will break through.
The thinking of Surinam
will bind all
into one.

We shall ponder the day
when preachers said:
once upon a time, once upon a time . . .
Buddha alone stood firmly erect
surveying the fields,
filled only with rice
and only with cows.
Above the bedsteads Christ was suspended,
stretched to full length
nailed in his own blood
on his cross,
so sad, so sad.
And he was still white.

But now
The fight is fought.
Peace has won.
Only together can we go
forward.
Only together
can we come to terms
with what nibbles at our souls.

Signal my words

Signal my words
to those who remain.
Open their eyes,
let them not lie.

Lekti den futu
abra den owru soro.
Dopu den dyodyo
nanga wan nyun bigin.

So un sa pusu
wisrefi go na fesi
ondro na star
di kari na nyun ten.

Dan un sa firi
unsrefi ala wan man,
wan kondre pipel,
pe prati no kan de.

Wi nengre

Way, nengre!
Te wi luku baka
fu si san ben pasa,
w'e krempi gwe
na ini a: "Frigiti."
Ma di mi dray,
mi si a se
e masi kon tapu a parwa,
na ini a weti skuma,
wan langa watra-ay,
mi geme na mi srefi:
Way, nengre!
Fa wi musu luku
na ini a spikri
fu historia, di blaka, blaka?

Koroni kawina

Kokronto koko, fa yu Losia Boy b' e froyti.

Lift up their feet
across the old sores.
Baptize their souls
with a fresh start.

Thus we'll go
forward
under the star
which heralds the new time.

Then we shall feel
all like one man,
people of a nation,
where no partition is found.

We negroes

Make way, negro!
When we look back
on that which has happened,
we shrink away
in "let bygones be bygones."
But when I turned around
and saw the sea,
mash of white foam
rolling over the parwa trees,[24]
one long, long tear,
I groaned inside:
Make way, negro!
How much we look
in the mirror of events,
which is black, black?

Coronie kawina[25]

Coconuts, how you used to whistle, young one from Leasowes.

24. *Parwa* trees grow in the flooded land near the sea.
25. Coronie is a district in Surinam that was brought under cultivation
only after 1800 by English and Scottish plantation owners during the interim
period of British rule. For this reason the plantations often carry British
names, like Leasowes in this poem. After emancipation the slaves of each
plantation jointly purchased the plantation from their former masters and
tried to keep it running. Consequently, Coronie remained a predominantly
Creole district, although small groups of Indonesians and Hindustani were

—Mi ben dape, Bato, gongote!
Fa den fremusu b'e lusu den srefi saka!
—Mi ben dape, Bato, gongote!
Plana, gowtu plana tapu a liba.
—Mi ben dape, Bato, gongote!
Den b'e poko, naki kaseko kon na syoro.
—Mi ben dape, Bato, gongote!
Kokronto merki b'e sweri leki Bosrokoman.
—Mi ben dape, Bato, gongote!
Leki wan gado oni nanga merki b'e rigeri.
—Mi ben dape, Bato, gongote!
Printa b'e feyri a loktu tron prasara.
—Mi ben dape, Bato, gongote!
Pantabusi b'e prati den kwikwi na ini fisi-olo.
—Mi ben dape, Bato, gongote!
Aleysi nanga watrakanu na ini den gotro.
—Mi ben dape, Bato, gongote!
Den kawinaman ay ben redi leki granaki.
—Mi ben dape, Bato, gongote!
Èn a oli b'e brenki tapu ala den skrufu.
—Mi ben dape, Bato, gongote!
Na ini kanari den skuna b'e monyo leki aleysi.
—Mi ben dape, Bato, gongote!
Gamelan nanga Tadya na ini a winti.
—Mi ben dape, Bato, gongote!
Ala di asege b'e boro den bon-ati.

I witnessed it, bato, gongote.[26]
How did not bats come flappingly down.
I witnessed it, bato, gongote.
Waves, gilded waves on the river.
I witnessed it, bato, gongote.
They are brought to a halt and then spend themselves jerkingly on the
                                                            riverbank.
I witnessed it, bato, gongote.
Milk of coconuts is extended like the bosrokoman.[27]
I witnessed it, bato, gongote.
Like deities did milk and honey the scepter sway.
I witnessed it, bato, gongote.
Spirits cascaded into the sky and were brooms.
I witnessed it, bato, gongote.
Shrubs kept the kwikwi[28] in the fishing ponds apart.
I witnessed it, bato, bongote.
Rice and watercress even in the furrows.
I witnessed it, bato, gongote.
The kawina drummers had eyes pomegranate red.
I witnessed it, bato, gongote.
And the oil glowed on all their joints.
I witnessed it, bato, gongote.
The canal was schooner-filled like mounds of rice.
I witnessed it, bato, gongote.
Gamelan and tadya carried on the wind.
I witnessed it, bato, gongote.
Meanwhile the beetle gnaws at the hearts of the trees.

---

settled there later on. Initially Coronie was only accessible by sea, and
schooners carried its products to the capital. The wealth of Coronie was
derived mainly from the cultivation of coconuts. In this poem we see coconuts
as a symbol for wealth. In later years the district deteriorated greatly. The
kawina is a popular dance.

26. This line is a good example of the almost ritual manner in which
stories are frequently interrupted by the audience. The poet has added
gongote to the original formula. This word is also used as an interruption
in a popular children's rhyme. It has a highly emotive connotation in
Surinam. It means literally "banana flour," formerly the staple diet of the
slaves.

27. Bosrokoman is the name of a little fish that swells up the moment it is
outside the water.

28. Kwikwi is a fish highly appreciated in Surinam.

29. Gamelan is the traditional music of the Indonesians. Tadya is a traditional Indian drum.

—Mi ben dape, Bato, gongote!
Drey anu fu switibonki lontu mi bere!
—Mi ben dape, Bato, gongote!
Baka den, angisa di b'e opo mi yeye.
—Mi ben dape, Bato, gongote!
Soso dati, no wan sorgu noso dyarusu trobi.
—Mi ben dape, Bato, gongote!
Èn den kaw b'e blo kwata fu soso breyti.
—Mi ben dape, Bato, gongote!
San ben libi, n'a singi fu den siksiyuru.
—Mi ben dape, Bato, gongote!

Gongote! Gongote!
Ay, gongote-bonu
nanga sten di srapu leki sewinti!
Ay, langa prasoro,
kokronto gongote-wenke na win!

EDGAR CAIRO

Wan pisi fu libi

Prakseri taki ofa a no switi fu de na mindri libisma. Fa yu ben e go
firi, efu den ben poti yu, yu wawan, na mindri fu someni swit' sani.
Yu sa wani fu didon yu wawan na tapu wan sula, nanga moy geri
èn broyn ston. Na watra e kowru yu. Na watra e datra yu ebi
prakseri. Na watra e dofu yu gi na sten fu konsensi. Efu yu sa firi
yu srefi yu wawan, dan na watra kan lekti yu srefi, opo yu, poti na
mindri soso santawan. Yu e kisi wan aparti presi. Na mindri fu den
yu kan de. Yu kan tesi na switi firi fu na santa dey. Ma yu no kan
taki nanga den, bika den no abi tongo moro fu ley. Soso farawe yu
kan si den. Mi abi na bribi taki so fasi yu no e tan wan dey na
Masra fesi. Dan yu e saka kon baka na yu sula, dorosey fu foto
b'bari. Te angri kiri yu, yu kan go na yu kampu. Tafra leki tafra e wakti
yu—ma no wan sma no de fu si. O langa yu e go tan so? Son sma e
go ori na libi disi wan wiki. Trawan wan mun langa. Wán enkri

I witnessed it, bato, gongote.
Dry peel of the sweet bean shaped into a cord around my waist.[30]
I witnessed it, bato, gongote.
And later on the kerchiefs which elevated my soul.
I witnessed it, bato, gongote.
That alone, no worry, barring a little jealousy.
I witnessed it, bato, gongote.
And the cows blew bubbles in pure delight.
I witnessed it, bato, gongote.
All that remained was the song of the cricket at the close of day.
I witnessed it, bato, gongote.

Gongote! Gongote!
O gongote, O portent[31]
with a voice sharp as the wind from the sea.
O tall parasols,
coconut gongote woman is like wine!

EDGAR CAIRO

Life

You might think that life among people isn't pleasant. How would
you feel if they had put you alone among so many delectable things?
You might want to lie down all alone in a rapid with beautiful yellow
and brown stones. The water cools you. The water heals all ponderous
thoughts. The water deafens you to the voice of conscience. If you
can feel yourself all alone you might be lifted up by the water and
placed amidst the pure and hallowed ones. One would have a separate
place. Among them it would be possible to live. One would be able
to sample the lovely feeling of the holy day. But one cannot talk to
the hallowed, because they have no tongues to lie with. One only sees
them from a distance. I believe that in this way it is only possible to
tarry before the face of God for one day. Then you would have to
descend to the rapids, far away from the din of the city. When
hunger assails you there is always the hut. What a feast awaits there
—but there is none around. How long can one stand up to it? Some
people would last for one week. Others one month. The exception

30. From the dry peels children fashion a cord that they wear round the
waist.
31. It is not quite clear whether the voice refers to "portent" or the
"crickets."

wan sa man fu libi so wan yari langa. Ma te fu kaba yu e go law.
Yu e go dede.
　　Dati meki son sma abi furu mati. Son wan abi pikinso. Ma mi
papa dati, wanwan a abi, fu taki reti, a abi wan nomo. Fu taki moro
reti, a ben abi wan. A ben de wan trutru, san den e kari: dip' bere
mati. Den tu so ben pasa skorobangi makandra. Takru nanga bun
fu wi Sranan, den ben prati. Efu foto ben e seki, den ben de na
bradyari tu, efu foto ben abi rostu, dan den srefi tu ben kowru. Edi,
na so a ben nen. Na mofo mi ben e kari en Basedi. Basedi ben de
sneyri. A ben fin'fini.
　　Wan takru sortu kosokoso di no abi kaba a ben gwenti e kisi.
Ala yuru wan pikin pisi tabaka ben e anga na en mofobuba. Mi ben
e kari dati en "tabakaworon." Te a ben tan, dan a ben ari wan dampu
fu na "lespeki tabaka." Nanga kosokoso a smoko e ari en srefi
komopo na ini en gorogoro. En mofobuba di ben srapu leki na
lanki fu wan udubaki, ben e lon wan pikinso tabaka watra. Dan
so a ben e ari en baka anu pasa. En fesi ben dipi leki gronmarki
pe pikinnengre prey. A ben gwenti tyari en wakatiki, fu di en wansey
futu no ben de leki fa gado meki di fu tra sma. Ay, Edi! Tide yu no
de moro, baya. Pe na ten go. Fa mi ben e si yu so krinkrin, tide mi
no mu si yu moro.
　　Te mi papa Nelis ben friyari, furu sma no ben e kon. Wanwan
kompe so, ben kan kon trus' ede pikinso. Ma es' esi den ben e ari
pasi, bika mi papa no ben e taki tori. A ben e sidon fow en anu na
ondro en kakumbe. Ma yu si, te Basedi ben doro, dan tori ben
dray. Now den ben de fu lo pondo. Den ben e nati den neki nanga
gindyabiri èn tesi wan mofo fiadu. Tranga sopi noyti ben e de,
bika no dringi, no smoko, mi papa ben e du. "Mi moni na mi sopi
èn mi wroko na mi smoko." Te den yonkuman fu wrokope yere
na tori disi, dan den e lafu. Dati na wan bigiman srefsrefi. Basedi
srefi ben e lafu tu nanga ala den tifi di blaka fu soso tabaka. Now
a ben de na en yuru. Nanga wan lekti geme a ben e opo en tori.
　　Sipiman di ben e kon nay krosi, noyti ben e pay. Ala fa en
uma ben owru-owru, toku den ben abi dek'ati e kon suku en. Wan
leysi wan fu den bigiskin kel opo na en tapu fu en umapikin ede.
Luku dyaso, Basedi grabu wan nefi, ma a no ben abi dek'ati,
someki a so esi leki fa a ben kan, lon go kibri na baka wan ston
peti. Di na man now—a no ben sabi na presi—dray en baka gi
Basedi, dati now fringi na wakatiki naki a man. Nanga den wortu:

would keep it up for one year. But in the end one would go mad.
One would die.

Therefore some people have lots of friends, others have few. But
my father had hardly any. To tell the truth, he had but one. To be
quite frank, he had had one. It was a real friend. What one would
call a bosom pal. They were together at school. They shared the
good and bad times of Surinam. When the city was in an uproar,
then were they also excited. When the city was calm, then were
they at ease. Edi he was called. Master Edi to me. Master Edi was a
tailor. He was very lean.

He used to get a cough that had no end. There was always a piece
of tobacco dangling from his lips. I used to call it his "tobacco worm."
He was always puffing at his very strong tobacco. Coughingly, the
smoke belched from his throat. From his lips, which were as sharp
as the edge of a wooden tray, drooled tobacco juice. He wiped the
back of his hand along them. His face was grooved like the stripes
that children leave in the earth when they play. He tried to walk
with a walking stick because one foot was not as God had made
those of other people. Oh Edi! Now you are no longer there, friend.
How time flies. I used to see you so clearly. Today I would rather
not see you any more.

When my father Nelis had his birthday, not many people turned
up. A friend or two popped in, but left soon afterward, because my
father did not like shop talk. He sat with his hands folded under his
chin. But when Master Edi came, then it was another story. Then
they made hay while the sun shone. They wetted their throats with
ginger beer and tasted a piece of the birthday cake. Never was there
any strong liquor around, because my father neither drank nor
smoked: "My money is my liquor and my work my smoke," he used
to say. When the boys at work heard this, they burst out laughing.
What a guy! Even Master Edi laughed, baring all his teeth, which were
black with the pure tobacco. Now his turn had come. With a slight
sigh he started talking.

Sailors who came to him to have their clothes sewed never paid.
Although his wife was very old, they couldn't refrain from making a
pass at her. Once one of these muscle men descended on him searching
for his daughter. Ah, look at Master Edi now! He grabbed his knife,
but he lacked guts, with the result that he ran away as soon as he
could to hide behind a stone wall. Now when the man—he did not
know the place—turned his back on Master Edi, he chucked his walking stick at him. With the words, "Come now, I shall strip you of

"Kon, mi e go puru krasi gi yu," a kari en gari, opo na nefi fu priti
na man poti na bonyogron. Na pôti matrosi ben lobi en libi, so meki
a teki diafutu. So na tori dati kon kaba.

Wan tra tori baka na fu sma di a ben gwenti nay gi. Na tan a
tan wan dey—a ben e nyan wan pisi sowtu lemki, bika korsu nomo
ben broko en mofo èn tapu en tesi—suma e broko kon dati fruku
mamanten: skowtu. SUKOWTU?! A ben weri wan pikin pisi blonsaka
ondrobruku. Es'esi a weri en bruku, en flanel bosroko, en trekbanti
èn wan gerigeri weti empi di no ben go na breki ete. Sito sito a ben
abi fu go nanga Kowlader. San ben pasa so dan? We, wan sma ben
tya krosi fu kon nay wan trowpaki. A ben si taki na krosi ben furu,
ma nanga en ay tapu na "wenste" di a ben e go meki, a no si taki
na krosi ben fufuru!

Edi gi tori, te a gi tori fa sma suku fu wisi en nanga moni. Ay,
ma a no waka leki fa na frufruktu ben prakseri! Koloku fu Edi, a
ben abi wan papamoni na ini en portumoni èn fu di leti na fesi a ben
bay lemki fu puru nanga asisi na smeri di ben kon tay fasi na en
ondro-anu, na eri wroko pori. A ben de so srefi taki na takru yeye
mandi. Fa na man e langa na moni so, so en anu tan fasi.

Ondrofeni tori ben e lolo go lolo kon te wan sani fu neygi yuru.
Dan Basedi ben e teki en felt-ati, nanga en wakatiki fu suku osopasi.
Te tra yari baka, nanga gado wani.

Te neti ben tapu, den bigisma fu mi ben e dribi den tu sturu di
den ben abi go na wan sey. Te sribi ben kiri mi, dan frukufruku
papaya ben abi fu bradi. Mi no ben kan tan arki den betiyesi tori
fu Basedi, bika na bigisma no ben lobi te pikinnengre mofo e warsi
na ini en tori efu den bradi den yesimama e arki. Yu! Dorfu ben waki
en leki paderij. Wan klapu ben sari yu! Ma mi dati a no ben kan fasi,
mi papa ben sa sorgu fu dati. Mi no ben kan sidon arki, so mi ben
e didon. Te na yuru ben doro, mi ben kan yere na wakatiki e gwe.
Tikó . . . tikótikó . . . ! Leki te yorka e prey mormo na neti.
Tikó . . . ! tikó . . . !

Dey na fesi mi ben e dren kaba taki so wan man e go kon. Na
neti dati mi pikinnengre tonton e stampu nanga tori. Ma tan mi ben

your lewdness," he wound himself up thoroughly and opened his knife
to help the man along to the graveyard. The poor sailor prized his
life and took to his heels. In this way did it end.

Another story again concerned someone for whom he used to sew.
One day he remained in bed longer than usual. He ate a salted lemon
because fever had dried his mouth and had affected his taste. And
who should stroll along on this early morning? The police. The police?!
He was wearing underpants made out of a flour bag. Quickly he put
on his flannel vest, his braces, and a type of yellow-white shirt
which had not yet been bleached. He had to go with Kowlader at
once. What had happened? Well, someone had brought along some
material from which to make a wedding suit. He had noticed that
there was a lot of material, but he was so preoccupied with his luck
that it didn't occur to him that it might have been stolen.

Edi kept on talking until he came to the story of how people
tried to bewitch him with money. But alas, it did not turn out the
way the damned guy thought it would. Luckily for Edi he had a
cowry shell in his wallet. And because he had just prior to that bought
a lemon to remove with the help of some ash the persistent odor from
his armpit nothing happened. It even happened that the evil spirit
became angry. When the man passed on the money, his hand remained
stretched out.[32]

Tales of experience rolled to and fro until about nine o'clock. Then
Master Edi took his felt hat and his walking stick to go home. Until
the following year, God be willing.

When night fell my parents pushed the two chairs to the side.
When I was sleepy the sleeping mat had to be unrolled early. I could
not stay awake to listen to Master Edi's savory stories, because the
man did not like children to interfere with the tale or prick up their
ears. You dare to look at him as if he is a circus! One smack and
you've had it. Me, he could not touch. My father would see to that.
I could not come to sit and listen, therefore I went to bed. When the
time came I could hear the walking stick going away. Tiko ... Tiko ...
Tiko ... as if spirits were playing marbles in the middle of the night.
Tiko ... Tiko.

Days ahead I dreamt that such and such would come.[33] That same
night my child's brain was buzzing with stories. Had it been possible

32. Cowry shells and lemons are used as protective medicines against
witchcraft. In this case the medicines turn the evil spirits against the user.

33. This whole passage is unreal and refers to nightmares which the child
had that night.

kan so, dan mi ben kan yagi en gwe. Te a ben opo mi, mi ben e kofu
ala en fesi, kofu ala en fesi, kofu en . . . te a no ben abi ay moro,
no noso, no mofo. Sma no ben mu sabi en moro, bikasi en wawan
ben de mi papa mati, en wawan ben sabi fu puru mi papa na mi
anu. Na a neti dati, mi no ben e sribi bun. Mi ben fasandruku.

Bakaten srefi, mi ben e kon kweki wan prakseri fa mi kan meki
na eri tori kon na wan kaba. Mi ben e ley gi na man srefi. Bakaten
Basedi siki sote. Saf'safri a no ben man wroko so bun moro. Na
kosokoso ben kon bigi en gorogoro, so meki a ben e spitispiti leki
bere-uma. Te a ben tan, a ben kan nay wan brukufutu moro bigi.
Mi papa ati ben e faya, bikasi sma ben sa prakseri taki na bimba a
abi. Leti dape mi ben wani en. Mi ben ogri. Mi ben pori. Mi no ben
lobi taki sani mu de tra fasi leki fa mi ben sa wani. So wan dey mi
bari krey kon na oso. Krosi ben pori agen. Na sneyri ben feni taki
mi e gro es'esi, èn fa mi ben langa gwe na loktu leki mansipari, a
nay den nyun skorobruku langa èn bigi. Mi e kon na ini oso so,
mi e watra! Wante mi papa ati teki faya. "Yu kan tyari na bruku go
baka. A kan ori en. A kan weri en!" Nanga dati wan kaba kon na
wan matiskap' di ben ori someni yari langa. Pe yu ben prakseri
taki na wan isrititey ben tay den tu sma, yu ley! Wan karuwiwiri
ben moro tranga!

Tide te mi e prakseri, mi e sidon saka mi ede, leki wan siki
fowru, sma mu ray san e ori mi ati so.

Edi siki. A go na at'oso. Fosi a go koti madungu. Bakaten
den ben abi fu puru en ston. Moro bakaten a ben abi fu du ete
wan koti na en manpe, ma leti dape/Fedi ben tanapu na en bedi-ede.
A komoto na nefidatra kamra, den saka en tapu na bedi, na so ba
Fedi frey na en ede wantron. No wan sma ben de fu nati en neki.

Sari na Ondrobon pe a ben e libi. A gersi na ini na wiki dati
den tamarenbon lasi moro furu wiwiri leki na ini wan eri yari. Na
a dey fu na beri, alen fadon moy fu en sey. Ala den krepsi ben
nati. Den ben gersi tingifowru. Koloku fu Edi. Mi papa waka na
en baka.

I would have chased him away. When he picked me up I beat him in
the face with my fists, struck him . . . until he had no eyes, no nose,
no mouth. I did not want him to be recognizable any more, because
he was my father's only friend. He alone could take my father away
from me. On this night I did not sleep so well.[34]

Later on I had an idea how to solve the problem. I even blackened
the man. Afterward Master Edi became very sick. As time went by
he could not work so well any more. His throat became so raw with
coughing that he vomited like a pregnant woman. It would happen
that he made the one leg of the trouser bigger than the other. My
father was angry, because people would think he had a swollen leg.[35]
This was where I wanted him. I was naughty. I was spoilt. I did not
want things to be different from the way I wanted them. Consequently
I came home crying one day. Once more the clothes were wrongly
cut. The tailor found that I was growing fast, and because I was
reaching for the sky like a mansipari,[36] he sewed the new school
trousers long and wide. I entered the house crying. All of a sudden
my father became very angry. "You can take back the trousers. He
can keep them. Let him wear them himself." Thus a friendship which
had lasted so long came to an end. If you had thought that an iron
cord bound these two together, then you were wrong. Corn silk
appeared to be stronger.

Now when I think back on it, I sit with my head bowed like a sick
bird. People don't know what depresses me so.

Edi was sick. He went to the hospital. First they operated on his
scrotum. Then they had to remove his testicles. Still later they
operated on his penis. But by then death winked at him. He came
from the operating room. They put him on the bed and at the same
time death got hold of him. There was no human being to give him
a draught of water.

It was sad at Ondrobon where he lived. It seemed as if the tamarind
trees lost more leaves in that week than in a whole year. On the day
of the funeral the rain added its portion. All the pallbearers were
thoroughly soaked. They looked like vultures. Edi was lucky. My
father was following the bier.

34. The expression *mi ben fasandruku* is left untranslated. The expression
is unknown to us but perhaps refers to a restless, nervous sleep.

35. Many inhabitants of Paramaribo formerly had legs swollen by elephanti-
asis.

36. We do not know what *mansipari* means. It may be a species of tree or
grass. It is used here to refer to a tall, thin youth.

Tide disi, Nelis e kosi den yonkuman fu en wrokope. Den e
teki den yesi èn arki. Dan wante so, wan lafu e broko kon tapu
den fesi. A no spotu. Na man disi na wan trutru man. Efu yu bigin
fu diki na ini en tori fu wrokope, yu e si dati a no lesi. A no e naki
wan bita nanga no wan fu den. Te den kon na wroko, dan a dape
kaba. Efu na seybi yuru a mu dape, teri tapu yu tin finga taki
siksi yuruten a dape kaba. Fu taki leti, den sabi en leki wan trutru
papa. Ma bigisma abi wan sani e taki dati kon waka nanga kon libi
a no wan. San di yu no si fu karu-wiwiri faya, na dati de leti so!
Na fu yu teki ay luku moro betre. So tu furu fu den yonkuman
no sabi, taki na lafu di mi papa e lafu, a no wan gron-ati lafu.

Te a de na oso, dan eri dey a e tapu en srefi na ini kamra. Dan
wan tapuskin a e ari tapu fu en bigindoy kon miti en ede wiwiri.
Te a de furfuru na strati, yuru no e teri gi en fu a kon na oso. Sonte
a e syen gi en srefi. Mi sabi den sortu sma di tan leki den yeye gwe
libi den. Wan grani papa leki en srefi e koti wiwiri gi en. Den tu
sabi den srefi leki tu finga fu wan anu. Dan so na tori e lolo tu.
Umatori no de na ini - ala fa na mi e prakseri dati. Tori fu ondrofeni
e waka. Fa libi kon diri. Fa den otopasi e furu dey na dey. Fa wan
sma mu tyari en srefi na ini na libi fu disiten. Dan . . . fu wan
momenti, mi papa sa wani opo en mofo, opo en gorogoro go te
na ini en ati fu bari fa problema e knufta en. Man na man! Ma ini
na afersi disi, man no man du fa a sa wani. A sani e trowe wan
span, wan ede-ati gi en. Fa Nelis kibri en srefi ini na makti bigi
sturu, a sa wani fu na skuma gro . . . gro . . . gro fu tapu en fesi.
Wan bergi. Wan bun bigi bergi fu tapu na winti fu en bro. A gersi
na sèm nefi sa koti en gorogoro . . . na lampu sa breni en. Faya . . .
na kamra e faya. A e opo gwe so esi leki a kan na ini na kowru
neti. Farawe wan sma e lafu. A e teki bro.

Mi papa no lobi mi moro. A no lobi mi mama tu. A no lobi mi
mama pikin tu. Mi tanta dati, fu mi mamasey, a no lobi srefsrefi.
Famiri fu papasey di e seni suku pikin gebroke a e yagi. "Meki
den suku masra efu go na lansigron! Mi no ben opo fraga seni
kari no wan sma!" Wan leysi wan famiri seni kari en fu kon na wan
fesa. Ma di na wan omu fu Nelis ben erken na lutu fu na famiri
dati, sobu fu di den no ben de trutru famiri, en ati teki faya.

Lately Nelis rails at the young laborers where he works. They
listen attentively to him. Then they suddenly laugh. Without being
funny, this man is a real man. If you observe his manner of working
closely, you will see that he is not lazy. He does not accompany
any of them for a drink. When they arrive at work, he is already
there. When he has to be there at 7 o'clock, count on it that he'll be
there at 6 o'clock. In truth, they know him like a real father. But
as the older people say: "There's more to a person than meets the
eye." It's what you don't see through the fire of corn husks that
causes the fire. You would have to look more closely. Therefore
many of these youngsters didn't know that my father's smile was not
from his heart.

When he was at home, he locked himself up in his room the whole
day long and pulled a blanket over his head. When he was in the mood
for an outing, he never paid heed to time, nor did he come home. Perhaps he was ashamed of himself. I know people who look as if their
spirit had deserted them. A man of his age used to cut his hair. They
knew each other like two fingers. They had many things to tell each
other. To my knowledge, they never spoke about women. They exchanged common experiences—that life has become so expensive,
that the streets are becoming increasingly fuller, how to cope with
present-day life.

Then at a certain point my father wanted to open his mouth, to
reveal his heart, to give vent to all his pent-up feelings. A man is only
a man, and in these things a man can't let himself go as he wishes. It
gave him tension and headaches. When Nelis planted himself in the
big and mighty chair, then he would have wanted the foam to grow,
grow, grow until it covered his whole face. A mountain, a mountain
to cover his breath. It seems as if the razor blade will cut his throat . . .
as if the lamp will blind him. It's hot, the room is hot. He stands up
as soon as it is possible and disappears into the cool night. In the
distance someone laughs. He takes a breath.

My father doesn't love me any more. He doesn't love my mother
either, nor does he love her children. My aunt on my mother's side,
he can't stand her at all. He sends away his own relations when they
come to ask for something. "Let them look for a man or go to the
almshouse. I have no flag at the mast inviting people to come and
fetch something." Once a member of the family invited him to a
feast. But because one of Nelis's uncles had recognized this branch
of the family,[37] so that, as far as he was concerned, they were not

37. In Surinam one can officially "recognize" a child, which makes him a

"Mi dati no bay famiri! Mi no sabi fu san ede den piki ebi poti na wi tapu!" Nanga dati a tori kaba. Na tanta di mi taygi yu taki a no lobi srefsrefi, na Kombe a e libi. Yere fa tori waka.
Na en kweki mi mama. Te a kon bigi. Fatu uma nanga bigi gogo so! Den sipiman di ben e komopo na Bedyan ben lobi mi mama. Sweet Mary, na so den ben e kari en, te a ben e go seri blokmowtu nanga tra sani moro gi den. Efu wanwan leysi den ben e fasfasi Sweet Mary, mi no ben de fu si. Efu den ben e pingi en gogo? A sa de so. Tronsu, yu mu sabi taki fu eri grontapu, efu yu kon na Sranan, dan nengre no abi noti. Ma san nengre tyari srefsrefi na: gogo! Wan tra tanta fu mi ben tya dati mor' ogri. Kande dati meki en nanga mi papa ben abi wan sani bakabaka. Na tori ben de so faya, taki na wenke ben e kon tan na ini oso ala fa mi mama ben de na uma fu na oso. Ma a ben loli. A ben logologo. A no ben abi dek' ati fu poti wan sma tap' strati. Mi yere dati di mi ben de na bere, mi mama ben sidon na sey oso e fanga winti. Fa a ben dungru so, dan a ari en yapon go pikinso na loktu, meki winti kan way fri kon na en ondrobere. Yere a yere wan sani fadon na en sey. A luku. Wan fu den fosten triki-isri dompu en srefi gi doti. Sma no ben de fu si na a sodro fensre. Ma mi mama kon sabi dati na a wenke ben suku fu kiri en, na ini en dyarusu. Ay, na didibri. A kisi en payman tu. Mi no sabi san pasa so soyfri, ma mi yere taki na busbusi den kon puru en nanga wan yonkuman. Lantiwagi ben abi fu tyari den gwe. Den no ben man lusu. Sma taki dati na wisi den wisi en fu di a ben de en wroko fu e teki sma man. Trawan taki dati na ini den krasi, den go didon leti pe wan akantamasu de, someki a strafu den. Mi no sabi suma mi mu bribi, ma mi sabi dati a feni en payman: suma du bun, na en nen; suma du ogri, na en nen!
Soleki fa mi taki, mi abi wan tanta na Kombe. En oso furu nanga gado prenki. A e strey leti kandra nanga kerki. Efu a kindi fu begi, a e fadon na sribi èn sofasi a e strey begi nanga pastoru, te kon miti wan sani fu mindri neti. Dan en skin e fasi. "E . . . e . . . e . . . mi yongudey gwe libi mi kaba!" A e dren ete dati wan bun dey wan sma sa du en na bun fu te a tapu wan bigi yari,

really family, he became angry. "I did not buy family. I don't understand why they cause us this trouble." And that was that.

As I've said, the aunt for whom he had no love lived in Combe. Listen to what happened. She took care of my mother until she grew up. A fat woman with a big bottom! The sailors who came from British Guyana loved my mama. "Sweet Mary" they called her when she came to sell delicacies to them. I was not there to see whether sometimes they did not make a pass at Sweet Mary, whether they did not pinch her bottom. Probably they did. In Surinam the negroes have nothing, but bottoms they certainly have in abundance.

Another of my aunts had an even bigger one! Perhaps for this reason there was something between her and my father. Things went so far that the girl came to live with us, even though my mother was the woman of the house. But my mother was weak. She did not have the guts to chuck someone out on the street. I have heard that when my mother was expecting me she sat on the side of the house, to catch the breeze. Because it was already dark, she pulled up her dress so that the wind could cool her belly. And then, dammit all, she heard something fall next to her. She looked. One of those old-fashioned irons had fallen to the ground. No one around in the window above, but my mother knew that the girl had tried to murder her out of sheer jealousy.

She's a devil and has got her deserts. I don't know exactly what happened, but I've heard that they fetched her and a youth from the bush. They had to transport them in an ambulance. They could not be separated. People say that she was bewitched because she specialized in stealing other women's husbands. Others say that in their lechery they went to lie precisely on the place where there was an akantamasu,[38] so that he had punished them. I don't know who to believe, but I know that she got what was coming to her: a person will reap what he sows.

As I've said, I have an aunt in Combe. Her house was filled with religious pictures. She vies with the church in the lighting of candles. When she kneels to pray, she falls asleep. In this manner she vies in prayer with the priest until about midnight. Her body then was benumbed: "E . . . e . . . e . . . I'm not so young any more." She still dreams that one day someone will do her a favor on a big anniversary

---

legal member of the family, although, from a biological point of view, he may not belong to the family at all.

38. *Akantamasu* is an evil spirit that lives in anthills.

a sa yuru wan syesi èn tyari en waka eri foto! Dan te a kon na oso,
piyano den mu prey gi en. Setdansi èn lanchey mu de na neti dati.
Na tanta lay trefu moro wis' man. Moro a e owru, moro a e bay
gowtu sani, bika na en yeye wani so. Wan bun dey yu sabi
umasma kaba, den no kan pasa wan sma di den sabi bun, sondro
fu dyompo kon na ini—mi mama go na mi tanta. Den taki den
tori sote, te a kon wan pisi. Now mi mama memre taki a ben abi
wan brifi nanga en, di a ben mu tyari go na mi papa wrokope. Na
man no ben wani go moro na wroko, bika na wroko ben kon ebi.
Di mi mama no ben sabi leysi kaba, so a gi tanta na brifi. Dati
no du moro leki reti, a dyompo na ini en frigikasi, teki en swarfu
èn bron na brifi. A taki wan tu moy mofo di mi no kan taygi yu
baka! Ala na ten dati, mi papa sidon na oso e wakti. En gogo e
faya, bika a e prakseri taki den e go gi na uma wan pikin gebroke.
Di dati doro so . . . d . . . , dan tori ben pori. Wan eri pisi ten den
no taki. Mi papa ori mi mama na ati. Dey langa a no ben e taki wan
wortu. A ben swa leki asin. Mi mama, kontrari, ben e suku taki ala
yuru. A no ben abi trobi fu bori tra nyanyan, te mi papa ben
trowe na fosiwan. Den tu sma ben kan go na Thalia go prey toneri,
fa den ben e meki.

San di tyari den kon taki, na wan toko di wan fu den prasiuma,
Syako, ben abi nanga en masra. A ben de fu wan tra wenke ede.
Syako ben abi wan fowru. So na tra uma ben abi kweki tu. Den
tu fowru ben gersi. Wan tu dey bifo Bedaki, na uma saka en
fowru na pan. Nanga ala en blakapepre èn nowtumuskati a smuru
a titi. Tantan . . . a yere wan sma e krutu. Na Syako. Nofo Syako
ben abi na sma na ati kaba, a no skuru en bowtu gi en! Ala sortu
mama! Disi nomo, bika na wenke ben teki na tra fowru leki di fu
en. Na eri mamanten, na so a toko waka. Go ari, go trusu. Na wenke
no du moro leki reti fu saka na eri pan gi Syako. Ma a gersi taki na
pikin di ben bigi Syako bere, ben lostu sutu faya, bika a teki na
eri pan so trowe gi dagu. Dan leti Syako masra komopo na wroko.

and hire a cab to take her for a ride around town.[39] And when she
returns home someone must play the piano for her. And on the same
night there should be square and barn dances.

My aunt harbors more taboos than a witch doctor. The older she
becomes, the more she buys golden trinkets, because her soul demands
it of her. One day, you know how women are, they can't pass by a
close acquaintance without popping in, my mother went to visit my
aunt. She sat talking for a while. Then my mother remembered that
she had a small note which she had to deliver at my father's place
of work. The man did not want to go to his work because he found
it hard. Because my mother couldn't read, she gave the note to my
aunt. She straight away went to the cupboard containing the provisions, took her matches and set fire to the note. She mumbled some
nice chants which I can't repeat to you. All this time my father was
waiting at home. He was sitting on hot coals because he thought they
would give some money to his wife. When she came home the fat was
in the fire. For a long time they exchanged no words. My father held
it against my mother. For days on end he uttered no word. He was
as sour as vinegar. My mother on the other hand tried very hard to
make up to him again. She had no objection to prepare other food,
if my father threw away the first dish. The way they behaved, the two
could have gone to act on the stage of the Thalia.[40]

The thing which caused them to be on speaking terms again was a
quarrel which one of the women of the yard, Syako, had with her
husband. It was about another woman. Syako owned a chicken. The
other also had one. The two chickens resembled each other. A few
days before Christmas the other woman started to prepare her chicken,
with all her black pepper and nutmeg. She stewed the chicken. Hold
on! . . . she heard someone abusing her. It was Syako. Syako had disliked her for a long time, but had never come to blows with her.
Everybody's mother's intimate parts were heard in the air.[41] Only because she had taken the wrong chicken. The quarrel lasted the whole
morning. Now the one had the upper hand, now the other. The woman
boldly pushed the whole pan into Syako's hands. But it seemed as if
the child in Syako's womb wanted to fan the fire, for she took the whole
pan and chucked it to the dogs. Precisely at that point Syako's husband

39. Every five years the so-called "big birthday" is celebrated, with more
festivities than the ordinary birthday party.
40. The Thalia is a well-known theater in Paramaribo.
41. Many common terms of abuse refer to the intimate parts of the mother
of the abused.

Na son ben faya. A trowe en baysigri na wan sey, grabu wan bowtu
san den ben poti nomo fu e kiri alata, èn seti lon na Syako baka.
Syako na ini en bradyari, opo futu! Na tan wi tan, un ben e konkru
pikinso, wi yere wan prit'bere bari. Na srefi momenti dati, na doro
broko opo. Wan emre watra naki trowe. Mi mama ben e krin kat'fisi.
Ala na watra fadon na Syako tapu, Syako, di broko kon na ini! Wi
yere wan sani naki na skotu so bow! Na a kodya. Na fasi fa na
wenke skreki, mi denki taki bakaten na pikin di a ben abi na bere
ben e go babaw. Den sma fu mi kon wasi Syako wan swit'watra. Den
kari en kra kon baka (so wan katiwatra). Na bere den ari nanga
abomafatu, di ben de na ini wan kastrolibatra. Na mi brada ben
koti en fu wan dyuka. Baka di na toko kowru, mi fruwondru. Mi
si dati den bigisma fu mi ben e taki baka leki noti no ben pasa. Ay
baya, nowtu nanga dede e tyari lobi kon.

Mi papa no ben lobi mi tanta, te dati kon dede. Ma di nowtu
naki un, pe un ben abi fu saka un tere? Leti dape! Wan bun tanpe
a no ben de, ma toku wi ben kan kibri un ede gi son nanga alen.
Te den ogri boy fu na birti ben e pasa, leti dape den ben e fringi
ston. Ala san den ben si na kino, leti dape den ben e kon du dati
baka, someki un no ben abi rostu. Efu yu poti, fu eksempre, pomerak
na strati, te yu kon baka, yu kan kisi wan gebre! Mi gudu! Ma na
baki dati no e kon baka! No nanga skowtu! Er'eri baki nanga swit'-
sani den ben kan lekti puru tapu yu ede. Gowtu sani na skin den
no ben e teri, funamku den Yampaneysi di ben e weri gowtusani
na ini den ede wiwiri. Kru nanga kru ben e feti.

Den bigisma fu mi no ben e tan dape. Den ben e tan na
Saramakastrati. Ala dey mi ben e tyari nyanyan go gi den. Na oso
fu den ben pikin. Dat' meki moro betre mi kan taki fu wan kampu,
wan afdaki. A no ben abi noti na ondro den senki, di ben e meki
wan sortu dri-uku nanga wan pikin loyki na bakasey. Te son ben
faya, yu no ben kan tan na tapu sodro efu yu no ben wani losi.

came back from his work. The sun was hot. He threw his bicycle
aside, picked up an iron bar used for killing rats, and ran after Syako.
In her excitement Syako took to her heels. While we sat gossiping
we heard a blood-curdling yell. At the same moment the door was
thrown open. A pail of water fell over. My mother was busy cleaning
catfish. All the water fell on Syako, who had entered unexpectedly.
We heard something falling against the partition. Bam! It was the
iron bar. The woman had such a fright that I think the child she
carried in her womb was bound to be dumb.

My parents bathed Syako in perfumed water. They recalled her
soul. No wonder, with all this catfish water on her.[42] They rubbed
her belly with boa fat which was in a caster oil bottle. My brother
had got it from a Djuka. After the quarrel I was amazed. I saw my
parents talking again as if nothing had happened. Yes, trouble and
death cement everything.

My father didn't love my aunt until she died. But when we were
in trouble, where were we forced to run to? Right there. It wasn't
the best solution, still we could find shelter there against the sun
and rain. When the hooligans in the area came along, they pelted
precisely this place with stones. Everything they saw in the cinema
they put into practice there, with the result that we had no peace
of mind. If, for example, you place some pomerak[43] on the side
of the road and you return a little later, it may drive you crazy, but
the tray is lost, my dear! Even the police can't help you. They would
steal the whole tray of nice things from your head. They had no
respect for the golden things on your body. Certainly not for the
Javanese who carry golden things in their hair. Gang and gang were
up against each other.

My parents did not stay there. They went to live at Saramacca
Street.[44] Daily I took food to them. Their house was small. For this
reason it's better to call it a hovel. There was nothing under the
corrugated iron, which formed a kind of triangle with a small opening
at the back. When the sun shone fiercely you could not sit above

42. Catfish is a taboo for many Creoles.

43. *Pomerak* is a pear-shaped purple fruit displayed for sale on the sidewalk.
The boys steal not only the fruit but also the wooden tray it is displayed on.

44. The story is not very clear at this point. The author first mentions that
the family had to live with the despised aunt in Combe (one of the quarters of
Paramaribo), and then says that the parents were living in Saramacca Street
(in another quarter of the town). Probably the boy (or children) stayed with
the aunt, who also prepared food for the parents.

Te na neti ben kowru, dan yu ben kowru leki dow. Tronsu, no wan
fu un no ben kan sribi tapu sodro. A ben e spuku, someki un puru
na trapu poti na dorosey. Na baka-oso yu ben abi wan sortu skotu
di mi ben meki fu kisiplanga, di mi go tan dape. Mi tapu en nanga
wan pisi seyri. Dati ben mu de wan was'oso. Na fosi dey di mi doro,
a ben de so fremder.

Memre wan skumaker bakadyari nanga soso pispis' leri. Broko
susu fu sma nanga kron futu, ala so ben de dape. Na trasey, yu ben
abi wan pindamiri pe dokun ben e meki. Dán baka yu ben abi wan
samiri di ben e kon trowe saksi de. Wan bun bigi mopebon ben
tanapu na prasi nanga wan pikin kumakoysi na ondro. A peti ben
de wan bari. So mi broko go na inisey. Foroysi ben de gadri, botri,
nyankamra, kari kon, ala sani wantron. Na bakadina ben lati pikinso,
someki un no tan langa fu go sribi. Mi bradi wan mamyo, papaya
srefi mi no ben abi. Mindrineti mi yere den sma fu mi e rigeri. Mi
prakseri taki bigisma mu lobi fa a fiti, so mi no ben abi noti fu
taki. Eri neti mi no sribi. Maskita! Mamanten di mi opo, mi si mi
skin lay nanga soso kundu-kundu. Ray san ben de na "duman?"
Fyo-fyo! Dat' meki den suma fu mi ben e rigeri so. Noti moro. Den
ben didon tapu wan gaba di ben lay fyofyo. Den kunsu-ede ben
weti fu eksi soso. Pe mi ben didon, den planga fu na gron ben abi
nâti. Den "doysri" now, ben e gwe go kibri na ondro na oso. Te
neti dan den be e lusu kon na doro leki den law. Ma mi du den
wan at' sani. Mi sorgu teki wan seyri, koti en opo moy, èn nay den
edesey sofasi, taki mi ben kan meki wan amaka. Ma mi ben drey èn
langa gwe na loktu leki manspari. Di mi wiki na tra mamanten tu,
mi no ben man opo. Eri neti mi ben didon fow mi srefi. Maskita!
Te na mira srefi ben abi wan sani fu kon suku.

Den taki dati te ay e lon watra, noso e lon en tu. Ma di mi ben
e feti nanga den someni problema disi, mi papa no ben e bada en
srefi moro, san di wani, efu san di no wani pasa nanga mi. A no
langa baka dati di un feni oso. Na tanta fu Saramakastrati dede.
Now mi mama feni wan tu sani baka! Na tori fu mi papa na dat'sey
kon moro ogri. Toku, fu di sensi den seti libi den ben didon na gron,
èn fu di den feni owru bedi, ala tu ben breyti. Mi mama lafu. Mi
papa no ari en fesi. Na bedi ben bigi. A ben lay wan l'lo kopro
pranpran. Fu tyari en go tapu na plata sodro, mi ben abi fu koti na
tapsey pisi komoto. Den feri ben kon ari, sodati na planga den
bigisma fu mi ben abi fu poti. Bigin bigin mi papa ati ben e bron. A
ben e fow en srefi go te na ini wan uku. Ma na mama fu mi, ke pôti
a no ben gwenti, ben e fadon-fadon. Bakaten mi papa kon teki

unless you wanted to be roasted. When it was cold at night you became as cold as dew. As a matter of fact, none of us could close an
eye in the loft. It was haunted there, so that we removed the ladder
and put it outside. At the back of the house there was a sort of protection which I made from planks when I came to live there. I put
a piece of canvas over it. It was supposed to be the bathroom. The
first day I came there it was so strange.

Imagine a shoemaker's backyard full of bits of leather. Club-footed
people's old shoes, all this type of rubbish was there. On the other
side of the house was a mill where peanut butter was made. Farther
to the back was a sawmill which had deposited sawdust there. A
tremendous mope tree stood on the plot with a small toilet under
it. Instead of a well there was a water barrel. The front of the house
consisted of a porch, kitchen, and dining room, all in one. So I came
to live there. It was already late, so that we didn't stay up too long.
I spread a cloth for a blanket. I didn't even have a sleeping mat. In
the night I heard my parents making a lot of noise. I thought that
grownups should know for themselves how to make love. It wasn't
my affair. I did not sleep that night.

Mosquitoes! When I woke up in the morning, I was covered with
lumps. Just guess what caused it. Bugs! It was for this reason that
my parents had been so restless, no other. They lay on a mattress
which was filled with bugs. Their pillow was white with bug eggs.
The floor planks had seams where I lay. The vermin hid under the
house. At night they looked like madmen. But I paid them back in
kind. I saw to it that I had a piece of canvas, cut it open and sewed
the ends in such a way that I could turn it into a hammock. But I
was thin and long like a manspari. When I woke up the following
morning, I couldn't get up. The entire night I lay folded up. Mosquitoes!
Even ants pestered one.

People say that it never rains but it pours. While I was struggling
with all these problems, my father never bothered one bit about me.
Not so long afterward we found a house. My aunt in Saramacca Street
died. Now my mother inherited a few things. Things seemed worse
on my father's side. Still, because they slept on the ground ever since
they started to live together and because they now got an old bed,
they were happy. My mother laughed, my father showed no emotion.
The bed was big. It was covered with copper decorations. In order to
get it to the loft I had to cut off part of it. The springs were worn out,
so that my parents had to put some planks on it. In the beginning my
father was angry. He curled himself up in a corner. But my mother,
poor soul, she wasn't used to it and kept falling off. Later on my

gwenti so, dati ala fa son ben e faya, a ben e tan didon tapu na
sodro. So wan pinaten, te lampugrasi srefi, te a ben broko, nanga
papira un ben e tapu na wansey gi winti. So wan pinaten. Nelis ben
sa mu abi wan ati fu ston, fu weygri so wan sani. Wan switi bedi
fu wan switi uma, na dati ben de wan fu den sani di a ben angri
gi someni langa. A no tru? Now en popki fu en ati ben sidon.

Eri foto lay nanga wrokope. Wan wrokope de, pe a e go de taki
wan man e wroko dritenti yari dape kaba. A no dri dey. So wan
dey na fu opo yu yeye, fu tagi Masra tangi, taki a tirtyari yu so
langa. Na man na mi papa. Ma dorfu opo na tori nanga en. "A
no de fanowdu fu sma kon sabi. Mi no ben go na wroko fu kon
na koranti," Nelis e piki. A no lobi op' opo kwetkweti. "Mi papa,
yu e go gi wan bigi poku no?" "Ayi, na so mi taki yèrè." Efu a
yere yu e taki na tori, a e bari: "Ak, no bari so tranga!—dan en
srefi e bari—a betre yu pay brotyasti en, efu poti en na konkruman
tongo! No wan enkri boda no e ori dya. Fu san so dan? Yu meki
en tide, yu meki en tamara. Tra tamara yu ari futu!" Nanga dati
a tapu na tori. Ay baya, trutru mi papa, mi no kon sabi yu.

Fa a de, awinsi yu abi wan alenkran na ini was'oso, nomo
nomo a sa tan wasi nanga en beki. Èn no dorfu taki, fu eksempre,
te mofoyari e kon so, fu go skuru en wasbeki. A e kisi wan atibron
gi yu, dati yu e aksi yu srefi efu tangi de na grontapu ete. A no
abi trobi fu naki na beki fow. En wanwan mu abi wán tepatu,
wán nyanyanpreti nanga so moro na in' oso.

Luku fa a tranga! Luku fa a swaki, luku fa a de libisma. Na
man di kan tanapu drikwarti yuru fesi wan singidosu nanga wan
babari-oloysi na ini en anu, nomo fu fanga na joysti yuru bifo a
go na waka.

Na man di e boro wrokope so fruku, no e rostu, bika te sirene
e bari, doro e bradi opo fu swari wrokoman, a sa wani fu lon, lon,
lon, ala den doro, ala den kamra, kibri en fesi, en baka, en skin,
lon ala den trapu, den oposaka, teki wan sikiman wagi, wan
skowtu-oto, opo sirene, bari, bari, krin en ati gi eri grontapu. . . .

father got used to it, so that he went to lie upstairs even when the
sun was shining. Such poverty! We even had to plaster the glass of
the oil lamp with paper when it was broken as a protection against
the wind. Such poverty! Nelis would have had a heart of stone to
refuse such a thing. A nice bed for a sweet woman, that was one of
the things for which he had yearned for such a long time. True or
not true? Something to his heart's content.

There were so many places to work in town, but there is only one
where a man had worked for thirty years. Not three days. That is
something to rejoice about, to praise God that He granted you this
for such a long time. That man was my father. But just dare to speak
about it. "People have nothing to do with it. I did not go and work
to get publicity," Nelis answered them. He disliked being cock of
the walk. "Father, you're going to hold a big feast, aren't you?"[45]
When he heard someone saying that, he called out, "Oh, don't shout
like that"—he himself was shouting—"Why don't you broadcast it or
spread it among the gossips? There won't be any feast here. What for?
You're successful today, you're successful tomorrow, the day after
tomorrow you're on the street." With this he put an end to it. Yes,
yes, truly father, how I came to know you.

He was such a type that if you had a tap in your bathroom, even
then he would still use only a bowl. And don't dare to scrub his bowl
at New Year, for example. Then he became so angry that you wondered
whether there was still gratitude left in this world. He was capable
of crushing the bowl. In the house he had a teapot all to himself, a
plate all to himself, and many other things.

See how strong he is, how weak he is, how human he is. The man
who could stand for three-quarters of an hour in front of the radio
with an alarm clock in his hand only to find out the right time before
he goes out; the man who arrived at his work so early, allowed himself
no time for pausing because when the siren goes off and the gates open
up to suck in the workers, then he would have run, run, run through
all the doors, all the rooms, conceal his head, his back, his body, run
up all the stairs, take all the elevators, take an ambulance, a police car,
put on the siren, yell, yell, pour out his heart to the whole world.

45. We have left untranslated the ironic reaction of the father, *"Ayi, na
so mi taki yèrè"* ("Of course, that is what I said"). This reaction does not fit
in with the next line.

The Origin of Surinam Creole

A *creole* language must by definition have its origin in a pidgin language (Hall 1966:xii). A *pidgin* originates in a situation in which no communication is possible in any of the existing mother tongues. In these circumstances, people try to communicate in one of the available languages (usually the language of the power group), although they have no opportunity to acquire a good command of it. A reduced, simplified language arises that is used only in restricted situations: in trading, in the market, in the factory, on the plantation, or in the army. In all other situations—at home, in religious ceremonies, in court, in education—the mother tongue is still used. Thus a pidgin has a restricted use and may be regarded as a reduced language when compared to the model from which it arose.

The process of reduction can be studied if one knows both the model language and its reduced pidgin form. The trade language employed between Trio Indians and Djuka bushnegroes can be regarded as a pidginized form of the creole mother tongue of the Djuka. Not much is known about this pidgin. De Goeje (1908:204-19) gives a short word list and some expressions. These few examples show that the vocabulary of the model language has been reduced in a more or less systematic way. The Djuka interrogative *sama* (who?) broadened its range of application to include also 'what?', 'which?', 'when?', and 'why?'. The Djuka demonstrative *disi* (this) is also used as the third person singular pronoun and as the adverb 'here.' The unmarked member of a pair of relational terms is taken from Djuka (in the case of adjectives with the addition of an 'essive' Trio suffix = *mee*), and the marked member adds the Trio negation *wa* ('no,' 'not'):

lánga-mee (far)	*lánga-mee wa* (not far, close by)
mooi-mee (beautiful)	*mooi-mee wa* (ugly)
hebi, hebee (heavy)	*hebee wa* (not heavy, light)

It seems as if the agents of the language change (the Trio in this case) reduced the vocabulary of Djuka at the expense of grammatical morphemes, which they took from their own language. This must be the basis of the concept of language mixing so often referred to in connection with pidgins.

A creole language develops from a pidgin as it becomes the native language of a group. If people speaking different mother tongues begin to intermarry and form a single community (as was the case, for example, when slaves of different origins were brought together on a plantation), and if a particular pidgin is the common language of this community, it will become the mother tongue of the children of mixed-language marriages and eventually of the whole community (though not of groups who do not intermarry with the others, such as the white settlers). As soon as this pidgin becomes the native language of a group, it must be used in many more situations than when it was only a contact language between people who had their own native languages, and we may thus assume that it undergoes a process of expansion to meet the new demands on it.

It is not possible to prove the reality of such a process in a direct way, because with the promotion of a pidgin to a creole status the pidgin ceases to exist. We can, however, find indirect evidence of it if, during the period of creolization, the speakers no longer had access to the original model language of the pidgin. This might be the cause of a remarkable distribution in the Zambuangeño lexicon of Spanish- and Philippine-based elements. Frake (1971) was struck by the fact that in this language a significantly greater number of un-marked lexical items had a Spanish origin and a significantly greater number of marked lexical items a Philippine origin. One must assume that, during the pidgin stage of Zambuangueño, the lexicon contained mainly unmarked lexical items and during the process of creolization, when the speakers no longer had access to the Spanish model, the marked items were added.

It is not, or not yet, possible to prove that the same development happened in Surinam Creole, although there is reason to believe that this language had a Portuguese pidgin origin and was creolized in contact with English.

Surinam Creole (also called Negro-English) is clearly an English-based Creole. In studying the origin of a large group of Creole verbs, the following results were obtained (Voorhoeve 1970):

English origin	Dutch origin	Portuguese origin	African origin	Unknown origin	Total
211	190	24	8	43	476

The influence of English is greater than this table suggests. The verbs of English origin are often very basic verbs, e.g. 'go,' 'come,' 'walk,' 'talk,' 'sleep,' 'want,' etc., certainly more so than the verbs of

Dutch origin. Verbs of African origin may also be basic, e.g. *nyam* 'to eat,' *fom* 'to beat,' *fufuru* 'to steal,' *koso* 'to cough,' *gonggosa* 'to gossip.' The same holds true for verbs of Portuguese origin, e.g. *sabi* 'to know,' *kaba* 'to finish,' *pina* 'to be poor,' *pasa* 'to pass.'

Surinam was under British rule for only sixteen years (1651-67). It is not absolutely necessary for the language of administration to serve as a model in the development of a pidgin or creole. The creole of Trinidad is French-based, although Trinidad has never been under French rule (Thomas 1869). The early history is of extreme importance. This type of language is used to try to bridge a communication gap between different components of the population. Once established, the language survives as long as it serves a useful purpose. It is therefore important to know as precisely as possible the growth of the population and the relative size of the different components during the formative period. The documents are often not very clear, and a certain amount of conjecture is necessary. Let me try to summarize the main facts (see also the population figures in the introduction, p. 3):

In 1661 there must have been about 1000 Europeans in the colony. In 1665 an epidemic eliminated many. Two hundred settlers left the colony that year, but 200 Portuguese Jewish planters from Cayenne, possibly with their own slaves, settled in Surinam. The colony was captured by the Dutch in 1667, recaptured by Barbados that same year, but handed back to the Dutch in 1668 in accordance with the terms of the peace treaty of 1667. Before Surinam was handed over, 67 of the most important English planters emigrated from the colony with 412 slaves. In 1671 a group of 517 people left the colony, followed in 1675 by a group of 250 whites with 980 slaves. In 1680 the last group of 102 Englishmen and slaves left, leaving only 39 Englishmen behind. The English planters were not allowed to take the slaves acquired under Dutch rule out of the colony, which meant that the ones who left were mainly the old slaves.

There are not many clues to the language of the slaves when they arrived from Africa. Slaves as far south as Angola were probably among the first groups (Daeleman 1973). The main contact language on the African coast in these early days was a Portuguese pidgin, although its influence was already declining in the seventeenth century. A distinction between old slaves (acquired before 1667) and new slaves (acquired after that date) seems important. After 1667 a rapidly increasing number of new slaves was brought in, and they soon outnumbered the old ones; this was already the case in 1671. The departure of the experienced slaves with the best command of English after 1671 forces us to assume that the original Surinam pidgin had already become firmly established among the slaves by about 1675. If this had not been so, it would have been impossible for the old slaves to pass on an English heritage to the new ones.

This short formation period (1651-80) might give rise to the hypothesis that an English pidgin had already been acquired by the slaves in Africa. There is no historical support for the existence of an English pidgin in Africa at such an early date, however, whereas the existence of a Portuguese pidgin has been established beyond doubt. Moreover, the creole of Surinam shows clear cases of early Portuguese elements. It is therefore worthwhile to consider the importance of early Portuguese influence.

The Portuguese Component

The existence of Portuguese elements in Surinam Creole is a problem, especially because of the preponderance of Portuguese elements in the language of the Saramaccan bushnegroes, the descendants of runaways to the central part of Surinam. In that language the Portuguese component is almost as strong as the English one. We must therefore consider the rather early Portuguese influence, which has not yet been accounted for by prevailing theories.

For a long time people have been satisfied to attribute the Portuguese influence to the presence in Surinam of Portuguese Jewish planters. Herskovits, however, pointed out that typical Jewish terms such as *trefu* (food taboo) and *kaseri* (ritually clean, kosher) are found in the coastal Creole, the language of the descendants of slaves, but not in Saramaccan Creole, the language of the descendants of the runaways (Herskovits 1930/31). There thus appears to have been no Jewish influence on the language that shows the strongest Portuguese influence, so the problem of the origin of the Portuguese influence remains. Herskovits also pointed out that newly imported slaves probably had the strongest tendency to escape to the bush, where they gathered in runaway tribes. These runaways did not get the opportunity to adapt themselves to the prevailing slave language spoken on the plantations. The English items in their vocabulary can easily be explained by the influence of their stay on the plantations or by later contacts with coastal Creole, especially after emancipation. The Portuguese items can have been adopted only in Africa.

Portuguese pidgin was in fact the most common contact language on the African coast during the seventeenth century. The slaves must have had contact with this language, even if it was only after they were transported to the African coast to be sold to European traders. They took this language with them to the New World. It might even have been the only means of communication with their fellow slaves and the crew on the ships. However, the same language was not used on the plantations in Surinam. Thus, after their arrival, the new slaves had to adopt the English-based pidgin, probably already in the process of becoming a creole.

If the Portuguese components in Saramaccan Creole are ascribed to the African period, then the few basic Portuguese items in Surinam Creole could possibly also have found their way into the language in essentially the same manner. This, in my opinion, would mean that one can no longer take it for granted that Surinam Creole originated only from an English-based pidgin. The oldest source was in any case an Afro-Portuguese pidgin, which might have developed into the English-based creole directly or via an intermediate English-based pidgin stage on the plantations. The whole process must have taken place in a remarkably short period of time (between 1651 and 1680). Thus it is possible that an English-based pidgin was not spoken by the newer slaves in Surinam but that they adapted their Portuguese pidgin to the language of their masters, and of the earlier slaves, and at the same time converted it to a more general use as their own mother tongue. This process by which a pidgin develops into a pidgin or creole with a different base may be termed *relexification.* The historical and linguistic arguments in favor of the relexification theory have been summarized in Voorhoeve 1973. Most of the Portuguese elements in the pidgin of the slaves were, as a result of this process, replaced by English elements without any great changes in the grammatical structure of the language.

The relexification theory explains the striking similarities in the structure of creole languages all over the world, which are based on different models (Thompson 1961). Taylor (1960) has drawn up quite a convincing list of these similarities. One of the most striking examples may be found in the verbal system of creoles. In Surinam Creole all (or nearly all) verbal tenses are formed by means of three verbal particles placed between the subject and the main verb: *ben* (past tense), *sa* (future tense or hypothetical), and *(d)e* imperfect tense or durative). These three particles, alone or in combination with each other, account for eight different verbal tenses and/or aspects. These eight tenses can be tabulated as follows (Voorhoeve 1957(a)).

	past	present	
nonconditional	ben-∅-∅- ben-∅-e-	∅↓∅-∅- ∅-∅-e-	⌐*perfect*
conditional	ben-sa-∅- ben-sa-e	∅-sa-∅- ∅-sa-e	⌐*imperfect*

There is no detailed description of all the creole languages on the basis of which a comparison of the verbal systems is possible. However, the verbal system always seems to operate essentially on the basis of three particles with roughly the same values, although the particles themselves have different forms and thus must have quite different origins:

	past	*future*	*imperfect*
Dominican Creole, etc.	te	ke	ka
Haitian Creole	te	ava	ape
Jamaican Creole	ben	wi	a
Surinam Creole	ben	sa	(d)e
Sarmaccan Creole	bî	sà	tá
Krio (Sierra Leone)	bîn	gò	dè
Negro Dutch	ha	lo	le
Papiamentu	taba	lo	ta
Philippine Creole	ja	de	ta
Indo-Portuguese	ja	di	ta
Macao Creole	ja	lo	ta
Malacca Creole	ja	ló (go)	ta

The similarities in the basic system are such that a common origin seems plausible. This common origin is not always reflected in the form of the particles but is hardly likely to be different from the trade language of the Portuguese sailors, widely used by different nations until the seventeenth century. This language was relexified in different directions, giving rise to differently based creole languages.

Evidence from Older Stages of Surinam Creole

Relexification of a more limited scope is a rather common phenomenon. In all languages, isolated lexical items are replaced by new ones with a different origin without affecting the grammatical structure of the language. This process is usually called borrowing, but in creole languages borrowing becomes such a massive phenomenon that it may completely change the affiliation of the language. It is possible to demonstrate the phenomenon in Surinam Creole, as we have access to old documents in the language. The oldest text, in *Beschrijvinge van de volksplantinge Zuriname* (Description of the Colony of Surinam), was published by J. D. Herlein in 1718. It is a curious document. It must have been constructed or elicited by a European, presumably the author himself, in any case by someone not aware of the subtle ways in which Surinamese Creoles show respect in their linguistic behavior. For example, the use of second or third person singular pronouns to refer to people of higher social position or people with whom one is not on intimate terms must often be avoided in Surinam Creole. This text used these forms freely and would therefore probably be jarring to modern Creole ears. It gives the impression of a European speaking with total disregard for polite Creole usage. It is possible that the author elicited the text from a Creole speaker, but in that case he has put the text consciously or unconsciously in a European mouth. It is highly unlikely that a Creole would have used such forms in everyday language. The lack of good manners should rather be attributed to the European author.

The text of 1718 has been criticized by Jan Nepveu, governor of Surinam from 1768 to 1779, in a manuscript of 1765. Nepveu made a few direct criticisms, mostly introduced by: 'Creoles would rather say . . .'. But he also added some vocabulary items and expressions that contain indirect criticisms of the 1718 text. Where Nepveu used different words for the Herlein items, we may assume that the Nepveu items were the normal ones in 1765. We reproduce here the original text from 1718 in the first column. The second column contains the corrections that can be deduced from the Nepveu manuscript of 1765. Corrections are introduced by a colon. If only one work in the Herlein text is corrected, this word is repeated in italics to the left of the colon. The third column presents the same text in modern Creole, between square brackets if the text lacks the necessary refinement. In that case an alternative polite rendering is added in parentheses. The fourth column presents as literal a modern English translation as possible. Italics in the original text draw attention to possible corruptions and printing errors. All translations of the original Creole text are based on the Dutch translation that accompanied it. For a later reprinting of the 1718 text with a Dutch translation, see Schuchardt 1914. For a reprinting with a literal English translation, see Rens 1953.

1718 Text	1765 Corrections	Modern Surinam Creole	English translation
1. Oudy.	: Ou fasi jou tan; *oe*: hoe.	Odi.	Hello.
2. Oe fasje jou tem?	: mi de boen.	Fa yu tan?	How do you do?
3. My bon.	*bon*: boen.	Mi de bun.	I am well.
4. Jou bon toe?	*ay*: aay.	Yu de bun tu?	Are you also well?
5. Ay.	: mi de belle wel, mi de belwel,	Ay.	Yes.
6. My belle wel.	mi de boen.	Mi de bun.	I am (very) well.
7. Jou wantje sie don pinkinine?	*wantje*: wanti, wandi; *pinkinine*: pinkinso. pekinini = my child.	Yu wani sidon pikinso?	Do you want to sit down a while?
8. Jie no draei?	*jie*: jou, joe; *draei*: drei, dreij.	[Yu (~I) no drey?] (more polite: Yu no wani dringi wan sani?)	Are you thirsty?
9. Ay mi wanto drinkje.	*wanto*: wanti, wandi; *drinkje*: drinki.	Ay, mi wani dringi (wan sani)	Yes, I could do with a drink.
10. Grande dankje no ver mie.	*ver*: for.	Grantangi [no fu mi] (more polite: watra no e kiri mi.)	Many thanks, not for me.
11. Jo wantje smoke Pipe Tobaki...ke?	*jo*: jou, joe; *wantje*: wanti, wandi.	Yu wani smoko wan pipa (tabaka)?	Do you want to smoke a pipe of tobacco?
12. Yo wantje loeke mie jary?	*jo*: jou, joe; *wantje*: wanti, wandi; *loeke*: loekoe	Yu wani luku mi dyari?	Do you perhaps want to see my garden?
13. Loeke mie *Druije se* hansum?	*hansum*: hansom, mooij.	Luku mi droyfi, fa den moy.	See my grapes, how beautiful they are.
14. Mie jary no grandebon?	:mi Jarie no mooij.	Mi dyari no moy?	Is not my garden beautiful?
15. Ay hantsum fo trou.	*hantsum*: hansom, mooij; *fo trou*: for troe.	Ay, a moy fu tru.	Yes, it is very beautiful.
16. Jo wantje gaeu wakke lange mie?	*jo*: jou, joe; *wantje*: wanti, wandi; *gaeu*: go; *wakke*: wakka: *lange*: langa.	Yu wani (go) waka langa (~ nanga) mi? (better: Yu wani kon waka nanga mi?)	Do you want to walk with me?
17. Oe plasje joe wil gaeu?	*oe plasje*: hoe plesi, hoe pleisi; *gaeu*: go.	Pe yu wani go? (~O presi yu wani go?)	Where will you go?
18. Mie wil gaeu na Watre-zy.	*w atre*: watra; *zy*: seij.	Mi wani go na watra sey.	I want to go to the riverside.
19. Oe tem wie wil gaeu na Riba?	*o..*: hoe; *gaeu*: go.	O ten wi sa go na liba?	When shall we go to the river?
20. Oe plesje tem.	: dá tem jou plessie.	Te yu wani.	Whenever you wish.
21. Mie missi take jou oudy.	*misi...si*: missi; *take*: taki.	Mi misi seni taygi yu (more polite: misi) odi (taygi = taki gi).	My mistress sends you her greetings.

1718 Text	1765 Corrections	Modern Surinam Creole	English translation
22. Akesi of joe tan an house?	ahakisi offi missie sa tan na Eosso.	[A aksi efi yu sa tan na oso] (better and more polite: A aksi efi misi de na oso.)	She asks if you will stay at home.
23. à Wilkom loeke joe na agter dina tem.	: a sa kom loeke jou, etc.	A wani kon luku yu di bakadina.	She will come visit you this afternoon.
24. No mie ben *benakase ta entre* ples à reddi *wen*.	: no mi sendi hakisi na tara plesi ε reddi; *à reddi*: a reddi, kaba.	No, mi (ben) seni aksi na wan tra presi kaba . . .	No, I have already inquired from another whether it would please her if I came to her.
25. As hem ples hem kon te maare.	*as* offi; *hem*: him, hem; *te maare*: ta mara.	Efi a wani, a kan kon tamara.	If it pleases her, she can come tomorrow.
26. Oe som bady Mastre vor joe?	*oε* hoe; *som bady*: so ma; *mastre*: masra; *vor*: for.	Suma na yu masra? (possible, but not natural: o suma na a masra fu yu?)	Who is your master?
27. Oe fasse nam vor joe Mastre?	*oε*: hoe; *fasse*: fasi; *nam*: nem; *vor*: for.	Fa yu masra nen?	What is your master's name?
28. Oe fasse kase joe Misisi?	*o*ɔ: hoe; *fasse*: fasi; *misisi*: missi.	Fa den e kari yu misi? (better: Fa yu misi nen?)	How is your mistress called?
29. Oe plesse jo liewy?	*oε*: hoe; *plesse*: plesi, pleisi; *jo*: jou, joe; *liewy*: libi.	Pe yu e libi?	Where do you live?
30. Klosse byna Forte.		Krosibey fu foto.	Close to the fortress.
31. Jie no love mie moore.	*j'e*: jou, joe; *love*: lobi; *moore*: moro.	Yu no lobi mi moro.	You do not love me any more.
32. Je wantje sliepe lange mie?	*ȷe*: jou; joe; *wantje*: wanti, wandi; *sliepe*: slipi; *lange*: langa. *wantje*: wanti, wandi.	Yu wani sribi langa (~ nanga) mi?	Do you want to sleep with me?
33. No mie no wantje.	*jie*: jou, joe; *bon*: boen.	No, mi no wani.	No, I do not want.
34. Jie no bon.		Yu a no bun suma.	You are not good (nice).
35. Jie monbie toe moussie.	*jie*: jou, joe; *toe moussie*: toe moussi.	Yu gridi tumusi.	You are too greedy.
36. Kom bosse mie wantem.		Kon bosi mi dan.	Come kiss me then.

1718 Text	1765 Corrections	Modern Surinam Creole	English translation
37. Na tappe.	*na tappe*: na tapce.	Na tapu.	Upward.
38. Na bie laeu.	*na bie laeu*: na bilo, na ondro, na gron.	Na ondro (to indicate a place: na bilo).	Downward.
39. Zon komotte.	*zon*: son.	Son opo.	The sun rises.
40. Zon gaeud on.	*zon*: son; *gaeud on*: go don.	Son dongo.	The sun sets.
41. Santje.	*santje*: santi.	Sani.	A thing.
42. Kaba.		Kaba.	Done (finished, ready).
43. Hause.	: hosso.	(H)oso.	A house.
44. Tappe.		Daki.	The roof.
45. Tappe windels.	: tappe fenstre; *wndels*: windau, finstre.	Tapu fensre.	Shut the windows.
46. Ope windels.	: oppo fenstre; *windels*: windau, finstre.	Opo fensre.	Open the windows.
47. Ver wate jie no ope windels?	*jie*: jou, joe; *ope*: oppo; *windels*: windau, finstre.	San ede yu no opo fensre?	Why do you not open the windows?

A careful comparison of the texts reveals that for a considerable period of time alternative possibilities of Portuguese and English origin coexisted in Creole. The clearest case is the pair *bun*/P. 'bom' vs. *belwel* / E. 'very well,' of which only the Portuguese-derived item survives in modern Creole. The Portuguese-derived item *grande* did not survive as a regular adverb, 'very,' or adjective, 'big,' but it is still present in composite nouns as *grantangi* (many thanks), *granmasra* (big master), *granman* (governor), *granmama* (grandmother), in the composite adverb *granwe* (long ago, in 1765 still found as *grandi wey*), and maybe also in the verb *grani* (to be old). The item *grandebon* may even have survived in the word *granbun* (holy communion). In modern Creole the regular adverb *heri* / D. 'heel' for the meaning 'very' can also be rendered by *fu tru* / E. 'for true.' The 1765 text contains the English-derived item *kweti* / E. 'quite' without indications as to its use. It is possible that this item replaced *grande* and survived for some time. It is still used in modern Creole but only in negative sentences. The pair *kaba* / P. 'acabar' and *a reddi* / E. 'already' also shows that the Portuguese item survived in modern Creole, although the English-derived item is still found in the dictionary of Focke in 1855, viz. *arede*. It appears that Portuguese items that managed to survive until 1718 were so firmly rooted in the language that it was no longer possible for them to be replaced by the coexisting English-derived item.

Alternative possibilities of items of English and of Dutch origin can also be found in the early texts. See the pairs *hansom* / E. 'handsome' vs. *moy* / D. 'mooi,' *windau* / E. 'window' vs. *fensre* / D. 'venster.' In both cases the English-derived item was eventually lost. The opposite occurred with the pairs *wani* / E. 'want' vs. *wil* (if *wil* is really from Dutch), *agterdina* / D. 'achter' and E. 'dinner' vs. *bakadina* / E. 'back dinner' (if *agter* is really from Dutch).

These alternative possibilities may reflect old dialectal differences. The unpublished dictionary by C. L. Schumann (1783) for instance contains the word *brens* / E. 'brains,' with the remark that this word is still used on the old English plantations but not in town (Voorhoeve Donicie 1963(b): 23). It is quite possible that Schumann or his Creole informant (whose oral comments he often cites in this diction-ary) had in mind the plantations that were first cultivated by the English pioneers before 1680. The English influence may in that case have been strongest and longest on the old English plantations and may have diminished only gradually with the spreading influence of the town language. Focke 1855 does not contain the word *brens*. A more detailed study of the Surinam Creole vocabulary in a historical perspective may reveal more about the development of the language.

If we accept the hypothesis that most slaves came from Africa during the seventeenth century with a basic knowledge of an Afro-Portuguese pidgin and in Surinam found a few slaves from Barbados with a more deeply rooted knowledge of an English-based creole or pidgin, we may assume that the English-based language quickly became dominant but that for some time there was a certain competition within it between Portuguese-derived and English-derived items with an identical meaning. The British planters, overseers, and indentured laborers reinforced the English, so that the English-derived items won the battle in most cases. The Portuguese-derived items that remained in the language after the English influence had ceased were so firmly rooted that they could not easily be replaced by subsequent developments. The English-derived items were in a much weaker position and many could thus be replaced by Dutch-derived ones.

APPENDIX 2

Orthographical Note

The Creole texts are presented in an ad hoc orthography that makes them easier for an English or American public to read. The following orthographic key should be kept in mind:

Nasals	m	n	ny	ng	consonant signs
Stops vcd	b	d	dy	g	
vcl	p	t	ty	k	
Fricatives	f	s	sy		
Lateral		l			
Trill		r			
Semivowels			y	w	
Close			i	u	vowel signs
Half-close			e	o	
Open				a	

The double orthographic symbols in this table represent simple phonemes. The distinction between the lateral and the trill is allophonic. A symbol *h* is used in the texts but represents only a free variant of a vowel not preceded by *h*. The palatal consonants are written with the corresponding alveolar consonant symbols plus *y*. The final close vowel of diphthongs is written as the corresponding semivowel. Nasalized vowels are written with *n* after the vowel. Noncreolized Dutch words have been written in the standard Dutch orthography. In some words the half-open front vowel *è* (an allophone of *e*) is written. The official Creole orthography writes *j* for *y*, *oe* for *u*, and has for diphthongs the following conventions: *ai, oi, oei* for *ay, oy,* and *uy; é* for *ey*.

The text of Johannes King in chapter 4 is not presented in this orthography. His work, written in a very idiosyncratic spelling, has been edited in the standard orthography by H. F. de Ziel, who bases his editing on a careful interpretation of the texts. We have used De Ziel's version without change.

HENDRIK SCHOUTEN

Een huishoudelijke twist

Kind lief, laat voort de Coffij geeven!
Tan Baija, jusno a sa kom.
Maak met de Slaaven dog geen leeven!
Den booijs den de toe moessie dom!
Spreek zagtjes! waarom zoo te schreeuwen?
Te mie no balie, den no doe.
'T was best jou bek maar toe te breeuwen!
Mekkie den tappou vo jou toe.
Kan een Creoole smoel wel zwijgen?
Da ogrie te mie pikkie dan?
Moet men dan altoos woorden krijgen?
Mie sabie, haksie tarawan.
Wat middel om die kop te breeken?
Jou no kan nak em langa ston.
Waar moet ik dan het vuilnis steeken?
Mie swerie Gado loekoe bon!
Wat zullen wij van middag eeten?
Na dienatem jou no sa sie?
Ik zeg, ik wil het aanstonds weeten!
Mie takkie jou no balie mie.
Wat schielijk, en niet lang te draalen!
Jou memmere mie fredde dan?
Moet ik de Bullepees ook haalen?
Fom mie, effe jou da wan man!
Zie daar . . . wijl gij mij dwingt te straffen!
De Diebrie moese nakkie jou!
Wilt nu maar Neeger-Engelsch blaffen!
Jou da wan schurke, dattie trou!
Moet ik dan hier de Baas niet weezen?
Nou mie no wannie gie jam jam.
De Slagter heeft meer Bullepeezen!
Eff jou goo Baij, jou moesse lam!
Hoor eens dat schelden! is 't geen schanden?
Jou memmere mie sa kaba?

Pas op! 'k heb 't stuur nog in mijn handen!
   Kaka vo soo wan Bakkera!
Wat schepzel zal dat wijf bedwingen?
   Doe san jou wannie, mie no kee!
Men breekt wel eerder staale klingen!
   Jou no sa brokke mie ti dee.
't Hart is door haat reeds ingenoomen!
   Jou takkie reijtie, da no kij.
Zij zal nog Hel nog Duivel schroomen!
   Da vo da hede wie sa scheij.

A domestic tiff

Dear child, come let's put the coffee out!
   Wait just a minim, man, anon it will be there.
Don't kick up such a fuss with the slaves!
   These creatures are awful for sure.
Speak softly please, why bawl so loud?
   If I don't yell they don't do aught.
Better then to shut your trap!
   Let them start at once with yours.
A Creole mouth can never stop!
   Am I wrong if I answer?
Must we always cross our swords?
   For all I care ask another.
How knock some sense into your obstinate head?
   You might perhaps try a stone.
What about the garbage if it bursts?
   I swear by God you better watch!
What will the pot today provide?
   Can't you wait till dinnertime?
I tell you I will know it now!
   And I tell you don't yell at me.
Move on, don't dawdle so!
   You think I am afraid of you?
Shall I get the cat of nine tails too?
   Beat me if you have the guts!
Here then, because you edge me on!
   Would the Devil flog you too!
Your negro-English, bark it now!
   God, you are a rogue for sure!

Am I not the master in here?
  Now I refuse to dish your food.
The butcher has more tails than one!
  If you go and buy, God strike you lame!
Listen to her, is it not a shame?
  Do you think I'll shut up now?
Hey ho! I have the reins in hand!
  I shit on such a white man!
What apparition would that shrew subdue?
  Do what you wish, I don't care!
Sooner it would be to break steel swords!
  Today you won't succeed in breaking me.
The heart's already eaten up with hate!
  How right you are, without a doubt.
She'll fear no devil, nor hot hell!
  That's why we'll part our ways.

Bibliography

Asjantenu Sangodare [Michaël Slory]. 1961 *Sarka. Bittere strijd.*
Amsterdam.
Bruma, Eddy. 1958. "Maswa," *Vox Guyanae* 3, 1:10-17.
Cairo, Edgar. 1969. *Temekoe.* Paramaribo.
———. 1970. *Kra. Wan bondroe powema.* Paramaribo.
Capelle, H. van. 1916. "Surinaamsche negervertellingen. Bijdragen
tot de kennis van West-Indische negerfolklore," *Bijdragen Taal-,
Land- en Volkenkunde* 72:233-379.
———. 1926. *Mythen en sagen uit West-Indië;* Zutphen.
Comvalius, Th. A. C. 1922. *Iets over het Surinaamsch lied. Een
bijdrage tot de kennis van de folklore van de kolonie Suriname.*
Paramaribo.
———. 1935/36. "Het Surinaamsche negerlied: de banja en de doe,"
De West-Ind. Gids 17:161-72.
———. 1938. "Twee historische liederen in Suriname," *De West-Ind.
Gids* 20:292-95.
———. 1939. "Een der vormen van het Surinaamsche lied na 1863,"
De West-Ind. Gids 21:355-60.
———. 1946. "Oud-Surinaamsche rhythmische dansen in dienst van
de lichamelijke opvoeding," *De West-Ind. Gids* 27:97-100.
Daeleman, Jan. 1972. "Kongo Elements in Saramacca Tongo,"
Journal of African Languages 11:1-44.
Dictionary of Jamaican English. 1967. F. G. Cassidy and R. B. Le Page,
eds. Cambridge.
Donicie, A. 1952/53. "Iets over de taal en de sprookjes van Suriname,"
De West-Ind. Gids 33:153-73.
———. 1963. See Voorhoeve and Donicie 1963(a) and 1963(b).
Drie, A. de. 1959. "Basja Pataka," *Vox Guyanae* 3, 6:18-20.
Encyclopaedie van Nederlandsch West-Indie. 1914-17. H. D. Benjamins
and Joh. F. Snelleman, eds. Den Haag and Leiden.
Focke, H. C. 1855. *Neger-Engelsch woordenboek.* Leiden.
———. 1858. "De Surinaamsche negermuzijk," *West-Indië* 2:93-107.
Foetoe-boi. 1946-56. Paramaribo.
Frake, Charles O. 1971. "Lexical Origins and Semantic Structure in
Philippine Creole Spanish," in Dell Hymes, ed., *Pidginization and
Creolization of Languages.* Cambridge.

Freytag, Gottfried A. 1927. *Johannes King der Buschland-Prophet, Ein Lebensbild aus'der Brüdergemeine in Suriname. Nach seinem eigener Aufzeichnungen dargestellt. Hefte zur Missionskunde,* 20. Herrnhut.

Goeje, C. H. de. 1908. *Verslag der Toemoekhoemak-expeditie.* Leiden.

Groot, Silvia W. de. 1969. *Djuka Society and Social Change: History of an Attempt to Develop a Bush Negro Community in Surinam 1917-1926.* Assen.

——. 1970. "210 jaar zelfstandigheid. Het verdrag van 10 oktober 1760," *De Gids* 133:410-13.

Hall Jr., R. A. 1966. *Pidgin and Creole Languages.* Ithaca.

Hellinga, W. Gs. 1955. *Language Problems in Surinam.* In cooperation with the staff of the Bureau for Linguistic Research in Surinam. Amsterdam.

Helstone, J. N. 1903. *Wan spraakkunst vo taki en skrifi da tongo vo Sranan.* Paramaribo.

Herskovits, Melville J. 1930/31. "On the Provenience of the Portuguese in Saramacca Tongo," *De West-Ind. Gids* 12:545-57.

——. 1936. *Suriname Folk-Lore.* New York.

——. 1937. *Life in a Haitian Valley.* New York.

Hoëvell, W. R. van. 1854. *Slaven en vrijen onder de Nederlandsche wet.* 2 vols. Zaltbommel.

Innes, Gordon, 1965. "The Function of the Song in Mende Folktales," *African Language Review* 4:54-63.

Jahn, Janheinz, ed. 1954. *Schwarzer Orpheus. Moderne Dichtung afrikanischer Völker beider Hemisphären.* München.

Kesler, C. K. 1927. "Spellingseenheid en taalverdeeldheid," *Neerlandia* 31:29-30.

Kesteloot, Lilyan. 1965. *Les écrivains noirs de langue française; naissance d'une littérature.* Bruxelles.

King, Johannes, 1973. *Life at Maripaston.* Edited by H. F. de Ziel. The Hague.

Koenders, J. G. A. 1943. *Foe memre wie afo. Het Surinaamsch in een nieuw kleed. Met oefeningen.* Paramaribo.

——. 1944. *60 (sieksie tin tien) moi en bekentie siengie na Sranan Tongo.* Paramaribo.

——. n.d. *Aksie mie, mie sa piekie joe foe wie skien.* Paramaribo.

Lichtveld, L. 1930/31. "Op zoek naar de spin," *De West-Ind. Gids* 12: 209-30, 305-24.

Lichtveld, Ursy M. and Jan Voorhoeve. 1958. *Suriname: spiegel der vaderlandse kooplieden. Een historisch leesboek.* Zwolle.

Naipaul, Vidia. 1962. *The Middle Passage*. London.

Penard, A. P. and T. E. 1917. "Surinam Folk-Tales," *Journal of American Folk-Lore* 15:239-50.

Rens, L. L. E. 1953. *The Historical and Social Background of Surinam Negro-English*. Amsterdam.

——. 1954. "Analysis of Annals," *Vox Guyanae* 1:19-38.

Renselaar, H. C. van. 1959. "Een laku-pree," *Vox Guyanae* 3, 6:36-48.

——. 1962. *See* Voorhoeve and Renselaar 1962.

——. 1963. "Colin, profeet van Coronie," *Uit Suriname's Historie* (Suriname), 20-24.

——. 1966. "Oude kaarten van Suriname," *De Nwe West-Ind. Gids* 45:2-13.

Schouten-Elsenhout, Johanna. 1963. *Tide ete. Fo sren singi*. Paramaribo.

——. 1965. *Awese*. Paramaribo.

——. 1974. *Sranan pangi*. Paramaribo.

Schuchardt, Hugo. 1914. *Die Sprache der Saramakkaneger in Surinam*. Amsterdam.

Shrinivasi [Martinus Lutchman]. 1970. *Wortoe d'e tan abra. Bloemlezing uit de Surinaamse poëzie vanaf 1957*. Paramaribo.

Slory, Michaël. *See also* Asjantenu Sangodare.

——. 1970. *Fraga mi wortoe* [Paramaribo].

——. 1971. *Nengre-oema* [Paramaribo].

——. 1971. *Bonifoto* [Paramaribo].

——. 1972. *Lobisingi* [Paramaribo].

——. 1972. *Vietnam* [Paramaribo].

Speckmann, J. D. 1965. *Marriage and Kinship among the Indians in Surinam*. Assen.

Taylor, Douglas. 1960. "Language Shift or Changing Relationship?" *Int. Journal of American Linguistics* 26:155-61.

Thomas, J. J. 1869. *The Theory and Practice of Creole Grammar*. Port-of-Spain.

Thompson, R. W. 1961. "A Note on Some Possible Affinities between the Creole Dialects of the Old World and Those of the New," in R. B. Le Page, ed., *Creole Language Studies II*, 107-13.

Trefossa [H. F. de Ziel]. 1957. *Trotji. Puëma. Met een stilistische studie over het gedicht Kopenhage, vertalingen en verklarende aantekeningen door J. Voorhoeve*. Amsterdam.

Tsjerne, De. 1952. Suriname-numer.

Valdman, Albert. 1970. *Basic Course in Haitian Creole*. The Hague.

Voorhoeve, Jan. 1950. "Repelsteeltje in Suriname," *El Dorado* 2: 95-96.

——. 1957(a). "The Verbal System of Sranan," *Lingua* 6:374-96.

——. 1957(b). "Missionary Linguistics in Surinam," *The Bible Translator* 8:179-90.

——. 1957. *See* Trefossa 1957.

——. 1958. *See* Lichtveld and Voorhoeve 1958.

——. 1958. "Op zoek naar de handschriften van Johannes King," *Vox Guyanae* 3, 1:34-40.

——. 1959. "Het vertalen van poezie," *Vox Guyanae* 3, 6:8-14.

——. 1960. "De handschriften van Mr. Adriaan François Lammens," *De Nwe West-Ind. Gids* 40:28-49.

——. 1962. *See* Voorhoeve and Renselaar 1962.

——. 1962. *Sranan Syntax.* Amsterdam.

——. 1963. *See* Voorhoeve and Donicie 1963(a) and 1963(b).

——. 1964(a). "Johannes King 1830-1899. Een mens met grote overtuiging," in *Biografieën Emancipatie 1863-1963.* Paramaribo.

——. 1964(b). "Creole Languages and Communication," *Symposium on Multilingualism* (Brazzaville, 1962), 233-42.

——. 1966. "Fictief verleden. De slaventijd in de Surinaamse belletrie," *De Nwe West-Ind. Gids* 45:32-37.

——. 1970. "The Regularity of Sound Correspondences in a Creole Language," *Journal of African Languages* 9:51-69.

——. 1971(a). "Church Creole and Pagan Cult Languages," in Dell Hymes, ed., *Pidginization and Creolization of Languages* (Cambridge), 303-15.

——. 1971(b). "The Art of Reading Creole Poetry," in Dell Hymes, ed., *Pidginization and Creolization of Languages* (Cambridge), 323-26.

——. 1973. "Historical and Linguistic Evidence in Favour of the Relexification Theory in the Formation of Creoles," *Language in Society* 2:133-45.

Voorhoeve, Jan, and Antoon Donicie. 1963(a). *De Saramakaanse woordenschat.* Amsterdam.

——. 1963(b). *Bibliographie du négro-anglais du Surinam. Avec une appendice sur les langues créoles parlées à l'intérieur du pays.* 's-Gravenhage.

Voorhoeve, Jan, and H. C. van Renselaar. 1962. "Messianism and Nationalism in Surinam," *Bijdragen Taal-, Land- en Volkenkunde* 118:193-216.

Waal Malefijt, Annemarie de. 1963. *The Javanese of Surinam: Segment of a Plural Society.* Assen.

Wooding, Ch. J. 1970. "Winti," *De Gids* 133:286-88.

Woordenlijst van het Sranan-Tongo (Glossary of the Surinam Vernacular). 1961. Paramaribo.

Ziel, H. F. de. 1957. *See* Trefossa 1957.

———. 1973. *See* King 1973.

Index